D0812564

Cultural Conservatism, Political Liberalism

Cultural Conservatism, Political Liberalism

From Criticism to Cultural Studies

James Seaton

Ann Arbor

THE UNIVERSITY OF MICHIGAN PRESS

To Sandra

Copyright © by the University of Michigan 1996
All rights reserved
Published in the United States of America by
The University of Michigan Press
⊗ Printed on acid-free paper

1999   1998   1997   1996   4   3   2   1

A CIP catalogue record for this book is available from the British Library.

Library of Congress Cataloging-in-Publication Data
  Seaton, James.
    Cultural conservatism, political liberalism : from criticism to
  cultural studies / James Seaton.
      p. cm.
    Includes bibliographical references (p.) and index.
    ISBN 0-472-10645-7 (acid-free paper)
    1. Criticism—United States—History—20th century. 2. Politics
  and literature—United States—History—20th century. 3. Literature
  and society—United States—History—20th century. 4. American
  literature—History and criticism—Theory, etc. 5. Political
  science—United States—Philosophy. 6. National characteristics,
  American. 7. United States—Civilization. 8. Culture. I. Title.
  PS25.S43 1996
  801'.95'0973—dc20   95-39785
                                              CIP

Contents

Acknowledgments

I would like to pay tribute to the example set by the work of the late Christopher Lasch, whose career exemplified the spirit of cultural self-criticism. I wish to thank Thomas D'Evelyn, Robert Garis, my brother William Seaton, and my colleague James Hill for their careful readings of sections of the manuscript. Roger Hornsby, professor emeritus of the Department of Classics at the University of Iowa, proofread the whole with care and speed. The faith and encouragement of LeAnn Fields of the University of Michigan Press have been invaluable. I am very grateful for the skillful copyediting supervised by Ellen McCarthy. The book was written with the aid of awards from the Department of English and the College of Arts and Letters at Michigan State University, whose assistance I am happy to recognize. My deepest gratitude is owed to my wife, Sandra Seaton, who has sustained me throughout this project, as she has since we first met. Her close reading of every draft of the manuscript saved me from many errors of judgment and style. Despite the help I have been lucky enough to receive from those mentioned and from many others as well, I alone am responsible for the content and the opinions expressed within.

Cultural Conservatism, Political Liberalism reflects my thought and work over the last ten years. I have incorporated material from the following essays into this book: "The Humanities and Cultural Criticism: The Example of Ralph Ellison," in *Rejuvenating the Humanities*, ed. Ray Browne and Marshall Fishwick, 101–108 (Bowling Green, OH, Bowling Green SU Popular P, 1992); Introduction, *Beyond Cheering and Bashing: New Perspectives on "The Closing of the American Mind,"* ed. William K. Buckley and James Seaton (Bowling Green: Bowling Green SU Popular P, 1992); "Innocence Regained: The Career of Leslie Fiedler," in *Politics and the Muse: Studies in the Politics of Recent American Literature*, ed. Adam J. Sorkin, 93-110 (Bowling Green: Bowling Green SU Popular P, 1989); "Irving Babbitt: Midwestern Intellectual," *MidAmerica* 18 (1991): 22–30; "A Pragmatic Look at the New Secularism: Rorty, Fish, and

Said," *New Oxford Review* 59 no. 3 (April 1992): 15–17. Copyright © 1992 *New Oxford Review*. Reprinted with permission from the *New Oxford Review;* "The Two Branches of the Law and Literature Movement: A Critique of Stanley Fish," *Legal Studies Forum* 15 no. 1 (1991): 65–74; "Edward W. Said: The Secular Critic as Revolutionary," *South Carolina Review* 23 no. 2 (1991): 168–180; "Cultural Conservatism, Political Radicalism," *Journal of American Culture* 12 no. 3 (Fall 1989): 1–10; "The Truth-Value of Bourgeois Hedonism: On H. L. Mencken," *Journal of American Culture* 8, no. 3 (1985): 53–58; "Beyond Masscult and Midcult: The Achievement of Dwight Macdonald," *Markham Review* 14 (1984–85): 7–12; "Marxism without Difficulty: Fredric Jameson's *The Political Unconscious*," *Centennial Review*, 28–29 nos. 4–1 (1984–1985): 122–42. Permission to reprint is gratefully acknowledged.

Introduction

This book makes a case for the continuing vitality of a tradition of cultural criticism obscured by the contemporary expansion of academic cultural studies.
The literary-cultural-political criticism reaffirmed in the following chapters may
be traced back in English at least as far as Samuel Johnson; Matthew Arnold is
its greatest examplar in the nineteenth century. Connecting literature to politics
without diminishing either, this tradition's commitment to the language of
public discourse fosters democracy even when the opinions of its practitioners
are unapologetically elitist. Often polemical, it finds little space for personal
confession but makes room for "cultural self-criticism."[1] Lionel Trilling, H. L.
Mencken, Irving Babbitt, Dwight Macdonald, Diana Trilling, Edmund Wilson,
and Ralph Ellison are among the successors of Johnson and Arnold in the
United States.

Jacques Barzun believes that the phrase "cultural criticism" appeared in
print for the first time in Lionel Trilling's 1942 essay "The Sense of the Past"
("Reckoning with Time and Place," 82). According to Barzun, the connotations of cultural criticism were then almost exactly the opposite of those conveyed by cultural studies today. Trilling and Barzun thought of the "spirit of
cultural criticism" as a kind of higher common sense informed by historical
understanding (83), a "non-method" that presupposed "the factitiousness of
theory and the unsuitability of system" (84). Their cultural criticism was not a
separate discipline, since it possessed no specific methodology or theory of its
own; its tools were judgment and tact, qualities that could be encouraged and
practiced but not systematized.

In "The Sense of the Past" Lionel Trilling finds a "charter to engage in
cultural history and cultural criticism" in David Hume's essay "Of the Rise and
the Progress of the Arts and Sciences." The great skeptic seems an unlikely
source for an affirmation of studies generally considered much more problematic than the natural sciences, whose pretensions to certain knowledge Hume

rendered suspect. But it appears that Trilling goes to Hume in search of "a charter to deal with a mystery" (185). Hume merely points out that creative artists
do not live in isolation; if it is impossible to penetrate the mind of the individual artist or writer, it is possible to learn something about the "gross, institu-
tional facts" (193) and make some reasonable inferences from these relevant to
the work of art itself.[2] Trilling seeks no more, since he is interested in cultivat-
ing a sense of the past rather than in devising a methodology.

Whether or not Jacques Barzun is right in claiming that the phrase "cultural criticism" first occurs in "The Sense of the Past," it is clear that the essays
that make up *The Liberal Imagination, The Opposing Self,* and *Beyond Culture* continue a tradition that began long before Barzun and Trilling's joint seminars at
Columbia. Trilling's loyalty to the example of Matthew Arnold, for example, is
evident throughout his career, from his first and longest book, *Matthew Arnold,*
to "Mind in the Modern World," his last major work. Today, of course, Arnold
himself is remembered most often as an advocate for the study of "the best that
is known and thought," a defender of a canon based on "high seriousness," a
traditionalist and a liberal humanist.

Matthew Arnold was indeed all these things. That is enough, for some
people, to condemn him and any tradition he might have inspired. Terry Eagleton generously dismisses the charge that the Victorian critic "supported nuclear
weapons," but he finds Arnold guilty of the moral equivalent; Arnold, like most
critics, "strengthened rather than challenged the assumptions of the power-sys-
tem" (195). If this accusation means that Arnold preferred reforming liberal
democratic society to taking his chances with Eagleton on the success of "the
socialist transformation of society" (211), Arnold is probably guilty as charged.
Eagleton, of course, has an advantage over Arnold, since the former is free to
attend to the consequences of several twentieth-century attempts to achieve
"the socialist transformation of society." Whether Eagleton has profited from
this advantage is open to question.

Terry Eagleton not only disagrees with what he takes to be the Arnoldian
position that "literature should convey *timeless* truths"; he suspects that Arnold
propagated this view primarily as a means of "distracting the masses from their
immediate commitments . . . and so ensuring the survival of private property"
(26). In one sense Eagleton's criticism does not go far enough. Arnold did not
restrict himself to arguing that literature was not primarily concerned with
immediate political issues; he insisted, much more scandalously for Eagleton,
that even criticism should aim at "disinterestedness" rather than engagement. In
his essay on "The Function of Criticism at the Present Time" Arnold calls for a
criticism whose governing attitude is *"disinterestedness,"* a criticism that refuses

to "lend itself" to "ulterior, political practical considerations about ideas" and, instead, attempts "simply to know the best that is known and thought in the world" (270). Even so, it would be a mistake to follow Eagleton in categorizing and then dismissing Arnold's critical practice as just another example of "middle-class ideology" (26).

Arnold urges critical disinterestedness not merely for its own sake but because he believes that criticism can thereby achieve its fullest social impact. Arnold argued that criticism should call attention to "the best that is known and thought in the world" in the belief that the dissemination of this "best" would disturb complacency, invigorate intellectual life, and thus contribute to the amelioration of social problems seemingly remote from the realm of high literature. "The Function of Criticism at the Present Time" refutes the allegation that Arnold urged immersion in great literature primarily as an escape from unpleasant social realities. Arnold quotes a politician expatiating on the virtues of "the old Anglo-Saxon race . . . the best breed in the whole world" (272) and another on the greatness of England:

> I look around me and ask what is the state of England? Is not property safe? Is not every man able to say what he likes? Can you not walk from one end of England to the other in perfect security: I ask you whether, the world over or in past history, there is anything like it? Nothing. I pray that our unrivalled happiness may last.

Arnold confronts the political speeches with a story "on which I had stumbled in a newspaper":

> A shocking child murder has just been committed at Nottingham. A girl named Wragg left the work-house there on Saturday morning with her young illegitimate child. The child was soon afterwards found dead on Mapperly Hills, having been strangled. Wragg is in custody. (273)

By itself the story would be terrible but without wider implication. Arnold draws on his literary skill to drive home how the newspaper story refutes the speechmakers:

> And "our unrivalled happiness;"—what an element of grimness, bareness, and hideousness mixes with it and blurs it; the workhouse, the dismal Mapperly Hills,—how dismal those who have seen them will remember;—the gloom, the smoke, the cold, the strangled illegitimate child! "I

ask you whether, the world over in past history, there is anything like it?"
. . . And the final touch,—short, bleak, and inhuman: *Wragg is in custody*.
The sex lost in the confusion of our unrivalled happiness; or (shall I say?)
the superfluous Christian name lopped off by the straight-forward vigour
of our old Anglo-Saxon breed! (273–74)

It is true that Arnold does not follow up with a call for "socialist transformation" or even any proposals for welfare reform. Critics, he argues, will per-
suade only by the exercise of a disinterestedness that will finally overcome the
suspicion of "the practical man." The wisdom of Arnold's strategy may be questioned; Jean-Paul Sartre and others have argued eloquently for a criticism of
engagement. Nevertheless, a criticism that can take account of the fate of a
Wragg while it attempts "to learn and propagate the best that is known and
thought in the world" seems worth salvaging.

The American critics who have continued Arnold's tradition often pay
serious attention to works outside any particular "canon" without losing sight
of the standards implicit in their own sense of "the best that is known and
thought in the world." Arnoldian cultural criticism, nevertheless, has lost
ground everywhere to cultural studies, a putative superdiscipline drawing much
of its appeal from its rejection of disinterestedness in favor of politicization.
Today college campuses in general and literature departments in particular are
key battlegrounds of the "culture wars." In 1965 Christopher Lasch noted that
the status of the intellectual as a "critic of society . . . is presumed to rest on a
measure of detachment from the current scene" (*The New Radicalism*, ix).
Today the "detachment" that could once be "presumed" is in short supply,
even in what used to be called the ivory tower. In English departments "race,
gender and class" have taken center stage, while questions of literary merit have
been rendered illegitimate—"marginalized," in the current discourse.

An upswing in the reputations of critics such as Lionel Trilling and the
writers discussed in part 2 would wreak no great change in U. S. society as a
whole. The revival of the tradition of discourse embodied in the works of such
writers, however, would at least contribute to the replacement of cultural warfare with debate. A revival would mean that the literary-cultural debates carried
on within literature departments would be accessible to others beyond the campus. At least some members of the general public might think it worth their
while to pay attention if literary critics today—following Trilling, Wilson, and
their peers—focused on conveying the insights of novels, plays, and poetry. On
the other hand, professors of literature unwilling to recognize the authority of
great writers are unlikely to convince anybody beyond their own graduate stu-

dents that their misgivings about contemporary society are based on anything more than the stereotypical hostility of academics to the "real world."

Richard Rorty suggests in "Professionalized Philosophy and Transcendentalist Culture" that the "highbrow culture" of Ralph Waldo Emerson, Edmund Wilson, and Lionel Trilling survives in the decentering impulse of contemporary cultural studies. In Rorty's account the attainment of a "culture which is transcendentalist through and through, whose center is everywhere and circumference nowhere" would be a victory for both old-fashioned "culture criticism" and his own pragmatism (70). Since Rorty's works offer the most persuasive rationale for cultural studies, a work affirming the older cultural criticism in preference to contemporary trends should take account of Rorty's very different narrative. Part 1, "Premises," considers the ideas about the relations between literature, morality and politics that shape the book as a whole. Chapter 1, "Richard Rorty: Pragmatism and Cultural Criticism," discusses Rorty's overall stance, while chapter 2, "Richard Rorty and Lionel Trilling: Liberalism and Literature," offers a critique derived from juxtaposing Rorty's views to those of a figure whom he claims as one of his predecessors in cultural criticism, Lionel Trilling.

After testing the premises of the argument in the first section, Part 2, "Examples," offers six portraits of critics whose work exemplifies the older tradition. Chapter 3, "Limits and Standards: Irving Babbitt and H. L. Mencken," suggests that these onetime adversaries had a great deal in common. Suspicious of grandiose political schemes supported by apocalyptic rhetoric, Mencken and Babbitt opposed both Prohibition and the Wilsonian notion of "a war to end war." Babbitt, like Mencken, observed that the high-minded rhetoric of American politicians such as Woodrow Wilson often served to justify the accumulation of power. Noting the affinities between democracy and imperialism, Babbitt debunked "the humanitarian-imperialistic cant of the 'white man's burden'" (*Democracy and Leadership* 155). Neither Babbitt nor Mencken joined in the 1920s celebration of the American status quo. Unimpressed by messianic reformers and undazzled by merely technological achievements, both were more than willing to judge contemporary society according to their own demanding intellectual and cultural standards.

In both his wit and his unapologetic championing of high culture Dwight Macdonald carried on the tradition of H. L. Mencken. In *Politics* and in his writings of the 1960s he demonstrated how Mencken's legacy could be allied with radical politics without compromising intellectual or aesthetic integrity. Chapter 4, "Beyond 'Masscult' and 'Midcult': The Achievement of Dwight Macdonald," argues that the common pigeonholing of Macdonald as a proponent of elitism misses the way in which his very pride as an intellectual prevented him from engaging in the condescension that is the token of truly pernicious elitism. Macdonald remains important not only for his insistence on judging both novels and movies according to equally rigorous standards but also for his ability in the 1940s to maintain a distinction between hating Nazism and hating all Germans.

During World War II Diana Trilling, like Dwight Macdonald, demonstrated in practice the independence of mind that almost all intellectuals approve in theory. Just as her reviews during the 1940s refused the temptation to approve of a novel just because it was "anti-Nazi," her later cultural criticism insisted on applying the same moral-cultural standards to all, including Beat poets, student protestors, and even liberal intellectuals like herself. Diana Trilling's anticommunism angered 1960s radicals, while their successors have portrayed her as an outdated cold war warrior. If the rereading of her work carried out in chapter 5, "Making Double Judgments: The Criticism of Diana Trilling," suggests her superiority to her detractors, it is not because she was right and they were wrong about politics (though that possibility should not be discounted), instead, it is because she never let politics overwhelm the fineness of her literary and moral discriminations. Unwilling to surrender her critical integrity to any single standard, she has continued to make "double judgments" throughout her career.

In *Patriotic Gore* Edmund Wilson managed to integrate his most severe criticisms of American culture with his deepest personal involvements. His criticism of U.S. society, North and South, is surely a self-examination; during his long book Wilson becomes both the Southerner, whose desire for individual self-assertion "is the cause of us all" (434), and the Northerner, whose loyalty to the state is also an assumption of responsibility. In writing on the Civil War, Wilson renounces the earlier excitement of *To the Finland Station*, where he celebrated the Bolshevik seizure of power as "the first time in the human exploit [when] the key of a philosophy of history was to fit an historical lock" (546). By the time he writes *Patriotic Gore* Wilson no longer expects to find truth in any "philosophy of history." His representative man is now Oliver Wendell Holmes Jr., who stoically carries out his responsibilities as a citizen of the republic but spends as much time as possible in the "great world of thought and art" (781). Chapter 6, "A Masterpiece of Cultural Criticism: Edmund Wilson's *Patriotic Gore*," celebrates Edmund Wilson as an American cultural critic and affirms *Patriotic Gore* as his greatest work.

Contrary to Richard Rorty's argument for the transcendental spirit of American cultural criticism, neither Lionel Trilling, H. L. Mencken, Irving

Babbitt, Dwight Macdonald, nor Edmund Wilson desire an Emersonian liberation from the past. Ralph Ellison has proven, however, that the spirit of Emerson can foster penetrating cultural criticism. Chapter 7, "The Example of Ralph Ellison," demonstrates Ellison's firm rejection of two standing temptations of Emersonianism: the readiness to dismiss the reality of daily life in favor of a vague spirituality and the antinomianism that rejects all principles beyond the self. Ellison's ability to draw upon proverbs and folklore from the African-American experience insures that the dimension of everyday life appears in his essays with a substantiality often lacking in Emerson himself. Against Rorty's celebration of a world in which nothing is sacred, Ellison urges a continuing struggle on behalf of the tenets of the American civil religion, those "principles—democracy, equality, individual freedom, and universal justice" that still "move us as articles of faith" ("Little Man at Chehaw Station," 17). Perhaps the fame of *Invisible Man* has distracted attention from Ellison's essays. No other factor seems capable of explaining the critical neglect of *Shadow and Act* and *Going to the Territory*, two collections that explore contemporary themes such as diversity, cultural pluralism, and the connections between political and cultural democracy with the flair of a novelist and the insight of a great cultural critic.

Contemporary cultural studies is often said to derive its radical impetus from the 1960s. In part 3, "Criticism and Cultural Radicalism," studies of Leslie Fiedler and Susan Sontag consider the impact of 1960s radicalism on criticism. Chapter 8, "Innocence Regained: The Career of Leslie Fiedler," presents the work of Leslie Fiedler as a case study of the collapse of the older cultural criticism under the impact of the 1960s. Fiedler's turn to political and cultural radicalism led to his renunciation of the allegiances he had once proudly affirmed, as "a liberal, intellectual, writer, American, and Jew" (preface, *An End to Innocence,* xiii), in favor of a pose of innocence as the eternal rebel. Ironically, it is Fiedler's "cold war" essays of the 1950s that remain valuable today, while his pronouncements decrying high culture are dated by their very attempt to keep up with the fashions.

Susan Sontag began her career by announcing the "obsolescence" of traditional humanism in *Against Interpretation*. In *Styles of Radical Will* she united avant-garde culture with her own brand of radical politics; in "What's Happening in America (1966)" she achieved an apocalyptic intensity impressive even for the 1960s. Today, however, Susan Sontag is best known for works tracing the relations between illness and literature. In both *Illness as Metaphor* and *AIDS and Its Metaphors* Sontag aims to calm rather than inflame; her goal is not the intensity of madness but, instead, the balance of sanity. Though she herself emphasizes the continuity between her earlier and later works, chapter 9,

"Susan Sontag and the Possibility of Humanism," argues that the discontinuities are more interesting.

Richard Rorty argues that contemporary cultural leftists such as Fredric Jameson, Edward Said, and Stanley Fish are carrying on the tradition of cultural criticism exemplified in the United States by critics such as those discussed in part 2. Yet Jameson, Said, and Fish, like Rorty himself, give up the claim to authority of the older cultural criticism, which based its standing on the prior authority of literature or history or religion—that is, the authority of the past. Political radicals such as Edward Said and Fredric Jameson and cultural radicals such as Fish and Rorty all agree that the past is not a corrective to the present but, rather, a source of error. All neglect Christopher Lasch's point that the past provides the only "political and psychological treasury from which we draw the reserves (not necessarily in the form of 'lessons') that we need to cope with the future" (*Culture of Narcissism*, 25). Section 4, "Cultural Studies," considers Jameson, Said, and Fish as progenitors and champions of cultural studies.

Chapter 10, "Fredric Jameson: Marxism without Difficulty," examines Jameson's attempt to validate his own political-cultural agenda after discrediting traditional forms of authority. Although Jameson argues that Marxism occupies a special, transcendent position among contemporary theories, he neglects what Karl Marx himself emphasized as the key criterion distinguishing his ideas from mere philosophizing: the unity of theory and practice. In *The Political Unconscious*, in which Jameson stakes out his most emphatic revolutionary claims, he offers, instead, the authority of the utopian vision. In *Postmodernism* Jameson reaffirms his Marxism, despite the cultural and political changes in the decade between the two books. Chapter 10 considers the ways in which *Postmodernism* responds to the difficulties with which the decade 1981–91 confronted Marxists.

Edward Said, to his credit, has at least one determinate goal, that of the Palestinian revolution. His clearest and most convincing writings, *The Question of Palestine* and *Covering Islam*, make the case for that revolution while appealing to traditional values such as justice and fairness. On the other hand, in *Orientalism* and in the essays in *The World, the Text, and the Critic* Said argues that such values are forever "contingent" and therefore without general validity. In challenging orthodoxies that inhibit revolution, Said seems unaware that he is also questioning the status of revolutionary ideals, including those of the Palestinians. Chapter 11, "The Critic as Exile: On Edward Said," argues that Said's insistence on posing as an "exile" from all cultures vitiates his understanding of Islam as well as Judaism and also impoverishes his literary criticism as well, even in such a major work as *Culture and Imperialism*.

Stanley Fish acknowledges that the political consequences of seeing power as the ultimate reality of human life are anything but revolutionary, yet he insists in presenting himself as a leftist, albeit a "cultural leftist." Fish's work does have the merit of admitting the logic of the deconstructive argument with which Edward Said begins but which Said drops whenever he wishes to make a political point. On the other hand, the consistency of Fish's logic leaves him with a view of the world even more barren than that of Said. Chapter 12, "The Two Branches of the Law and Literature Movement: A Critique of Stanley Fish," considers the limitations of Fish's use of "rhetoric" as a totalizing concept for both cultural and legal studies.

The concluding section, "Cultural Conservatism, Political Liberalism," begins with a consideration of two recent attempts to make past culture available to contemporary society. Chapter 13, "Best-sellers of Cultural Conservatism: E. D. Hirsch and Allan Bloom," examines E. D. Hirsch's *Cultural Literacy* and Allan Bloom's *The Closing of the American Mind* in light of the possibility of linking cultural conservatism with an expansion rather than a contraction of democracy. Hirsch throughout claims that the carrying out of his proposals, especially the teaching of a set of core texts throughout the country, would expand democracy in a variety of ways. "Cultural literacy" would be particularly valuable for those now termed the "culturally disadvantaged" in achieving individual economic mobility. The spread of cultural literacy would also promote political democracy, since discussion can only take place on the basis of at least some shared assumptions and common vocabulary. Hirsch concludes that some version of cultural conservatism is necessary if any version of political radicalism or leftism is to gain a hearing.

Allan Bloom's formidable cultural literacy aided him in offering a sharp critique of contemporary institutions and attitudes in the name of "the philosophers." In *The Closing of the American Mind*, however, Bloom does not turn to the accumulated wisdom of the past, but, instead, to the controversial interpretations of that past inspired by Leo Strauss. In its radical dismissal of opposing opinions *The Closing of the American Mind* sometimes parallels those whom Bloom attacks most sharply. It is not difficult, for example, to find echoes of Herbert Marcuse in his ideas or, in his appeal to the force of his own personality as a basis of authenticity, to a 1960s document such as Eldridge Cleaver's *Soul On Ice*. It is Bloom's romanticism, finally, that both powers the considerable accomplishment of his best-seller and limits its achievement.

Bloom and Hirsch together, then, suggest that cultural conservatism may be compatible with "Left" as well as "Right" politics. On the other hand, neither has articulated a version of cultural conservatism that allows a substantive critique of the present; Hirsch's demystification of culture lends itself to a debunking that deprives literature and art of critical authority, while Bloom's view of culture allows for critique only by an elite few. In neither is the most important capacity of cultural conservatism allowed to function freely: the ability to criticize ourselves and our own time by standards that transcend our immediate interests.

Chapter 14, "On Cultural Self-Criticism," argues that the ability to move beyond the alternatives offered by Hirsch and Bloom, on the one hand, and cultural studies on the other, depends on a revival of a once-flourishing tradition of cultural self-criticism. Ralph Waldo Emerson speculated in 1841 that the cultural war of his own time was simply the current version of a struggle endemic to human society: "The two parties which divide the state, the party of Conservatism and that of Innovation, are very old . . . It is the opposition of Past and Future, of Memory and Hope, of the Understanding and the Reason. It is the primal antagonism." Most important, Emerson noted what it is all too easy to overlook today; the battle lines are drawn not only between generations, regions and classes but shift within each individual's "bosom . . . every hour" (173).

Theodor Adorno, whose own cultural pronouncements have the authoritative ring of papal bulls, noted that the cultural critic "speaks as if he represented either unadulterated nature or a higher historical stage. Yet he is necessarily of the same essence as that to which he fancies himself superior" (19). A good point. If critique of one's own culture is not to be mere sermonizing, then it must be self-criticism, since the critic is indeed "of the same essence"—part of the same culture—as that which he or she criticizes. It follows that in intellectual and cultural matters total victory and unconditional surrender are rarely either possible or desirable. The cultural critic is wise to remember that a willingness to point out the limitations of others does not insure that one will not suffer from similar flaws of tone, rhetoric, and implication.

Chapter 15 includes a consideration of the intellectual history of diversity as an ultimate value that raises questions about its contemporary use in cultural studies and elsewhere. The title of *Cultural Conservatism, Political Liberalism* announces the agenda of the book as a whole, and both the conservatism and the liberalism are reaffirmed in the final chapter. Nevertheless, both the critique of the contemporary cultural Left, and, especially, the affirmation of the older cultural criticism must stand or fall on their own merits. The goal throughout is not to polarize but to clarify, not to contribute to the victory of one side over another in the culture wars but to aid in the revival of a tradition in which critique was tempered by a recognition that the best cultural criticism involves self-criticism. Revival and tradition are themselves, of course, fighting words to some. Perhaps it is impossible to find a spot above the battle in the culture wars. The author writes, then, as a partisan, but as one who aspires to the larger partisanship T. S. Eliot shared with Matthew Arnold and the philosopher F. H. Bradley against the reigning utilitarianism: "we fight rather to keep something alive than in the expectation that anything will triumph" (52–53).

Part 1

The Premises

Chapter 1

Richard Rorty: Pragmatism and Cultural Criticism

Unlike Fredric Jameson, Richard Rorty does not grant a privileged, foundational status to any metanarrative, including the Marxist. Unlike Edward Said, Rorty does not claim any special insight as an outsider, victim, or exile. Unlike Stanley Fish, who argues that there really isn't any difference between being persuaded by rhetoric and being compelled by force, Richard Rorty believes that the difference is so important that it provides a yardstick for measuring human progress ("Cosmopolitanism without Emancipation," 216).

Even for critics of Rorty, such differences between his outlook and that of the cultural Left in general are worth emphasizing. Jameson, Said, and Fish are representative in presenting the postmodernist consensus as the achievement of rigorous thought. Failure to agree indicates either a weak mind or willful, self-interested hypocrisy. Ideological adversaries, that is, are either fools or knaves. Rorty, a professional philosopher despite himself, is not so impressed with the logic of postmodernist discourse. According to Rorty, the prestige of the postmodernist consensus has little to do with logic.

Rorty believes that Derrida and his allies are right when they refuse to provide reasons for their views:

> When philosophers like Derrida say things like "there is nothing outside the text" they are not making theoretical remarks, remarks backed up by epistemological or semantic arguments. Rather they are saying . . . that a certain framework of interconnected ideas . . . ought to be abandoned. They are not . . . claiming to have discovered the *real* nature of truth or language or literature. ("Nineteenth-Century Idealism," 140))

Rorty criticizes Derrida and his American disciples when they succumb "to the lure of philosophical system-building" ("Philosophy as a Kind of Writing," 99).

Derrida, and, a fortiori, his exponents and vulgarizers, lack "any interesting arguments" for their proposals (98). The proposals themselves are interesting not because they solve philosophical puzzles, but because they suggest that we can get away with ignoring the puzzles and go on to other things. Whereas many American commentators present Derrida as a philosopher of language, a kind of postmodernist Ferdinand de Saussure, Rorty argues that

> Derrida is in the same situation in regard to language that many of us sec-
> ularists are in regard to God. It isn't that we believe in God, or don't
> believe in God, or have suspended judgment about God, or consider that
> the God of theism is an inadequate symbol of our ultimate concern; it is
> just that we wish we didn't have to have a view about God . . . We just
> regret the fact that the word is used so much. (97–98)

One of the effects of Rorty's presentation is to encourage those readers who share his views to retain a certain respect for those who dissent. The dissenters need not be regarded as either weak-minded or culpably biased. As Rorty points out in the introduction to *Consequences of Pragmatism*, there are no "fast little arguments" against foundationalism or even against belief in God (xxxvii). Objectors to postmodernism, therefore, cannot be dismissed as mere obscurantists or irrationalists.

Stanley Fish and Richard Rorty agree that there is no direct link between "antifoundationalism" and any particular politics. Unlike Fish, however, Rorty wants to connect his philosophy to his politics—if not by the ties of logical implication, then by some other means. Rorty is willing to acknowledge that pragmatism as a mere theory of truth may be a tool for dictators. He remembers Mussolini's attraction to pragmatism and concedes that pragmatism provided no logical device "to answer Hitler." In response Rorty argues that Mussolini's knowledge of pragmatism was sketchy and that pragmatism's lack of usefulness against Nazism is not the fault of pragmatism itself but an illustration of the limitations of philosophy in general:

> this inability to answer Hitler is not the result of pragmatism being
> a wicked or an inadequate philosophy. *Philosophy* is just not the right
> place to look for responses to mad tyrants, or Nietzschean bully-boys, or
> complacent, heartless Thatcherites and Reaganites. ("Just One More
> Species," 6)

Rorty goes on to claim, however, that a belief in "universal, objective truths," a point of view he calls "anti-pragmatism," serves the purposes of "governments which have no use for social democracy" (6). This thesis seems to be special pleading. Yes, the Spanish Inquisition based its authority on the certainty of Catholicism, but in the twentieth century the most egregious dictatorships have demonstrated a marked hostility to "universal, objective truths." Totalitarian governments seem to view such truths as an implicit challenge to their rule. Both the Fascists and the Nazis emphasized their break with idealist philosophies and indeed with all fixed standards against which the conduct of government or party might be measured, while dialectical materialism, the official philosophy of Stalinism, rejected any fixed morality and emphasized that the essence of the cosmos is change.

As *1984* suggests so vividly, a belief in the malleability of the past is an aid to totalitarian rule, while a conviction that what has happened cannot be altered provides a refuge for individual resistance to the mobilization of the self. If pragmatism can be taken to mean that the truth is whatever works, its influence must sometimes have strengthened the impulse to justify whatever means might be necessary for a ruling party (fascist, Nazi, Stalinist, or any other) to accomplish its objectives. On the other hand, if the "universal, objective truths" Rorty worries about are, for example, the "self-evident truths" of the Declaration of Independence, their influence seems much more likely to work on behalf of freedom rather than tyranny. Abraham Lincoln, at least, believed that the Declaration's assertion that "all men are created equal" was written precisely in order to interpose "a stumbling block to those who in after times might seek to turn a free people back into the hateful paths of despotism." Lincoln did not suppose that the Declaration in itself could prevent tyranny, but he did assert that the "plain unmistakable language of the Declaration" would provide would-be tyrants with "at least one hard nut to crack" ("Speech on Dred Scott Decision," 398–99).

Richard Rorty emphasizes the strong affinities between left-liberalism and American pragmatism, especially the version promulgated by John Dewey. Rorty makes the case for such links in a number of sometimes contradictory assertions. He describes Deweyan pragmatism as "a philosophy tailored to the needs of political liberalism, a way of making political liberalism look good to persons with philosophical tastes" ("Cosmopolitanism without Emancipation," 211). Elsewhere he makes the more limited claim that pragmatism provides the service of "clearing the ground" for "democratic politics" ("Introduction: Anti-representationalism" 13). On another occasion, Rorty finds that connections between American pragmatism and "social democracy" derive from "the entirely contingent fact" that many American pragmatists have discovered "the romance of American democracy" by reading Emerson and Whitman ("Just One More Species" 6).

These conflicting claims arouse the suspicion that the relation between Dewey's pragmatism and democracy is more equivocal than Rorty would like to think. The usual criticism of Dewey's pragmatism as a political influence has not been that it is insufficiently in tune with American democracy but that it provides no principled basis for criticisms of what the democratic majority may decide. This criticism is important if, with Lincoln against Stephen Douglas, one assumes that democracy means not merely the rule of the majority but also the protection of individual rights. It is not clear that Dewey's thought, especially as interpreted by Rorty, allows or encourages the checks on government available in other American traditions. Rorty's version of Deweyan pragmatism both undermines the civil religion's belief in moral standards that transcend even American self-interest and removes the restraints built into the natural law tradition invoked in the Declaration of Independence. Furthermore, the limitations on governmental power that a written Constitution has so far imposed would vanish if Rorty's "textualist" acceptance of theories that preclude offering the words of a text as evidence for or against interpretation becomes accepted doctrine.

Rorty points to pragmatism's affinities with romanticism as the strongest evidence for its contemporary usefulness for American democracy. He argues that John Dewey himself is best understood as a romantic who throughout his philosophical career was in "romantic pursuit of a fully, egalitarian, fully democratic America" and whose most important political accomplishment was keeping "Emersonian romance alive in a period when people like Walter Lippmann . . . were pooh-poohing it in the name of 'practical politics'"("Just One More Species" 6). Rorty answers Dewey's critics by arguing that he possessed a "bolder philosophical imagination, and a more passionate social hope" than any of them:

> Dewey was as romantic a communitarian as Frank and Mumford were, or as Alasdair MacIntyre and Robert Bellah are. But his romanticism was more radical. His vision was of a community bound together by romance alone, by a shared quest rather than shared principles, a shared willingness to experiment rather than settled convictions. (7)

One may accept Rorty's thesis that Dewey was indeed a radical romantic and still question whether a tendency to inflame romantic enthusiasm is necessarily a recommendation for a political philosophy. In an essay praising Roberto Ungar and Cornelius Castoriadis as romantic radicals, Rorty does stop to consider that romanticism in politics has had catastrophic consequences in the twentieth century:

> Romanticism, after all, was common to Mussolini, Hitler, Lenin, and Mao—to all the leaders who summoned a nation to slough off its past in an act of passionate self-renewal, and whose therapy proved far worse than the disease—as well as to Schiller, Shelley, Fichte, and Whitman. ("Unger, Castoriadis," 189)

The enormous disproportion between the evil done by the first four mentioned as against any possible good achieved by the second quartet would seem to demand that any political attitudes susceptible to identification as romantic should be regarded with extreme suspicion. This suspicion grows the more one reflects on the politics of Schiller, Shelley, Fichte, and Whitman—four writers whose careers are presumably supposed to provide the strongest evidence available for demonstrating the beneficient influence of romanticism on politics. But Fichte's nationalism was virulently anti-Semitic and Whitman's expansive view of America involved an imperialist program far beyond any the capitalist politicians themselves ever implemented, while Shelley and Schiller were generally ineffectual as politicians. A comparison of the two foursomes might suggest that romanticism in politics has great power to do evil but is largely impotent when it is, allegedly, benign.

Milan Kundera, an author whose "account of the novel as the vehicle of a revolt against the ontotheological treatise" seems exemplary to Rorty ("Heidegger, Kundera, and Dickens" 68), warns in *Life is Elsewhere* of a particular affinity between totalitarianism and romantic poets. The intellectual atmosphere that Rorty himself believes most suitable for democracy does not seem particularly romantic:

> What is needed is a sort of intellectual analogue of civic virtue—tolerance, irony, and a willingness to let spheres of culture flourish without worrying too much about their "common ground," "their unification," the "intrinsic ideals" they suggest, or what picture of man they "presuppose." ("Habermas and Lyotard," 171)

Rorty's attraction to romanticism, and particularly to its American sources in Emerson and Whitman, colors and arguably distorts his notion of "culture criticism" when it leads him to take Emerson as the central, defining example of the cultural critic. The point is important, since Rorty argues that one of the central results of the triumph of the pragmatic outlook would be to supplant "Philosophy"—that is, the tradition of European thought in which Plato, Descartes, and Kant are central figures— with "what is sometimes called 'culture criticism'" ("Introduction: Pragmatism and Philosophy," xl). Rorty argues that "culture criticism" is a product of "transcendentalist culture," of which Ralph Waldo Emerson is the great American representative. Culture criticism is transcendental, according to Rorty, not so much because it "transcends" disciplinary boundaries, though it does that, but because its practitioners adopt a viewpoint that transcends the concerns of moral and aesthetic judgment:

> In this form of life, the true and the good and the beautiful drop out. The aim is to understand, not to judge. The hope is that if one understands enough poems, enough religions, enough societies, enough philosophies, one will have made oneself into something worth one's understanding. ("Professionalized Philosophy," 66)

For Rorty the "transcendentalist point of view is the mark of the highbrow" (67), the intellectual who may lack the knowledge of the scholar or the methodology of a researcher but who writes about philosophy, literature, and politics with equal authority.

The transcendental culture criticism described by Rorty may very well take the place of traditional philosophy, as Rorty predicts and hopes. It is a historical error, however, to assert, as Rorty does, that the attitude he describes accurately characterizes the cultural criticism to which he refers, specifically "the sort of writing done by T. S. Eliot and Edmund Wilson, by Lionel Trilling and Paul Goodman" (68). Whatever may be the case with Emerson, it is not accurate to suggest that questions of morality and aesthetics "drop out" in the writings of T. S. Eliot, Edmund Wilson, Lionel Trilling, and Paul Goodman, the writers mentioned by Rorty. It would be equally inaccurate to suggest that morality and aesthetics drop out of the work of any of the cultural critics discussed in part 2 of the present study.

The issue here is not simply a matter of terminology. The older tradition of cultural criticism can still provide a valuable example that can aid Americans in debating their conflicting ideas about religion, politics, morality, and literature. The cultural criticism of figures like Lionel Trilling and Edmund Wilson, to mention two figures cited by Rorty and also featured in this book, deserves to be reconsidered, in large part because such criticism provides examples of the way in which considerations about the beautiful (for example, in literature) may throw light on the good (for example, in personal morality) and how such thoughts about the good and the beautiful may lead to insights about the just (for example, in national politics). If these critics merely allowed questions about the true, the good, and the beautiful to drop out—if this tradition itself were, that is, already "transcendental," in Rorty's sense of the word—then it would provide no alternative to the postmodernist versions of cultural studies that now provide the "cutting edge" of humanistic studies and exert their influence in the larger culture as well.

Lionel Trilling, H. L. Mencken, Irving Babbitt, Dwight Macdonald, Diana Trilling, and Edmund Wilson might be thought of as forming an anti-Emersonian, antiromantic tradition, in that they all oppose the set of attitudes—boundless optimism, the rejection of limits, lack of interest in contingent, material facts—that have made up popular Emersonianism. In Ralph Ellison's work the influence of Emerson emerges filtered through the prism of African-American experience, resulting in an individual perspective that yokes Emersonian hope to a confrontation with the realities of everyday life. These critics, including Ellison, are cultural conservatives in that they acknowledge the authority of literature, especially the literary works generally acknowledged as classics, as a source of truth about the human condition. They are public critics in that their authority is derived from nothing more mysterious than the presumption, which they share with at least part of the public, that a close and thoughtful reading of literature and of belles lettres generally—history, philosophy, biography, etc.—can throw light on moral issues and political dilemmas. It is one of the purposes of this book to suggest that this older tradition of cultural criticism provides insights about society, culture, and politics that even those on the political Left today might find valuable. For academics and critics a revival of interest in this tradition might provide a notion of cultural criticism as something distinct from the cultural studies associated today with figures such as Fredric Jameson, Edward Said, and Stanley Fish. The following chapters attempt to make good this claim not by presenting theoretical arguments but by providing examples, in accord with Rorty's own preference for "examples rather than principles" ("Pragmatism, Relativism, Irrationalism," 173).

Before going on to consider some representative works of the earlier tradition, the relation between the overall argument and Richard Rorty's pragmatism should be clarified. In his essay on "Nineteenth-Century Idealism and Twentieth-Century Textualism" Rorty emphasizes that textualism—antifoundationalist, postmodernist thought—is vulnerable to criticism not on the basis of a theory of reality but on the question of its possible socio-political effects. In Rorty's words, "The serious objections to textualism, I think, are not episte-mological but moral" (156). There are, indeed, some serious moral-political objections to be raised. It is not clear that Deweyan pragmatism has been as beneficient politically as Rorty finds it. Rorty's defense of American pragma-tism as a version of romanticism raises even more questions, since political romanticism has a checkered history, to say the least. Furthermore, Rorty's characterization of culture criticism seems wildly misleading as a description of the outlook of Lionel Trilling and the writers considered in chapters 3 through 7.

Rorty acknowledges that there is a good deal to be said on behalf of the traditional humanism which textualism—or pragmatism or postmodernism—seems to be displacing. Although he usually emphasizes the democratic affinities of Dewey's pragmatism, in his essay on "Nineteenth-Century Idealism and Twentieth-Century Textualism" Rorty admits, in a passage whose generous eloquence demands extensive quotation, that it is the other side, the nontextu-alists, the traditional humanists, whose "view" is favorable to democracy, since theirs is

> the view that, in the end, when all the intellectuals have done all their tricks, morality remains widely shared and available to reflection—some-thing capable of being discovered rather than created, because already implicit in the common consciousness of everyone . . . It is the side which is democratic rather than elitist, which regards culture as in the service of the people. Trilling and Abrams and Graff [Rorty is referring to the Ger-ald Graff of *Literature Against Itself*] do not want there to *be* a sacred wisdom which takes precedence over the common moral consciousness. . . . Because they want criticism to bring an antecedent morality to light, enlarge upon it and enrich it, they resist the suggestion that there is no common vocabulary in terms of which critics can argue with one another about how well this task has been performed. (157–58)

With honesty that is more impressive than any dialectical turn, Rorty admits his own perplexity: "I think that this moral objection states the really important issue about textualism and about pragmatism. But I have no ready way to dis-pose of it" (158).

The search for a "ready way to dispose" of either the objection or textual-ism will continue, but the prospects for a definitive solution are not encourag-ing. In the meantime a thoroughgoing pragmatist might discover that when the strengths of the cultural criticism of Lionel Trilling and Edmund Wilson are balanced against the virtues of postmodernist discourse, the pragmatic advantage lies with the older tradition. Contrary to Rorty, that tradition does not depend on assent to the "Kantian conviction" that "morality" is "already implicit in the common consciousness of everyone" ("Nineteenth-Century Idealism," 157). Trilling, Wilson, and their peers did expect that their readers would share with them a frame of reference broad enough to allow discussion. Despite laments about the loss of a common culture, that expectation is still possible today, as Rorty himself suggests in essays such as "The Priority of Democracy to Philosophy" and "On Ethnocentrism." The issue is not one of traditional metaphysics v. textualist-pragmatic skepticism but, rather, "a matter of cultural cost-accounting," as M. H. Abrams puts it in a passage quoted by Rorty in his essay on "Nineteenth-Century Idealism and Twentieth-Century Textualism" (Abrams 295; Rorty 157). Rorty concludes that, on balance, the cultural Left is a good thing for American culture and that postmodernism is, overall, a good thing for the contemporary world.

Should we welcome the advance of a "post-Philosophical" culture? In the introduction to *Consequences of Pragmatism* Rorty himself emphasizes that this is the question that needs to be discussed, whereas theoretical questions about the nature of ultimate reality will get us nowhere:

> The question of whether the pragmatist view of truth—that it is not a profitable topic—is itself *true* is thus a question about whether a post-Philosophical culture is a good thing to try for. (xliii)

One way in which Rorty tries to focus the question is to describe the kind of intellectual that the new culture would produce; in an essay on "Freud and Moral Reflection" he makes explicit his own "assumption that the ironic, playful intellectual is a desirable character-type" (158). It would be easier to share Rorty's assumption if he would offer examples of the intellectuals he has in mind. Does he mean "ironic, playful" figures such as Jacques Derrida and Stanley Fish, or does he mean critics such as H. L. Mencken and Dwight Macdonald? By his own account, Rorty seems to mean both. In his essay on "Professionalized Philosophy and Transcendentalist Culture," in *Consequences of Pragmatism,* Rorty presents T. S. Eliot, Edmund Wilson, and Lionel Trilling, among others, as early versions of Derrida and Lacan, even though in a later essay in the same volume, "Nineteenth-Century Idealism and Twentieth-Century Textualism," he acknowledges that the triumph of postmodernism would mean the end of the culture that sustained Trilling and his like.

Another way in which Rorty tries to address the question of the desirability of the post-Philosophical world is through a comparison to the work of the Enlightenment. Although the *philosophes* indeed drastically reduced the cultural effect of traditional religion, their work was, overall, in the interests of civilization. Thus, Rorty argues in the introduction to *Consequences of Pragmatism*, the Enlightenment provides a historical example that can reconcile us to the loss of traditions that today seem irreplaceable:

> If Philosophy disappears, something will have been lost which was central to Western intellectual life. . . . But the Enlightenment thought, rightly, that what would succeed religion would be *better.* (xxxviii)

From Rorty's point of view the intellectual revolution involved in postmodernism is simply the Enlightenment's critique of religion taken one step further.

One may seek to preserve the heritage of the Enlightenment and still feel, however, that the wisest Enlighteners were those who did not make war on religion but, instead, made their peace with it. The Anglo-American Enlightenment, which created the institutions of bourgeois liberalism that Rorty rightly celebrates as the most reasonable form of social organization so far achieved, made a point of conserving religion while criticizing fanaticism. The tradition of the French Revolution, on the other hand, attempted the kind of "extirpation" that Rorty sometimes seems to favor, as when he asks the rhetorical question:

> And what should we *do* about such [metaphysical or religious] intuitions— extirpate them, or find a vocabulary which does justice to them? (xxxi)

Rorty's own answer is supplied a few pages later, when he criticizes Thomas Nagel for holding on to these same intuitions:

> For the pragmatist, the *only* thing wrong with Nagel's intuitions is that they are being used to legitimize a vocabulary (the Kantian vocabulary in morals, the Cartesian vocabulary in philosophy of mind) which the pragmatist thinks should be eradicated rather than reinforced. (xxxvii)

A pragmatist who looked at history for hints about the possible cultural and political impact of a total break with past spiritual and moral traditions would find little justification for wishing another such break upon humanity. Twentieth-century attempts at such a break include the Russian Revolution, the Nazi regime, Maoism, and, on a smaller but comparably horrendous scale, the Cambodian revolution of the Khmer Rouge. The terrible political deeds that the revolutions mentioned carried out were all justified in advance by intellectuals, who dismissed the constraints of morality and, especially, constraints based on traditional religion. Rorty tells his readers that "the pragmatist is urging that we do our best to *stop having* such intuitions, that we develop a *new* intellectual tradition." One of the intuitions that he suggests should be dropped is "If God does not exist, everything is permitted" (xxx). Based on the historical examples just reviewed, it might be prudent for contemporary intellectuals to look for the kernel of truth that might be hidden in that "intuition."

Rorty's failure to see any great difficulties attending the "extirpation," or "eradication," of traditional moral and cultural ideas seems to be connected to his desire to see the Left, including the Marxist Left, as basically well intentioned but perhaps occasionally somewhat excessive in its zeal. This desire seems odd, given Rorty's own preference for liberal institutions. He admires Sidney Hook as the most persistent voice of the "anti-ideological liberalism" that Rorty calls "the most valuable tradition of American intellectual life" ("Pragmatism without Method," 64). That characterization appears in a contribution to a festschrift for Hook published in 1983, but the sentiment is not just a matter of politeness. In 1991 Rorty asserted that the notion that John Dewey was a bit of a cold war warrior didn't bother him at all, since he believed that "the Cold War was a good war" ("Just One More Species," 6).

Nevertheless, often in his writing Rorty seems to suggest that the Left, including the Marxist Left, is A Good Thing. For Rorty "any leftist political movement—any movement which tries to call our attention to what the strong are currently doing to the weak—is a lot better than no left" ("De Man and the American Cultural Left," 137). Rorty follows that problematic characterization with one that is even more questionable: "Dialectical materialism was a pretty incoherent and silly philosophical system, and it eventually fell into the hands of mad tyrants. But it got quite a bit of good done while it lasted" (137). But "dialectical materialism" came into its own with the Bolshevik seizure of power and emerged as a full-fledged philosophy only with Stalin. Social democracy did not need dialectical materialism to justify its reforms. Where is the "quite a bit of good" that dialectical materialism did, this philosophy that provided the vocabulary for justifying the incalculable crimes of the Stalin era? One of the main functions, perhaps the central function of "dialectical materialism" during its heyday, "while it lasted," was to provide a way of justifying "what the strong are currently doing to the weak." It is difficult to imagine what historical calculus Rorty can be using when he suggests that this philosophy, because, apparently, it was leftist, must somehow have "got quite a bit of good done while it lasted."

It is likewise difficult to understand what could have led Rorty to couple Bentham and Marx in the following way: "Bentham and Marx—philosophers who have been responsible for much good in the public sphere but who are useless as advisers on the development of one's moral character" ("Freud and Moral Reflection," 156, n. 22). Bentham and Marx may be lumped together plausibly enough as figures who had a great deal to say about politics and society and very little about personal morality, but it betrays a casual attitude about human history to describe both as parallel figures "responsible for much good in the public sphere." The assertion that Marx contributed "much good in the public sphere" is scarcely intelligible without at least a qualifying statement that he was also responsible for much evil, so much that there is simply no comparison with a figure like Bentham, even if one detests utilitarianism and even if one shares Foucault's view of Benthamite reform. The view of Marx Rorty presents here—Marx as a reformer on the order of Bentham—makes sense only if one restricts one's view to the internal affairs of the United States and a few other Western democracies and avoids turning one's attention to Eastern Europe, to Asia, to Africa, to all those countries in which "Marxism" has been an ideology justifying wholesale massacre. To suggest some sort of moral equivalence between Jeremy Bentham and Karl Marx requires an extraordinarily frivolous attitude toward great historical calamities.

Rorty's characterization of the American cultural Left is also inaccurate, but at least the phenomenon at issue, a "Left" virtually powerless in the larger society but mighty at the Modern Language Association, here seems material for comedy and satire, whereas the state power of the Marxist Left in much of the world has been a matter for tragedy or for some genre beyond tragedy. Rorty believes that this Left has its heart in the right place, after all, and, even if some of its members talk rather foolishly at times, "they are still doing a lot more good than most of their critics are doing." If the latter are simply "bashing liberals," as Rorty sometimes intimates, then the point is well-taken ("De Man and the American Cultural Left," 137). If "their critics" are rethinking and reaffirming the cultural heritage that the Left wants to purge or drop entirely, Rorty's point is arguable.

Furthermore, it is not as clear as Rorty seems to suppose that the impact of the cultural Left has been or will be entirely benign. Rorty assumes that the main social effect of the cultural Left is the discouraging of prejudice against homosexuals and racial minorities. The basis for this assumption, however, is not as obvious as Rorty wishes to believe. After all, one doesn't need to be a cultural leftist to be against discrimination on the basis of sexual preference or race. As Rorty knows well, the equality of individuals is a basic precept of liberalism itself. Partisans of the cultural Left often suggest, however, that a commitment to mere equality is not enough; eager to view themselves as a moral avant-garde, cultural leftists often insist on esoteric definitions of "sexism" and "racism" that leave everybody except themselves guilty as charged. They find protofascist ethnocentrism when one defines Western culture without reference to the uniquely diabolical qualities of "logocentrism" and "phallogocentrism." Without some such assertions it would be difficult to see in what way cultural leftists might be morally superior to ordinary liberals.

Rorty assumes the sincerity and the good intentions of those on the cultural Left and supposes that their impact on society will be positive as well. One may question, however, the political and social consequences of cultural radicalism without impugning the motives of any putative avant garde. It might very well be that the news that a commitment to the equality of individuals makes one a sexist and a racist might lead many to conclude that sexism and racism are not so bad; many called upon to denounce Western culture wholesale or be called bigots might decide that bigotry seems rather reasonable. Rorty is willing to offer "Two Cheers for the Cultural Left"; this may be at least one cheer too many.

In summary, there are good pragmatic reasons why even someone who shares Rorty's textualism might very well wish to encourage the development of cultural traditions that antedate the arrival of postmodernism—not extirpate or eradicate them. What we have seen so far of the new approaches is not nearly as cheering as Rorty seems to think, and there are resources in the old that he neglects. The following chapters make a case for the continuing relevance of a tradition of cultural criticism that provides an alternative to the new superdiscipline of "cultural studies." Just because American society has often aroused high aspirations, there has never been a shortage of those willing to offer shortcuts to impossible satisfactions—personal, political, and even theoretical. Cultural critics from Mencken to Ellison, in reaction, have emphasized all the more strongly the need to take account of the realities that postmodernist discourse discounts as mere "texts" to be "rewritten."

Chapter 2

Liberalism and Literature: Richard Rorty and Lionel Trilling

Richard Rorty is on safe ground in recognizing the importance of "culture crit-icism—the sort of writing done by T. S. Eliot and Edmund Wilson, by Lionel Trilling and Paul Goodman" ("Professionalized Philosophy," 68) but on thin ice in suggesting that his own work may be viewed as a continuation of the efforts of such writers. Rorty's conception of the transcendentalism of such cul-tural critics is arguable when applied to Emerson, but it seems downright wrong in relation to, for example, Lionel Trilling. Some parallels between Rorty and Trilling are evident, however, and they are significant enough to make an extended comparison worthwhile. Both share a concern about the state of lib-eralism, and both propose the same remedy: the renewal of liberalism through literature. Rorty echoes Trilling in stressing that literature can stimulate an awareness of "contingency" (what Trilling called "the conditioned"). Both Rorty and Trilling stress that literature fosters an "ironic" perspective, for both a mark of intellectual maturity. Despite these important similarities, Trilling and Rorty differ fundamentally on the relation of literature to liberalism. The for-mer looks to literature for cultural self-criticism, the latter for reinforcement.

Trilling's doctoral dissertation on Matthew Arnold became his first book. *Matthew Arnold*, published in 1939, presented Trilling's own view of cultural criticism as well as Matthew Arnold's. Ten years later, in his preface to the sec-ond edition, Trilling declared that he felt "an even enhanced sense of his [Arnold's] standing for the intellectual virtues that are required by a complex society" and reaffirmed his own belief that "openness and flexibility of mind" were the most important of such virtues. Rorty would agree that "openness and flexibility" are peculiarly desirable attributes for the cultural critic. Trilling, however, connects such "virtues" not to a transcendentalist rejection of referentiality but, instead, to Arnold's eagerness "to see the object as it really is" (5). Here the disagreement is sharp, since in Rorty's scheme only "lowbrows" believe in an independent reality that serves as a criterion for distinguishing truth and lies; admission to conversation with Rortyian "highbrows" requires the recognition that what is important is not what is true but what is interesting. Trilling, with Matthew Arnold, thinks otherwise.

In *The Liberal Imagination* Trilling praises literature for its ability to dramatize the complexities political doctrines inevitably neglect. In later works such as *Sincerity and Authenticity* and "Mind in the Modern World" Trilling warns that literature itself can mislead. Throughout his career, however, he never stopped arguing that both literary critics and politicians should try their best "to see the object as it really is." In his 1955 collection, *The Opposing Self*, Trilling praises Keats for his "sense of the stubborn actuality of the material world" ("Poet as Hero," 37) and quotes with approval Keats's view that poetry "is not so fine a thing as philosophy—For the same reason that an eagle is not so fine a thing as a truth" (27). Rorty's intellectuals achieve transcendence through a "textualism" that frees them from the constraints of referentiality, but in "Mind in the Modern World" Trilling defends Matthew Arnold's notion of referential objectivity as the very essence of the intellectual enterprise. Although Trilling concedes that this effort "can never wholly succeed," he argues eloquently that the ideal remains central to intellectual life at its best:

> It has always seemed to me that the simplest and best definition of objectivity is contained in that phrase of Matthew Arnold's . . . objectivity is the effort "to see the object as in itself it really is." The object, whether it be a phenomenon of nature, or a work of art, or an idea or system of ideas, or a social problem, or, indeed, a person, is not to be seen as it, or he or she, appears to our habitual thought, to our predilections and prejudices, to our casual or hasty inspection, but as it really is *in itself*, in its own terms, in these alone. Objectivity, we might say, is the respect we give to the object as object, as it exists apart from us. Eventually we will probably, and properly, see the object in more terms than its own—what in itself it is seen really to be will make it an object of admiration, or an object of affection or compassion, or an object of detestation. This way of seeing the object, as something we move toward or away from, even as something we wish to destroy, is not precluded by the ideal of objectivity, which requires only that, before the personal response is given, the effort to see the object as in itself it really is be well and truly made. (122)

The notion that there is some sort of "external" reality, inescapable even if changeable, is for Trilling an important truth easily overlooked by many intellectuals. Trilling defines this reality as "the *conditioned*," that which opposes "the demand for life as pure spirit" ("William Dean Howells," 79). Trilling argues that it is a characteristic of American culture in particular to conceive of "unconditioned spirit" not as a mystical dream but as "a realizable possibility." Trilling even offers the yearning for "unconditioned spirit" as an explanation, if not an exculpation, of the Stalinist currents on the American Left. Americans who yearned for unconditioned spirit were drawn to Communism because "to the modern more-or-less thinking man, Communist society is likely to seem a close approximation to the unconditioned, to spirit making its own terms" (80).

Trilling associated himself with what he took to be George Orwell's essential criticism of the "liberal intelligentsia"—that they refused to understand the conditioned nature of life." Trilling associates "the conditioned" with the everyday world, the realm of the "familial commonplace" in which one must cope with "the hardness of the cash and the hardness of getting it, the inelegance and intractability of family things." These difficulties detract from the dignity of the intellectual, since they are all "so absurdly *conditioned*—by things, habits, local and temporary customs, and the foolish errors and solemn absurdities of the men of the past" ("George Orwell," 144).[1]

A comparison between the rhetorical uses that Trilling and Rorty make of two notions whose denotations are quite similar, Trilling's "the conditioned" and Rorty's "contingency," brings out important differences between them. For Trilling an awareness of "the conditioned" is a moral achievement even more than an intellectual one, since it requires intellectuals to recognize the limits of their own intellectuality. Trilling connects the conditioned with those realities that intellectuals of the "adversary culture" find most frustrating: the limitations of verbal manipulation, and, even more important, the close ties between the intellectuals themselves and the bourgeois world their writings condemn.

In contrast, the recognition of Rorty's contingency costs intellectuals very little and, indeed, may seem positively desirable. Rorty admires "the sort of person who faces up to the contingency of his or her own most central beliefs and desires" (*Contingency, Irony, and Solidarity* xv). In practice, however, literary intellectuals' acknowledgment of the "ungroundable" character of all beliefs is often liberating rather than frightening. It makes things easier, not more difficult. The awareness that principles are really nothing more than preferences facilitates changing one's "preferences" whenever the old ones become inconvenient. For a professional intellectual, furthermore, the news that there are no "grounds" allows a welcome latitude in devising interpretations or fashioning meanings. Rorty's contingency does not lead to a recognition of forces beyond symbolic discourse but to the postmodernist slogan that "there is nothing outside the text."

The irony of Rorty's "liberal ironist" is largely theoretical. Liberal ironists work for the diminishment of suffering, even while they recognize that there are no grounds—no "noncircular theoretical backup" (xv)—according to which cruelty can be condemned. Rorty does not suggest, however, that liberals question the quality of their organized compassion. Trilling's irony strikes closer to home. Just as Trilling told liberals that liberalism loses the truth of its original vision as it becomes institutionalized, so he insisted that the success of the "adversary culture" in the academy and the media should arouse suspicion about the oppositional quality of its projects. Writing in the milieu of literary New York, in which cultural status was based on the capacity to identify oneself with an avant-garde defined by its opposition to bourgeois culture, Trilling asks "how can irony be withheld from an accredited subversiveness, an established moral radicalism, a respectable violence?" ("Fate of Pleasure," 75). This sort of irony is beyond Rorty's liberal ironists, whose irony is only theoretical—only directed at the theoretical basis of liberal ideology, not at a consideration of the ideology itself in light of the emotional and cultural needs of its proponents.

Both Rorty and Trilling believe that literature has particular importance for political liberalism, but the function that each assigns literature illustrates a characteristic difference: for Rorty literature confirms, while for Trilling it tests and questions liberal assumptions. The fundamental assumption of liberalism, according to Rorty, is that "cruelty is the worst thing we do" (*Contingency*, xv). The Rortyian liberal turns to literature to reiterate what he or she already knows—that cruelty is evil. People who are "victims of cruelty" cannot speak for themselves, "so the job of putting their situation into language is going to have to be done for them by somebody else. The liberal novelist, poet, or journalist is good at that" (94). Although Rorty says "Literary merit is not a matter of reinforcing a widely used final vocabulary, not a matter of success in telling us what we have always known but could not express satisfactorily," what he gets out of literature is precisely a confirmation of his own philosophy, a "reinforcing" of his own ideas (167).

For Rorty the moral function of literature is exhausted by its relevance "to the avoidance of either social or individual cruelty" (141). Literature stirs self-criticism in only one, rather limited way; some books "help us see the effects of our private idiosyncrasies on others" (*Contingency*, 141). Novels, for example, are "socially useful" when they "help us attend to the springs of cruelty in ourselves" (95). A novel can "show how our attempts at autonomy, our private obsessions with the achievement of a certain sort of perfection, may make us oblivious to the pain and humiliation we are causing" (141). Liberals, that is, may learn from literature to change their private behavior, but liberal political assumptions are not questioned.

According to Rorty, literature encourages "solidarity" despite differences in "religion, race, customs" (*Contingency* 192). In an essay entitled simply "*The Princess Casamassima*" Trilling pointed out that Henry James's novel includes characters who are poor but nevertheless as "proud and intelligent" as the middle-class readers of *The Princess Casamassima* (84). Trilling argues that literature can teach liberals not merely compassion but also the harder lesson of respect, the lesson that those who suffer misfortune can be as "proud and intelligent" as those who send aid. Rorty's solidarity, in contrast, focuses on "similarities with respect to pain and humiliation" (*Contingency* 192). In Rorty's view literature should arouse "sensitivity to the pain and humiliation of others" (198). Arguing that conceptions of human equality derived from belief in "a common human essence" are no longer persuasive (91), Rorty argues that what human beings have in common is simply "the ability to feel pain" (88). Compassion, or solidarity, arises in a straightforward way from the kind of imaginative identification with "others" that literature encourages.

For Rorty solidarity becomes morally complicated in only one way, when the compassion one extends to "us" is intensified by our anger at "them." The solution, however, is not difficult: Rorty notes that it is "characteristic of liberals" like himself—"people who are more afraid of being cruel than of anything else"— to "try to extend our sense of 'we' to people whom we have previously thought of as 'they'" (192). The "ethnocentrism" of liberals is not really ethnocentrism at all: "It is the ethnocentrism of a 'we' ("we liberals") which is dedicated to enlarging itself, to creating an ever larger and more variegated *ethnos*. It is the 'we' of the people who have been brought up to distrust ethnocentrism" (198).

As postmodernists, Rortyians reject religious absolutes, but, as liberals, they claim superior moral standing based on their opposition to cruelty. The implications of this unexceptionable position are dramatized by a figure not usually recognized as a voice of liberalism—Blanche DuBois of *A Streetcar Named Desire*. In scene 10 Blanche declares her creed to an underwhelmed Stanley Kowalski: "But some things are not forgivable. Deliberate cruelty is not forgivable. It is the one unforgivable thing in my opinion and it is the one thing of which I have never, never been guilty" (146). Like Rortyian liberals, Blanche is sure that there is nothing worse than cruelty. She has been "guilty" of many things and neglectful of many more, but she can tell herself and Stanley that she has never been guilty of "the one unforgivable thing." Whatever happens, Blanche knows that she is innocent of the only crime that really matters. Leslie Fiedler found a yearning for innocence at the heart of post–World War II liberalism; the desire to assert one's innocence in a corrupt world remains an important impulse throughout American culture and perhaps especially on the Left, as the phenomenon of "political correctness" suggests. Despite Rorty's celebration of irony, his definition of liberals as the people who hate cruelty encourages the seductive (for liberals) notion that the expression of liberal opinions guarantees personal innocence in a cruel world.

Rorty seems unaware of a difficulty that bothered Trilling throughout his career: "liberal novelists" and "liberal poets" rarely write anything memorable, while the great literature of the twentieth century has been produced by figures whose hostility to liberalism is intense and virtually unanimous. In "The Function of the Little Magazine" Trilling admitted that he could not find "a single first-rate writer" who affirmed liberal ideas in their imaginative work. There is something wrong, Trilling asserted, when "there is no connection between the political ideas of our educated class and the deep places of the imagination" (94). What is it that is wrong? Because liberalism is an orthodoxy, vigorously individual thought is suspect; because it is a leftist orthodoxy, vigorous thought is politically incorrect. In the opening essay of *The Liberal Imagination*, "Reality in America," Trilling muses that on the Left stupidity seems to be valued as an indication of political soundness: "It is as if wit, and flexibility of mind, and perception, and knowledge were to be equated with aristocracy and political reaction, while dullness and stupidity must naturally suggest a virtuous democracy" (11). Trilling is explaining why the very flaws of Theodore Dreiser attract liberals while the greatness of Henry James leaves them cold. Beyond James's possession of "wit" and "flexibility of mind" and "perception," however, there is another and a more important reason why liberals are uncomfortable with Henry James.

Trilling suggests that liberals' definition of themselves as compassionate benefactors of the less fortunate prevents them from viewing those who are the objects of their compassion as complex human beings. Literature can provide a corrective to such narrowness. In *The Princess Casamassima*, for example, Henry James presents a novelistic world in which poor people are granted a full humanity. The result, argues Trilling, bruises liberal prejudices:

> That James should create poor people so proud and intelligent as to make it impossible for anyone, even the reader who has paid for the privilege, to condescend to them, so proud and intelligent indeed it is not wholly easy for them to be "good," is, one ventures to guess, an unexpressed, a never-

to-be-expressed reason for finding him "impotent in matters sociological." We who are liberal and progressive know that the poor are our equals in every sense except that of being equal to us. ("*Princess Casamassima*" 83–84)

Whereas Rorty's liberals are defined by a simple, humane opposition to cruelty, Trilling's intellectuals are more complicated beings, whose most noble aspirations are linked to morally questionable impulses. In "Manners, Morals, and the Novel" Trilling warns that "we must be aware of the dangers that lie in our most generous wishes," since "when once we have made our fellow men the objects of our enlightened interest [we] go on to make them the objects of our pity, then of our wisdom, ultimately of our coercion" (208). Trilling calls this corruption of goodness "the most ironic and tragic that man knows." Against it human beings must summon a wary "moral realism" educated by "the free play of the moral imagination." He argues further that "the most effective agent of the moral imagination has been the novel of the last two hundred years" (209). The moral task that Trilling requires of literature is considerably more difficult than Rorty's simple evoking of sympathy, but then Trilling believes that politics involves considerably more difficult moral dilemmas than the straightforward Rortyian choice between cruelty and compassion.

Trilling finds the yearning of liberal intellectuals for some absolute peace, for some utopia in which the work of moral vigilance may cease, to be not praiseworthy but positively dangerous. Trilling is not referring to a Rortyian desire for self-creation but, rather, to a seemingly opposed impulse, a yearning for the extinguishing of self in the peace of union with all. The Princess Casamassima, says Trilling, seems "the very embodiment of the modern will," since she is one of those "that despises the variety and modulations of the human story and longs for an absolute humanity, which is but another way of saying a nothingness" ("*The Princess Casamassima*" 87–88). According to Trilling, literature's unique importance derives from the inducements it offers to delight in "the variety and modulations of the human story."

Throughout his career Trilling engaged in cultural self-criticism. Writing as a liberal, he pointed to the limitations of liberalism; writing as an intellectual, he explored the self-deceptions characteristic of intellectuals. A cultural critic, he refused to accept culture itself as an ultimate standard. Like Richard Rorty today, he connected culture and politics, literature and liberalism. His work, however, may be seen as an implicit critique of Rorty's program rather than an anticipatory endorsement. The parallels between Rorty and Trilling only emphasize the continuing force of Trilling's cultural self-criticism as an alternative to the cultural studies of which Rorty imagines Trilling to be a pioneer.

Part 2

Examples

Chapter 3

Limits and Standards: Irving Babbitt and H. L. Mencken

H. L. Mencken and Irving Babbitt commanded opposing forces in the culture wars of the 1920s. Mencken led the attack on fundamentalism, Puritanism, and the genteel tradition. He viewed Babbitt as a leading proponent of the latter two and gave him no credit for avoiding the first. Babbitt, in turn, regarded Mencken as a vulgar mocker of civilized values, whose enormous popularity provided another symptom of the decline Babbitt was trying to stem. During the 1920s Mencken and his allies won most of the battles, but today the difference between victor and vanquished seems unimportant compared to the ways in which both differ from contemporary trends. While the historian may focus on the conflicts between Mencken and Babbitt, their vital significance today derives from what they shared.

They shared, for example, an ability to criticize without self-righteous vindictiveness. Mencken made fun of his satiric targets, but he rarely became morally indignant; he did not claim to be better than other people, just smarter. Irving Babbitt spoke for civilized values without professing personal sainthood, even by implication. He went to great pains to distinguish his "humanism" from "humanitarianism," arguing that only sentimentalists could expect most human beings to be guided by universal love. Self-styled humanitarians were either fooling themselves or trying to fool others. Most people, including himself, were likely to find themselves fully occupied in attempting to live up to the ordinary norms of social conduct.

Rejecting what Mencken called the "messianic delusion" that society could be transformed into an harmonious paradise through social engineering, Mencken and Babbitt both opposed prohibition and attempts to legislate morality in general. Both Mencken and Babbitt criticized Woodrow Wilson as a self-proclaimed humanitarian who employed grandiose slogans to manipulate his country into world war and, not so incidentally, to amass great power for himself. Both emphasized the importance of decency and common sense, qualities they found increasingly undervalued at a time when prohibitionists on the Right and Communists on the Left wanted nothing less than a new human being.

The reputations of Mencken and Babbitt have suffered similar vicissitudes. Both were at the peak of their influence in the 1920s, and in the 1930s both lost their audiences as literary intellectuals turned Left. The rehabilitation of the two has proceeded slowly, though there are signs of a renewed interest in both. One suspects that neither will find his way into many required reading lists in departments of cultural studies.

H. L. Mencken was probably the most influential American writer of the 1920s. He began writing as a journalist for the *Baltimore Herald* in 1899 and joined the *Baltimore Sun* in 1906, remaining with the *Sun* for the rest of his life. His intellectual career began with an interpretation of Nietzsche as an iconoclastic social Darwinist much like Mencken himself. With George Jean Nathan, Mencken edited *Vanity Fair* from 1914 to 1924 and the *American Mercury* from 1924 to 1933. Realizing that the audience for his criticism was dwindling as the Depression continued, Mencken turned to autobiography in the 1930s and to revisions of *The American Language*. While still a working newspaperman, he suffered a stroke in 1948; James T. Farrell recounted Mencken's own assessment of his situation after the stroke: "If I could read and write, I'd be content . . . I'm out of it . . . I'm a hell of a mess." Farrell added that Mencken suffered through his last days "with courage" (intro., *Prejudices: A Selection,* xvi–xvii). Mencken died in 1956 in Baltimore, on Hollins Street, in a house next to his birthplace. The great iconoclast had avoided change in his personal life.

The impact of Mencken's writings has always been more important and far different from what a rehearsal of his ideas might lead one to expect. Many of Mencken's opinions (especially the social Darwinism that he found confirmed in Nietzsche) are morally suspect as well as dated, but it is indisputable that the effect of his writings has not been to increase prejudice or reinforce conformity but, instead, quite the opposite.[1] James Farrell, a serious political leftist, admired Mencken so much that he edited a selection of Mencken's essays, *Prejudices: A Selection.* Mencken is perhaps best known for his vituperative attacks on Americans in general, but a study of his representative works, including especially his language studies, reveals Mencken's populist side. Any simple classification of him as an elitist defender of power is misleading at best.

Mencken never renounced his political and economic conservatism. His continuing championship of the "American language" as opposed to English in new and expanded editions of *The American Language* nevertheless affirmed the creativity and intelligence of the same people Mencken denounced in "On Being an American" as a "timorous, sniveling, poltroonish, ignominious mob of serfs and goose-steppers" (10). While praising American slang for its intelligence and vigor, Mencken denounced the "multitudes of American pedagogues" who continue to believe "that the natural growth of the language is wild and wicked, and that it should be regulated according to rules formulated in England" (51). The Americans who produced a term like rubberneck have little in common with the "booboisie" that Mencken berated so heartily:

> Such a term as *rubberneck* is almost a complete treatise on American psychology; it reveals the national habit of mind more clearly than any labored inquiry could ever reveal it. It has in it precisely the boldness and contempt for ordered forms that are so characteristically American, and it has too the grotesque humor of the country, and the delight in devastating opprobriums, and the acute feeling for the succinct and savory. (92)

Mencken shrewdly contrasts slang, which derives from "a kind of linguistic exuberance, an excess of word-making energy" and which at best "embodies a kind of social criticism" with "cant" (557), whose chief purpose "is to make what is said unintelligible to persons outside the group." On the other hand, says Mencken, "The essence of slang is that it is of general dispersion" (556). Before adepts in academic jargon condemn Mencken as an elitist, it is well to remember that everything he wrote was for "general dispersion." A study of several of Mencken's characteristic productions—his short book *In Defense of Women*, his essay on Theodore Roosevelt, "Roosevelt: An Autopsy," and his essay "On Living in Baltimore"—brings out the critical perspective often concealed by Mencken's surface bombast.

On the basis of Mencken's current, and largely deserved, reputation as an apologist for some of the most outrageous social and political ideas of the late nineteenth century, one might suspect that, with such a defender as the author of *In Defense of Women*, women need no enemies. The book demonstrates a number of Mencken's congenital prejudices, expressed in his usual vigorous language—for example, his view that the leaders of the women's movement of his time are not truly feminine: "The suffragette . . . represents that abnormal sub-species of woman which is almost male in its credulity and emotionality" (136).

Mencken takes it for granted that marriage is almost wholly to the advantage of women rather than men. For a woman, "getting a husband means, in a sense, enslaving an expert, and so covering up her lack of expertness, and escaping its consequences" (63). Mencken is even contemptuous of the physical beauty of women:

> This so-called beauty, of course, is almost always a pure illusion. The female body, even at its best, is very defective in form; it has harsh curves and very clumsily distributed masses; compared to it the average milk-jug, or even the average cuspidor, is a thing of intelligent and gratifying design—in brief, an objet d'art. . . . The average woman, indeed, is ungraceful, misshapen, badly colored and crudely articulated, even for a woman. (44–45)

Despite such passages, the book reveals Mencken's own identification with what he considers the superior intelligence and wisdom of women, an intelligence manifested in their practical hedonism as against the romantic illusions of men. For Mencken so-called feminine intuition is, in reality, the opposite of mysticism. Mencken argues that the doctrine of "intuition" was developed as a "refuge" that allows men to acknowledge the superior abilities of women without admitting their intelligence:

> Being disinclined to accredit this great sagacity to a mere competent intelligence, he [the average man] takes refuge behind the doctrine that it is due to some impenetrable and intangible talent for guessing correctly, some half mystical supersense, some vague (and in essence, infra-human) instinct. (25)

Feminine intuition is simply critical intelligence:

> All this intuition of which so much transcendental rubbish is merchanted is no more and no less than intelligence—intelligence so keen that it can penetrate to the hidden truth through the most formidable wrappings of false semblance and demeanor, and so little corrupted by sentimental prudery that it is equal to the even more difficult task of hauling that truth out into the light, in all its naked hideousness. (27–28)

For Mencken this capacity to see through the illusions promoted by organized society, the myths of marriage and of noble ideals in the name of which the individual is supposed to sacrifice sensual happiness, is the mark of genuine intelligence, of which women "have almost a monopoly" (9).

Mencken, however, does not believe that either sex has a monopoly of ability. High intelligence in both men and women requires a bisexual constitution: "The truth is that neither sex, without some fortifying with the complementary character of the other, is capable of its highest reaches of human endeavor" (11). Men of genius, therefore, must possess feminine qualities:

Find me an obviously intelligent man, a man free from sentimentality and illusion, a man hard to deceive, a man of the first class, and I'll show you a man with a wide streak of woman in him. . . . The essential traits and qualities of the unpolluted masculine, are at the same time the hallmarks of the numskull. (10)

The phenomena surrounding modern marriage reveal the superior critical abilities of women. The romantic idealization of marriage is a product of masculine illusions, argues Mencken. The average man possesses a set of beliefs that "makes him, above all, see a glamour of romance in a transaction which, even at its best, contains almost as much gross trafficking, at bottom, as the sale of a mule" (33). A typical man, says Mencken, sharing the "common masculine illusions about elective affinities, soul mates, love at first sight, and such phantasms" (84), succumbs immediately "to a pair of well-managed eyes, a graceful twist of the body, a synthetic complexion or a skillful display of ankles without giving the slightest thought to the fact that a whole woman is there" (48). Women, on the other hand, possess a "sagacious apprehension of the relatively feeble loveliness of the human frame" (44). Women marry primarily for economic security, and they take the initiative in courtship, contrary to male assumptions, in order to make the best deal for themselves. Mencken also notes that the male doctrine that the typical female "shies modestly at the banal carnalities of marriage itself" is merely another example of male sentimentality (35).

Mencken writes that a woman "seeks a husband, not sentimentally, but realistically" (67). She is concerned primarily about "economic security" (66), but the desire for sexual pleasure is also present. Women, then, act like intelligent hedonists who desire maximum pleasure over the long run and are not diverted from their calculations by either superficial physical attractions or by the myths of romantic love. In the important issues of everyday life they reveal their inherent superiority to men, who actually believe the illusions that sustain organized society and submit willingly to its institutions, including marriage. Women, on the defensive because of their "physical and economic inferiority," look at life with the "merciless perspicacity" otherwise found only in "men of special talent for the logical, sardonic men, cynics" (29)—men like Mencken himself. Women make use of institutions such as marriage without succumbing to the myths that sanctify them.

In politics, too, women share Mencken's values, despite his dislike for professional reformers and hence for the leaders of the women's suffrage movement. Although Mencken dislikes suffragettes, he agrees with them about the importance of their cause: "My own belief . . . is that the grant of the ballot to women will mark the beginning of an improvement in our politics, and, in the end, in our whole theory of government" (139). Eventually, says Mencken, the enfranchisement of women will lead not to the further extension of the franchise but to the restriction of the ballot to those who are really qualified: "to the small minority that is intelligent, agnostic, and self possessed—say six women to one man" (133). Unlike men, women will not be bemused by "schemes for the instantaneous overhauling of the world," since the typical woman's "experience of the impossibility of instilling sense and decency into one or two actual men, even on the most modest scale, is enough to convince her that the reformation of the whole race is hopeless" (136). In politics and society, as in marriage, women refuse to accept the traditional social myths: "They are quite without that dog-like fidelity to duty which is one of the shining marks of men . . . their fundamental philosophy is almost that of the I. W. W." (208). Mencken's assumption that men and women are born with certain definite mental traits derived from their sexual identity may have little scientific basis, and many of his assertions simply reveal his acceptance of current beliefs. It is all the more striking, then, to observe how his identification with the supposed outlook of women enables him to criticize illusions, particularly about sexuality, promulgated by established society. Throughout his career Mencken's values remained remarkably similar to those that *In Defense of Women* he identified as peculiarly women's.

An illustration of the tenacity of those values can be found in his essay "Roosevelt: An Autopsy." Mencken shared Theodore Roosevelt's basic beliefs—distrust of democracy, desire for a strong government, even the insistence that "the American people, during the next century, will have to fight to maintain their place in the sun" (131). Yet when World War I seemed to offer an opportunity to put such ideas into practice in the United States, Roosevelt and Mencken reacted in precisely contrary ways. Roosevelt, according to Mencken, simply ignored his former intense admiration for Germany and became the foremost advocate of war against the Central Powers. Roosevelt's desire for the presidency and his militarism triumphed over any intellectual consistency. Mencken, on the other hand, refused to disguise his admiration for

German society—but his admiration led him to attack the war, war propaganda, and particularly Woodrow Wilson's justification of the war in the name of "brummagem ideas . . . to the edification of a moral universe" (109). In practice Mencken's avowed Nietzscheism, with its glorification of war, gave way to a practical and shrewd refusal to accept the justifications for individual sacrifice in the name of the grand principles that Wilson specialized in promulgating.

The essay on Roosevelt also offers clues about the significance of the middle-class, bourgeois virtues for Mencken. Mencken emphasizes that Roosevelt, despite his pretensions to aristocratic virtues, was thoroughly bourgeois. Nevertheless, says Mencken at the end of the essay, Roosevelt also "had all the virtues of the fat and complacent burgher": "His disdain for affectation and prudery was magnificent. He hated all pretension save his own pretension. He had a sound respect for hard effort, for loyalty, for thrift, for honest achievement" (135). Mencken here clearly identifies with his subject, as he did in *In Defense of Women*. The complacent burgher, like the typical woman, sees the world as it really is; the freedom from any desire to reform it liberates one from illusions about its actual imperfections. Throughout his writings Mencken emphasized his fundamental contentment with both himself and his immediate environment. It was this basic security that allowed him to criticize the world around him with such abandon.

"On Living in Baltimore" explores what city life, bourgeois life, means to Mencken. For him New York is the antithesis of Baltimore:

> What makes New York so dreadful, I believe, is mainly the fact that the vast majority of its people have been forced to rid themselves of one of the oldest and most powerful of human instincts—the instinct to make a permanent home. . . . The very richest man, in New York, is never quite sure that the house he lives in now will be his next year—that he will be able to resist the constant pressure of business expansion and rising land values. (238–239)

Whereas New York is a city of apartments, Baltimore is a city of private homes, where stability is cherished. As Mencken says, "I have lived in one house in Baltimore for nearly forty-five years" (241).

It is not merely stability that makes for the virtues of bourgeois life; otherwise, the despised "husbandman," the farmer, would be at least the equal of the bourgeois. What is important for Mencken is the human relations that are possible in a city in which stability is cherished:

Human relations, in such a place, tend to assume a solid permanence . . .
His contacts are with men and women as rooted as he is. They are not
moving all the time, and so they are not changing their friends all the time
. . . But of the men I knew best when I first began going to New York,
twenty-five years ago, not one is a friend today. . . . In human relationships
that are so casual there is seldom any satisfaction. It is our fellows who
make life endurable to us, and give it a purpose and meaning; if our contacts with them are light and frivolous there is something lacking and it is
something of the very first importance. (242–43)

The last sentences of this passage seem especially moving, lacking as they do
Mencken's usual verbal fireworks and revealing a core of values very different
from the aggressive Social Darwinism he so often preached. A bourgeois for
Mencken, then, is preeminently a householder, whose personal stability and
security make possible an independent scrutiny of society and its institutions. In
Baltimore Mencken found "a tradition of sound and comfortable living" but
also something more:

A Baltimorean is not merely John Doe, an isolated individual of *Homo sapi-
ens*, exactly like every other John Doe. He is John Doe *of* a certain place—
of Baltimore, of a definite *house* in Baltimore. It is not by accident that all
the peoples of Europe, very early in their history, distinguished their very
best men by adding *of* this or that place to their names. (243)

Mencken, of course, abominated all reforms and considered reformers the
chief enemies of the good life. He reveled in his own complacency. Nevertheless, his entire body of work reveals a constant struggle against the cultural status quo. His writing never stagnates into the mere connoisseurship of pleasures;
he is always acting as "one of the bringers of light to 'the Republic,'" in
Edmund Wilson's words ("Aftermath of Mencken," 104). Mencken's tribute to
Roosevelt was all the more significant in the light of his disagreement with
Roosevelt's attempt to draw the United States into World War I. The passage
seems implicitly autobiographical and suggests again why the popular image of
Mencken as a reactionary elitist is so misleading:

What he [Roosevelt] stood most clearly in opposition to was the superior
pessimism of the three Adams brothers—the notion that the public problems of a democracy are unworthy of the thought and effort of a civilized
and self-respecting man—the sad error that lies in wait for all of us who

hold ourselves above the general. . . . There was no aristocratic reserve about him. He was not, in fact, an aristocrat at all, but a quite typical member of the upper bourgeoisie. (134)

Here, as often in his writings, Mencken transcended the elitist philosophy in which he thought he believed. Mencken surely deserves to be regarded as "dated" if his writings present little more than a comically simple-minded translation of Nietzsche into early-twentieth-century American. But that view of Mencken, to which he himself contributed not a little, has always been misleading.

Mencken was one of the great polemicists. Those interested in preventing debate from degenerating into cultural warfare might well pause to consider how Mencken integrates the strongest vituperation with the most evident good nature. Mencken's essays do not encourage hatred, nor do they divide people into the saved and the damned. Mencken considers himself intellectually superior to others, but he makes no claims to moral superiority. The result is that one leaves his essays refreshed, impressed by Mencken's own exuberance, his obvious pleasure in writing and in life. Leaving aside his callous comments on the death of William Jennings Bryan and perhaps a few other pieces, Mencken's tone in his published writings is not mean-spirited; if his opponents are presented as fools, he never intimates their wickedness; and, given his general picture of the follies to which humanity is congenitally susceptible, any individual example scarcely implies any stupidity below the norm—while Mencken is often surprised by the occasional instances of intelligence and common sense that he does run across. With self-righteousness rampant on both Right and Left Mencken is more relevant today than he has been for a long time.

In 1942 Alfred Kazin was emphatic about the datedness of Irving Babbitt, describing him and his ally Paul Elmer More as "the spiritual, if not the intellectual, children of the last Brahmins in New England" (223). George Santayana had already argued in 1931 that the "New Humanism" of the two was merely the last gasp of "The Genteel Tradition," whose sources he had identified in 1911 as the Puritanism and transcendentalism of New England. The characterization of the New Humanism by reference to declining local traditions made it plausible to assume that the memory of the New Humanism would scarcely outlast Irving Babbitt's death in 1933. In 1933 Ernest Hemingway felt that his reference in "A Natural History of the Dead" to "any self-called Humanist" required a footnote. Hemingway supplied one revealing more about the author than the New Humanism; Hemingway asked "the reader's indulgence" for referring to an "an extinct phenomenon," then justified the allusion in the story on the grounds "of its mild historical interest and because its omission would spoil the rhythm" (102). In 1939 the *New Yorker* commented that "Professor Babbitt is gone, and Humanism is forgotten, except for its incidental importance to the rhythm of Hemingway's prose" (26), while in 1942 Kazin announced confidently that the New Humanism "has passed into history" (220). These verdicts now seem premature.

Irving Babbitt was born in Dayton in 1865 and grew up in Madisonville, Ohio. As a teenager he worked on a farm, as a reporter, and as a ranch hand in Wyoming, where he was known as the Long Kid. After graduating from Harvard College with a major in classics in 1889, he taught at the College of Montana, earning enough money to enable him to return to Harvard for graduate study, where he received an A.M. degree in 1893. After teaching at Williams College for one year, Babbitt was offered a position at Harvard, where he remained the rest of his life. From the beginning of his career his relationship with Harvard was less than harmonious; he had wanted to teach in the classics department but had to settle for French. His differences with Harvard, however, could not have been resolved by a simple change of department. Throughout his career Babbitt opposed the reigning trends in American education, and he was not afraid to begin by criticizing Harvard itself. If Babbitt was to be a champion of culture, he would redefine culture itself as an arena for debate and confrontation rather than a source of genteel refinement. Just as the Irish Burke once defended and thereby reconstituted the English heritage, so Irving Babbitt, the midwestern outsider, took it upon himself to defend and redefine high culture as a vital force rather than an inducement to genteel spirituality.[2]

In his first book, *Literature and the American College*, Babbitt took on the new elective system championed by Charles W. Eliot, the president of Harvard. Harvard, Babbitt says, promotes both a Baconian "training for power, training with a view to certain practical or scientific results" (100), while its elective system reveals its acceptance of "Rousseau's idea of liberty" (98). Noting that Eliot had defended the elective system on the grounds that the "youth of eighteen is an infinitely complex organization" whose needs could not be met by any prescribed curriculum no matter how carefully selected, Babbitt comments that "the wisdom of all the ages is to be as naught compared with the inclination of a sophomore." After identifying Bacon and Rousseau as the twin founts of everything wrong with contemporary culture, Babbitt, an untenured assistant professor, sums up his president as both "a good Baconian" and "a disciple of Rousseau" (96).

Babbitt's criticism of the elective system was important in itself, but his dispute with contemporary society went beyond educational issues. To Babbitt,

President Eliot's notion of an education whose ideals were "Power and Service" only embodied the larger confusions of an era in which reason and feeling were distorted into a worship of technology, on the one hand, and the cult of sentimentality, on the other. Babbitt's humanism opposed the extremisms of both "those who mechanize life and those who sentimentalize it," as Babbitt put it in *Democracy and Leadership* (255). Babbitt had few doubts about the perniciousness of the extremes he opposed; he was unwilling, however, to convert his own approach into a competing creed. Arguing that it was the error of neoclassicism to substitute rules for judgment, Babbitt refused to define his humanism by adherence to any particular set of religious dogmas, philosophical theories, or even specific moral taboos. He did advocate adherence to a "law of measure" that warns against the extremes of either heart or head. In *Literature and the American College* Babbitt explained why no formula could provide moral answers:

> Man is a creature who is foredoomed to one-sidedness, yet who becomes humane only in proportion as he triumphs over this fatality of his nature, only as he arrives at that measure which comes from tempering his virtues, each by its opposite. (83)

Allen Tate, among others, deplored Babbitt's unwillingness to turn to religion for authority. Babbitt, however, refused to turn to any authority as a way of foreclosing the debate over the consequences of modernity. In "What I Believe" he referred to himself as a "thorough-going modern" (9). He not only refused to take anything on faith but insisted on experience as the final judge of all truth. Where Babbitt differed from other moderns—how, in his own formulation, he was more "thorough-going"—was in his broader view of both experience and the self. He was willing to consider not only his own experience but also that of past generations in looking for standards of art and conduct and, in considering the self, to note the reality not only of impulse but also of "vital control" (14).

In "What I Believe" Babbitt called his position a "positive and critical humanism" (14), differentiating it both from traditions depending on the prestige of a social class and those derived from the certitudes of authority. He respected Christianity and classical antiquity, but he refused to accept the affirmations of either on faith alone. In a 1920 essay on "English and the Discipline of Ideas" he argued that "our most urgent problem just now is how to preserve in a positive and critical form the soul of truth in the two great traditions, classical and Christian, that are crumbling as mere dogma" (69). The importance of this task has been affirmed not only by conservative thinkers but by the critical theory that is one of the most important sources of today's cultural radicalism. In the late 1930s Herbert Marcuse argued that critical theory, by which he meant an intelligent Marxism, differed from ordinary sociology in just this respect:

> When critical theory comes to terms with philosophy, it is interested in the truth content of philosophical concepts and problems. It presupposes that they really contain truth. The enterprise of the sociology of knowledge, to the contrary, is occupied only with the untruths, not the truths of previous philosophy. (147–48).

Not only Babbitt's method but also his conclusions often suggest striking parallels to contemporary radicals who regard Babbitt, if they notice him at all, only as an adversary. Babbitt's critique of imperialism, for example, today sounds like a critique from the Left, yet it is straightforwardly derived from the basic tenets of Babbitt's humanism. Furthermore, Babbitt makes a convincing argument that it is precisely "left" democratic idealists who are most likely to find excuses for empire. Babbitt criticizes President Eliot's view of education as "training for service and training for power" (*Literature,* 63) in part because he believes that "the will to power is, on the whole, more than a match for the will to service" ("What I Believe," 8). Power unchecked by either traditional religion or the *frein vital* of the humanist would have little trouble using the most idealistic and democratic sentiments to justify imperialist actions. In *Democracy and Leadership* Babbitt notes that "to be fraternal in Walt Whitman's sense is to be boundlessly expansive" (267). Babbitt adds that the political consequence of such expansiveness, no matter how idealistic the motive, is simple imperialism:

> If we go, not by what Americans feel about themselves, but by what they have actually done, one must conclude that we have shown ourselves thus far consistently expansive, in other words, a consistently imperialistic, people. (268)

A look at Walt Whitman's *Democratic Vistas,* usually considered a central text of American democratic idealism, confirms Babbitt's point. Whitman prophesies:

> Long ere the second centennial arrives, there will be some forty to fifty great States, among them Canada and Cuba. The Pacific will be ours, and the Atlantic mainly ours . . . The individuality of one nation must then, as

always, lead the world. Can there be any doubt who the leader ought to be? (981)

You [America] said in your soul I will be empire of empires, overshadowing all else, past and present . . . I alone inaugurating largeness, culminating time. (990)

The point of noting such passages is not so much to quarrel with Whitman as it is to suggest that the language of romantic idealism, however democratic, can easily be converted into a defense of imperialist expansion. Babbitt's emphasis on the need for self-scrutiny and self-restraint, his distrust of the expansive impulses of both the individual and the nation, seem necessary correctives for a society all too ready to believe in its own innocence.

If Babbitt's critique of imperialism makes an argument congenial to the political Left, his distinction between humanism and humanitarianism raises pertinent questions that leftist rhetoric usually leaves unexamined. What could possibly be wrong with humanitarianism, with a movement based on love for all human beings? Babbitt's emphasis on the "law of measure" suggests that any emotion or movement, if carried to an extreme, turns into its opposite. Thus, Babbitt argues in *Literature and the American College*, "An unrestricted application of the law of love to secular affairs will lead, not to love, but to its opposite, hatred" (106). The rhetoric of the "humanitarian crusader" both justifies and conceals "the will to power" (*Democracy*, 286). Babbitt's insight is supported by allies whose thought is otherwise far removed from his own. Sigmund Freud, for example, observed that any generalized love is inevitably balanced by the opposing impulse toward aggression, so that, for instance,

once the apostle Paul had laid down universal love between all men as the foundation of his Christian community, the inevitable consequence in Christianity was the utmost intolerance towards all those who remained outside of it. (65)

Likewise, Thomas Mann, in *Reflections of a Nonpolitical Man,* notes that "humanitarian is not always the same as humane" (43) and asks, "Could it be true that universal love, loved directed far away, only flourishes at the cost of the ability to love 'closer at hand,' there, you see, where love has its only reality?" (138).

Babbitt's critique of humanitarianism does not mean that the humanist should be entirely self-absorbed. It is true that Babbitt observes that the humanist attempts self-reform while the humanitarian tries to reform others. But humanistic culture for Babbitt is never merely a source of aesthetic pleasure for the individual. Although he was suspicious of attempts to legislate morality—such as the prohibitionist Eighteenth Amendment—Babbitt did believe that the cultural critic served an important public function as a mediator between the heritage of the past and the problems of the present. The critic should speak to the public at large, reformulating the insights of the past in the language of the present and rethinking them as well. For Babbitt this meant an unending attempt to study literature and to analyze critically both religion and philosophy in search of truths that could withstand the criticism of a modernism that rejected all appeals to authority. Babbitt undertook this search because his own critical sense required it but also because he felt that only one who spoke the language and accepted the assumptions of modernity could hope to influence contemporary society.

For H. L. Mencken, Babbitt's emphasis on the moral implications of literature reduced him to just another puritanical crusader, despite Babbitt's sharp critique of the crusading impulse. Mencken argued that the civilized critic should simply sit back and enjoy the show provided by the United States. Surveying "The National Letters," Mencken viewed humanism's criticisms of U.S. society as nothing more than "the alarms of schoolmasters" (22). Mencken declared that he himself took positive pleasure in "the whole, gross, glittering, excessively dynamic, infinitely grotesque, incredibly stupendous drama of American life" (23).

In "The Genteel Tradition at Bay" George Santayana offered much the same critique as Mencken in more measured language and in a more comprehensive way. Like Mencken, Santayana argued that a genuine humanism would avoid moral criticisms of the contemporary but would seek, rather, to understand it and, as well, to enjoy the show: "Why not frankly rejoice in the benefits, so new and extraordinary, which our state of society affords? . . . at least (besides football) haven't we Einstein and Freud, Proust and Paul Valéry, Lenin and Mussolini?" (163). Irving Babbitt, however, was not ready to simply enjoy "Lenin and Mussolini" as dramatic figures in an exciting play, nor was he ready to view the excesses of U.S. society as entertainment. He was worried that the United States might be subjected to the rule of "humanitarian crusaders" who, in their zeal for the crusade, would be only too eager to reject the limitations of the Constitution for the "direct action" of a charismatic leader (*Democracy*, 183). Babbitt's humanism resists channeling into the service of any self-proclaimed savior. In "What I Believe" Babbitt offered the unheroic, everyday virtues of "moderation, common sense, and common decency" as the central humanistic virtues (13). For Babbitt one of the dangers of romanticism was precisely its tendency to glorify violence for its own sake. Today, when Nietzsche and Heidegger are venerated as spiritual seers, it is well to recall Babbitt's prescient warning, written in 1924, well before the rise of Nazism: "The Nietzschean . . . expansion of the will to power . . . would lead in practice to horrible violence and finally to the death of civilization" (*Democracy*, 259).

In the Great Depression it seemed reasonable to assume that the New Humanism was dead. Almost sixty years after Babbitt's death, however, his stature as a cultural critic seems evident. His refusal to accept the progress of science and technology as an unmitigated good, his critique of imperialism, and his emphasis on the need for limits have all been vindicated by events. Nor did Babbitt's search for "standards" involve an unexamined ethnocentrism; in "Buddha and the Occident" he specifically condemned any Western "assumption of superiority" (225). Babbitt praised Eastern thought not, in stereotypical fashion, for its mystical intuition, but, rather, for the rationality and self-criticism often associated exclusively with the West. Babbitt rejected the parochialism and blandness of the genteel tradition for an unsparing, still pertinent analysis of the dominant trends of modern culture. It is easy enough for us to spot his prejudices and limitations; we might better, however, allow his writings to point us to the self-criticism that Babbitt championed as the central activity of the true humanist.

In another, more personal way Babbitt was vindicated long ago. In 1933 Hemingway, or at least the narrator of "A Natural History of the Dead," asserted "So now I want to see the death of any self-called Humanist"; Hemingway (or the narrator) voiced the hope that he would "live to see the actual death of members of this literary sect and watch the noble exits that they may make" (102), apparently in the belief that the nearness of death would shake the "decorum" that Irving Babbitt claimed to live by. Irving Babbitt died of ulcerative colitis on 15 July, 1933. Through the middle of April Babbitt insisted on continuing to lecture, and he continued to grade exams and theses at home almost until his death. When urged to quit he responded, "When a man has been hired to do a job, it's only decent to stick to it to the end." Given ulcerative colitis, it is accurate to describe such a resolve as "definitely heroic."[3] Babbitt defined the humanist virtues as "moderation, common sense, and common decency." These are usually considered unheroic, but perhaps that deserves reconsideration too.

Mencken and Babbitt alike emphasized the virtues of peaceful, daily life— moderation, civility, good manners—as distinct from the virtues associated with those attempting to save the world by force or otherwise, such as unbending principle, total commitment, absolute sincerity. Both rejected the self-righteousness so typical of American militants of both the Right and the Left. Their cultural criticism was based on both common sense and on the authority of a cultural heritage validated by experience. Neither was willing to accept the authority of a genteel tradition that simply ignored large aspects of human life. Both were cultural conservatives ready to criticize the present in the light of the experience made available in literature and history; today their objections to imperialism and to "messianic delusions" in general make their criticisms relevant to the contemporary follies of both Left and Right.

Chapter Four

Beyond "Masscult" and "Midcult": The Achievement of Dwight Macdonald

In the essays that make up *Against the American Grain* (1962) Dwight Macdonald formulated the positions on mass culture, or "masscult" (his own preferred term, since he denied that the phenomena designated constituted any sort of culture at all), often taken as his entire intellectual legacy. Since *Against the American Grain* is typically remembered as an example of "traditional elitist" criticism, to use Michael Real's representative phrasing (17), it is only too easy to "place" Macdonald himself, grant his historical importance, and then ignore him. Even John Simon's eulogy, published as the introduction to the 1983 edition of *Against the American Grain*, asks us merely to remember Macdonald as a "hard-working elitist" rather than one of "the lazy sort." Although Simon's point is that Macdonald was an elitist who "would eagerly help others join the club" (vi), it is a point likely to be lost on those for whom the term elitist carries a moral charge roughly equivalent to fascist. Those who have never read anything by Dwight Macdonald but have only heard about him in cultural studies classes are likely to think of Macdonald as a sort of customs official examining the documents of those wishing to enter the realm of High Culture. Those who go on to read *Against the American Grain* are likely to discover a writer whose prose is marked by nasty glee when, as almost always happens, he finds the documents insufficient for entry. Some such caricature seems to be the general picture of Macdonald that remains available in the general culture; its influence, unfortunately, is likely to deter many from seeking out the insights that Macdonald's works still offer.[1]

It is true that much in *Against the American Grain* encourages the pigeonholing of Macdonald as a "traditional elitist," hard-working or otherwise. Although he declares at the beginning of the book that "it is precisely because

I do believe in the potentialities of ordinary people that I criticize Masscult"
(11), in practice he seems uninterested in "masscult" and quite willing to leave
"ordinary people" to their own devices:

> The great majority of people at any given time (including most of the rul-
> ing class for that matter) have never cared enough about such things to
> make them an important part of their lives. So let the masses have their
> Masscult, let the few who care about good writing, painting, music, archi-
> tecture, philosophy, etc., have their High Culture. (73)

The "liberal-cum-Marxian hope for a new democratic, classless culture" has
proved fallacious (70); the best one can hope for, according to Macdonald,
"would be to revive the spirit of the old avant-garde, that is to re-create a cultural—as against a social, political, or economic—elite as a countermovement
to both Masscult and Midcult" (70).

Macdonald thus takes his place with Ortega Y Gasset and others who
argue for the legitimacy of cultural elitism while disavowing political or economic elitism.[2] Macdonald apparently considers masscult to be beneath the
need for critical scrutiny: "It is not just unsuccessful art. It is non-art. It is even
anti-art" (70). It is the pretensions of midcult that call for debunking, whereas
mass culture should simply be recognized for what it is and then ignored: "let
the masses have their Masscult, let the few . . . have their High Culture, and
don't fuzz up the distinction with Midcult" (73). Macdonald's opening historical description of the origins of mass culture, short on examples and unoriginal
in theory, seems perfunctory, especially next to his incisive critiques of such
midcult favorites as Thornton Wilder's *Our Town* or James Gould Cozzens's *By
Love Possessed*.

If Macdonald had never written anything except *Against the American
Grain*, he would remain an important cultural critic. It is, however, fundamentally misleading to see Macdonald's work through the prism of the opening
chapter of *Against the American Grain*. Macdonald's essays in *Politics*, written during and in the aftermath of World War II and collected in *Memoirs of a Revolutionist* (1956), remain central documents for any discussion of the dilemmas facing intellectuals who attempt to analyze their own culture. More surprisingly,
the film criticism collected in *Dwight Macdonald on Movies* (1969), most of which
was written after *Against the American Grain*, reveals that Macdonald's working
involvement with popular entertainment implicitly repudiated the rigid categories of the earlier book. A reconsideration of the *Politics* essays and the later
film criticism brings out the complexity of Dwight Macdonald's achievement

and demonstrates the folly of dismissing him as a textbook example of "traditional elitism."

Politics, which was edited and published by Macdonald himself (his wife was the business manager), deserves discussion on its own merits. The journal's first issue was published in February 1944, when almost all shades of political opinion were agreed on a moratorium on debate until the war was won. In this atmosphere Macdonald and his contributors asserted their moral and political independence, refusing to reduce the issues surrounding the conduct of the war to tactics alone. Macdonald raised the strategic question about whether the Allied policy of "unconditional surrender" prevented the growth of dissident groups within Germany and Japan. He used his talents as a literary critic to analyze General George Patton's "flat and theatrical, brutal and hysterical, coarse and affected, violent and empty" D-Day speech to his troops, arguing that Patton's speech was "typical of the style of this war" ("My Favorite General," 96).

In a series of articles on "The Responsibility of Peoples" Macdonald analyzed the question of war guilt and, at a time when all Germans were being condemned by both Left and Right as war criminals, argued that the concept of moral responsibility could not be applied to an entire people. Indeed, Macdonald demonstrated that the attempt to identify Nazism with the German people, although presenting itself as the expression of ultra anti-Nazism, led to the conclusion that actual Nazi officials were not to be singled out for blame: "All are guilty; therefore no one is more guilty than another; therefore the Nazis and the *junkers* are no more guilty than their opponents" (67). Macdonald noted that the argument had the effect of transforming "the most extreme anti-Nazism . . . into its dialectical opposite" ("Responsibility of Peoples," 69).

Macdonald's essays on "The Responsibility of Peoples" reveal his ability to maintain the moral and intellectual independence to make critical distinctions at a time when many on both Right and Left were eager to prove their anti-Nazi credentials by condemning everything and everybody German. These writings retain their moral and intellectual importance, not only in regard to war guilt but also in the discussion of individual and collective responsibility in other areas, such as popular culture. In response to criticism from readers of *Politics*, Macdonald changed and deepened his conception of collective responsibility in a way that illuminates his later writings on best-sellers and movies.

Although editorially *Politics* was a one-man operation, one of its great strengths was the intellectual community fostered by Macdonald's willingness to publish articles and letters criticizing his own ideas. In "The Responsibility of Peoples" Macdonald insisted that the entire population of Germany could not be held morally responsible and thus punishable for the terrible crimes of the

Nazi regime. In retrospect his emphasis provides a humane corrective against a policy of collective responsibility that justified saturation bombing, including the firebombing of Dresden, and almost led to mass starvation in the years after the war. In the discussions on war guilt within *Politics* that followed the original articles, however, Macdonald clarified his ideas. In a reply (not reprinted in *Memoirs*) to a correspondent who seemed to object that his "article does not draw a sufficiently sharp line between the Nazis and the German people," Macdonald replied:

> If anything, on reflection, I think my article . . . gave too much the impression that the German people have no responsibility of any kind for Nazis. This was because the problem I was dealing with was that of moral responsibility . . . in that sphere responsibility can only be an individual matter. . . . But the German people have a political responsibility for Nazism, both in that they permitted Hitler to come to power, and in that they endured his rule without revolt. For to absolve the German people of this kind of responsibility is to regard them simply as victims, dupes, or slaves, with slavish irresponsibility. . . . But if one believes . . . that the masses are not the inanimate raw material which Fuhrers and demagogues mould at will . . . then they must also be held responsible. ("Reply to Reimann," 155)

After distinguishing between political and moral responsibility in answer to one correspondent, Macdonald was pressed by others to make explicit his view not only of German responsibility but also of his own. His response is worth quoting at length:

> Since political responsibility is something that can only be voluntarily assumed by a class or a people *itself*, something distinct from any notion of guilt or punishment, it follows that one can assign it only if one identifies one's self with the people one holds responsible. It is a *criticism made from inside*, and when I wrote of the German people's political responsibility I was venturing to identify myself with them and thus criticize their ("our") behavior from within. Cork [one of the letterwriters] points out that "by similar logic" I myself bear some responsibility for military Jimcrow. He thinks this is absurd, since I have personally written a lot against Jimcrow. But I do accept responsibility, inasmuch as my efforts have been ineffectual; and as a member of that group in American society which seeks racial democracy, I say we have failed and must blame our failure on our own

incompetence and lack of energy and devotion as well as on economic-historical factors. We did our best, perhaps, but our best was not good enough. And who among us can say he has done all he could have done? Not I, at least. ("Comment," 207)

> Morally, I regard the masses, with whom I identify myself, as having some possibility of choice in politics and hence as bearing some responsibility if they make what seem to me bad choices . . .; I include myself in this responsibility, as I indicated, and do not conceive it as a matter of "crime and punishment" but rather of "self-criticism." (209)

To summarize Macdonald's final position: although on the question of moral responsibility, of guilt and punishment, it is necessary to discriminate, to punish individuals rather than groups, collective responsibility nevertheless does exist. It has meaning, however, only when applied from within, as a measure of self-criticism. What, then, "collective responsibility" might there be for the existence of popular or mass culture, masscult and midcult?

Macdonald himself never related his analysis of political and moral responsibility to the question of the responsibility of the "masses" for popular culture. Indeed, in the historical and theoretical essay that provides a framework for *Against the American Grain* Macdonald seems to take a position analogous to his original argument in "The Responsibility of Peoples." The shallowness of mass culture cannot be blamed on ordinary people, since mass culture, unlike folk culture, is not "an autochthonous product shaped by the people to fit their own needs" but, instead, "Masscult comes from above. It is fabricated by technicians hired by businessmen" (14). The difficulty of envisioning any historical alternative to masscult leads quickly, however, to the resigned observation that "the great cultures of the past have all been elite affairs" (56) and the proposal that the masses be left alone with their kitsch while the "few who care about good writing . . . have their High Culture." The absolution of the masses thus turns quickly into its "dialectical opposite," the assertion of the unalterable and eternal dullness of "the great majority of people at any given time" and the clear distinction from this great majority of the author himself and, presumably, the reader as well (73).

In *Politics* Macdonald had declared his own identification with the masses. This identification, which he made in passing as though it were something to be taken for granted, never prevented him from exercising the full range of his intellect and sensibility nor from voicing unpopular—some would have called them treasonable—opinions. In *Against the American Grain*, however, Macdonald is no longer able to maintain a vision of "the possibilities of ordinary people" (11). The people are, after all, merely masses, despite occasional protestations to the contrary and despite his own observation that membership in the masses is determined more by social forces than by personal traits.

The point is not simply a moral one, although one's moral sensibility must be blunted if one denies to any group a recognition of their full humanity. Macdonald's writing was never more incisive, his formulations more provocative, than in his writing for *Politics*. In contrast, the long essay on "Masscult and Midcult" that opens *Against the American Grain* comes alive only when Macdonald analyzes particular works; the historical and theoretical discussion has little of the verve of the earlier writing. As Macdonald himself suggested, his lost appetite for abstract thought reflected the disillusionment of an entire generation of intellectuals, who came to believe that the "end of ideology" had finally occurred with the apparent collapse of Marxism and the seeming stability of the postwar West. In Macdonald's own case this disillusionment resulted in the sterile categories of masscult and midcult. Macdonald's cultural essays have few parallels to the turns of thought in "The Responsibility of Peoples," in which, for example, a consideration of German war guilt could suddenly point to the moral deficiencies of the writer himself. One condition for a revival of criticism on popular culture and in other areas might be a willingness to renew the kind of self-criticism that Macdonald carried out in his earlier work.

Whatever the limitations of the theoretical framework of *Against the American Grain*, Macdonald's analyses of particular works often achieve devastating brilliance. His deflations of the artistic pretensions of such works as Archibald MacLeish's *J.B.* or Hemingway's *The Old Man and the Sea* remain as witty and telling as when they were written. Although parodies of Hemingway's style are common enough, Macdonald's rises beyond burlesque to insight:

> He wrote a novel called *Across the River and into the Trees*. It was not a good novel. It was a bad novel. It was so bad that all the critics were against it. Even the ones who had liked everything else. The trouble with critics is that you can't depend on them in a tight place and this was a very tight place indeed. They scare easy because their brains are where their *cojones* should be and because they have no loyalty and because they have never stopped a charging lion with a Mannlicher double-action .34 or done any of the other important things. The hell with them. Jack Dempsey thought

Across the River was OK. So did Joe Dimaggio. The Kraut (Marlene Diet-
rich) thought it was terrific. So did Toots Shor. But it was not OK and he
knew it and there was absolutely nothing he could do about it. (169–170)

What makes this parody so effective is that the cruel accuracy of the stylistic
burlesque does not prevent Macdonald from granting to Hemingway the
recognition of his own failing powers. Macdonald, audaciously, ends the essay
with a description of Hemingway's suicide in the same style. Yet the effect is
not one of viciousness but, rather, of a compassion that sharpens rather than
blunts the awareness of Hemingway's artistic decline. The criticism of Hemingway then, is a kind of self-criticism; its power results from Macdonald's ability
to identify himself with Hemingway even while he parodies Hemingway's
mannerisms.

The Hemingway piece illustrates that, despite Macdonald's loss of theoretical appetite, his individual critical studies retain a perspective—that of implicit
self-criticism—that Macdonald seemingly abandoned in his division of human
beings into the elite few and the insensitive masses. Macdonald's criticism of the
movies, for example, often succeeds in transcending the dichotomy of elite v.
masses in a way that adherence to his own proclamations would have rendered
impossible.

Film criticism is often vitiated by two contrasting but complementary syn-
dromes, each deriving from the critic's self-consciousness as an intellectual.
Sometimes the critic feels called upon to defend his or her status by burdening
practical criticism with theories whose elaboration does not so much illuminate
the particular observations as serve to establish the author's credentials as an
intellectual. On the other hand, critics may feel defensive about their putatively
refined sensibility, and, instead of developing their own insights and observations about a film, attempt to guess what the mass audience would consider
entertaining.

Macdonald's criticism, despite his self-consciousness as an intellectual,
avoids both tendencies. Indeed, it is precisely because Macdonald is comfortable
with his own status as an intellectual that he feels no need to neglect his own
insights in search of the elusive masses. Macdonald's early career on *Fortune*
apparently cured him of the American intellectual's congenital sense of inferiority to the rich and powerful. If, in the process Macdonald acquired a few illusions of his own, at least he was freed from the defensiveness and envy that
occasionally distort the prose of literary radicals. In *"Massachusetts* vs. *Mailer"*
both the illusions and the justifiable pride are in evidence. Macdonald com-

ments that Norman Mailer's ability to act as his own lawyer in defending himself against charges of drunk and disorderly conduct provided further evidence
for Macdonald's longheld view that

> any intellectual worthy of the name could run a railroad or a bank better
> than the pros because he would be smarter and because making money and
> such "practical" activities are child's play compared to constructing a good
> paragraph. (209)

Macdonald's satisfaction with his own status as an intellectual does not
lead him to ignore the virtues of popular movies, while he notes their
flaws—contrary to his own labeling of all cultural phenomena into the separate, inviolable categories of masscult, midcult, and high art. A few examples of his criticism from *Dwight Macdonald on Movies* demonstrate the point.
After noting that *Gone with the Wind* contains "all the humors and heartaches
and glamour and stereotypes of women's magazine fiction," Macdonald separates himself from the doctrinaire "highbrow" position by his willingness to
rely on the evidence of his own experience, however "incorrect" it may
seem; whatever the movie's faults, he concludes "it is not boring" (477). In
attempting to explain the gap between the disdain a certified highbrow
might be expected to feel for *Gone with the Wind* and the reaction he himself actually feels, Macdonald provides an example of the insights his freedom
from conventional categories can provide:

> It has the courage of its bad taste. At the same time, it is quite tough-
> minded. Scarlett and Rhett are stock characters, but they are also individ-
> uals; she is selfish, greedy, unscrupulous, and these qualities are not glossed
> over any more than Rhett's cynicism and worldly callousness are. In this
> respect *GWTW* is superior to the Tennessee Williams uncolored spectac-
> ulars—*Suddenly, Last Summer, The Fugitive Kind*—which divide the Saved
> from the Damned with Calvinistic rigor. The dialogue in *GWTW* is less
> literary, but at least there is some doubt as to whether the heroine is a
> bitch—or rather, as to whether she is *only* a bitch. This makes it more
> interesting, more grown-up. Adult entertainment, that's what I like about
> *Gone with the Wind.* (478)

Nor does Macdonald's unrepentant intellectuality lead him to stress the literary aspect of film over the images on the screen. Macdonald's sharpest comments on Hollywood movies often concern the visual impact of movies that
Macdonald, according to his own categories, would have to consider specimens

of masscult. For example, Macdonald captures the quality of Jimmy Cagney's performance in *The Public Enemy*:

> It is, of course, James Cagney's picture. His performance is as great as any-
> thing I've seen in movies; his balletlike control of his body, every move-
> ment at once precise and free. . . . He expresses everything physically, as
> when, after successfully dating Jean Harlow, he does a little double-shuffle
> dance step before getting back into his sports car; or the animal grin as he
> ducks behind a wall with the machine-gun bullets chipping out the corner
> and his partner dying on the sidewalk, the reflex grimace of a fox who has
> escaped the hounds, and also the smile of I am Alive and He is Dead.
> (454–55)

Again, on the impact of color:

> In *Home from the Hill*, for instance, it amounted to a visual rape; a super-
> market glowed like Vermeer, overalled farmers sitting around a town
> square looked like figures from the Sistine Chapel, shots of a barbecue
> reminded one of Rubens (or one of those full-color pornographic close-
> ups of roast beef in magazine ads). Here the color is milder, but still the
> family dinner table comes out like the setting for an orgy and a stained-
> glass chandelier takes the play away, visually speaking, from the actors. It is
> also a matter of the kind of color one gets in Hollywood films, a color so
> rich and intense that nothing looks shabby or everyday. (459)

Macdonald can even become lyrical over movie credits:

> Credits have been getting more and more important. Since they are over-
> printed with text, they must be simple and striking, and since they try to
> summarize the mood of the film, they must resort to stylization, which is
> at least a precondition of art . . . Lately a variation has been introduced: the
> action begins at once and often continues for some time before the credits
> come on. This precredit footage, also, is likely to be much better than the
> rest, for here we are in the magical world of art where meanings are not
> literal and not easily identified—Eden before Adam got around to naming
> the animals. (458–59)

Such passages reveal the kind of insights that Macdonald's implicit perspective—as distinguished from his official platform—makes possible: because
he is untroubled about his status as an intellectual, because he does not feel that

such a status divides him from others, he is free to find his pleasures and make his discriminations without reference to the labels enshrined in *Against the American Grain*. Macdonald says of himself:

> I have been accused of "not liking movies," which is nonsense: my difficulty is I like them too much so cannot bear to see the medium's wonderful, infinite possibilities not used to the utmost; I still think as I did in the twenties that the cinema is *the* great modern art—potentially.

It was apparently easier to withstand the tension between what movies could be and what in fact they were than the related tension between what people could be and the masses that actually existed—although not all that much easier: Macdonald made this comment in his last film column for *Esquire*, in which he also wrote that he just couldn't "face having to grapple" with any more bad films (176).

Dwight Macdonald's legacy for cultural criticism is twofold. His practical criticism of particular works, both literary and cinematic, embodies the work of a critical intelligence willing to risk individual judgments without the protection of a supporting doctrine, an intelligence that, in dealing with popular culture, can discriminate in its judgments and judge by the highest relevant standards. Such criticism remains exemplary. Second, Macdonald's work in *Politics*, particularly in his essays and comments on "The Responsibility of Peoples," suggests at least the outlines of an approach that would avoid the blank opposition of mass and elite culture on which Macdonald himself later insisted: an approach based on a recognition of one's kinship with nonintellectuals in which one's own intellectual identity is not relinquished. His stubborn insistence on the integrity of individual experience and his willingness to revise and correct his own judgments remain touchstones of cultural criticism.

Chapter 5

Making Double Judgments:
The Criticism of Diana Trilling

In an era of "neoliberals," "neoconservatives," and "progressives" Diana Trilling's long allegiance to an unadorned liberalism, reaffirmed in her 1993 memoir, *The Beginning of the Journey*, does her honor. She has not been tempted to prove her contemporaneity by changing her ideas or even by switching labels. There are those who would dismiss Diana Trilling as an outdated cold war warrior whose polemical anticommunism deprives her literary-cultural criticism of more than historical interest. Others consider not merely anticommunism but liberalism itself obsolescent in a postmodern world. A rereading of Diana Trilling's work, however, confirms both her intellectual integrity and her complementary recognition of moral-political complexity.

On the few occasions when Diana Trilling offered an explicit characterization of liberalism, she defined it straightforwardly as a political philosophy stressing individual rights. In 1967 she argued that the affirmation of "basic human and civic rights" would necessarily remain at the core of liberalism "so long as the word is in use." This simple claim enabled Trilling to make the key point that a liberalism that was more than a sentimental effusion could not adopt the slogan "no enemies to the left." A liberal could not, at least not "in the name of liberalism," defend any system, "whatever its professed idealistic goals," that deprived its people of "basic rights." It followed that "no one can call himself a liberal who is not an anti-Communist" ("Two Symposiums" 49). Today the term progressive is often used to indicate general agreement with enlightened opinion and to signal that history is on one's side; liberal is avoided, apparently because it seems to signal commitments in an awkwardly specific way. Diana Trilling, in contrast, regarded the former term with some disdain. In a 1967 symposium she distinguished her own position from "what calls itself liberal opinion but which I less honorifically prefer to call progressivism" (65).

Trilling's forthright liberalism may be compared favorably not only with the professional vagueness of contemporary politicians but also with Richard Rorty's contemporary reworking. The contrast is not political but philosophical; Rorty shares Trilling's anticommunism, but he identifies liberalism with feelings like compassion or solidarity rather than with the principles Trilling emphasizes.

On occasion Trilling herself seemed to suggest that liberals have a corner on idealism and decency. In "A Memorandum on the Hiss Case" she warned, "Whoever thinks Hiss guilty but would still think of himself as a person of liberal conscience has the duty of bringing to that case his most finely tempered understanding of its complexities" (68). The notion that the possession of a "liberal conscience" is an accomplishment rendering one morally superior to those whose conscience is not politically attuned is not perhaps a necessary implication of Trilling's phrasing, but it seems a plausible one. In "After the Profumo Case" (1964) Trilling refers to the Labor Party as "the party which in England is supposed to speak most firmly for the liberal—by which we mean the decent—values." (19). It is true that Trilling offers this characterization as a means of emphasizing the contrast between the party's ideals and its actions; she finds that Labor "opportunistically manipulated" the Profumo case for electoral advantage (18). That such behavior should disturb Trilling points up her own belief that liberal and decent are, or should be, synonymous terms.

References to a "liberal conscience" may seem unexceptionable and even redundant if one believes that the available political alternatives require consciencelessness. Diana Trilling seems to think that is the case; Communists have sold their souls to the revolution, and conservatives are meanly satisfied with things as they are. Both characterizations may be reductive, but the first is more plausible than the second. Many revolutionaries, Marxist or otherwise, trumpet their rejection of traditional ethics in favor of a revolutionary morality that judges every action by the sole criterion of its effect in bringing the revolution closer. To claim that these radicals lack the standards of traditional morality requires only taking them at their word. Conservatives, on the other hand, usually make a point of their adherence to traditional moral values. To make a plausible case that this claim is a false one—and thus provide evidence for the special moral status of liberalism—would require a great deal more argumentation than Diana Trilling ever provides.

In the United States, of course, those who call themselves "conservatives" are usually believers in the political liberalism that descends from John Locke and Edmund Burke. American conservatism is not to be identified, except opportunistically, with a defense of feudalism, fascism, or monarchism. How, then, to distinguish American conservatives from American liberals? Although Diana Trilling makes a convincing case for her principled opposition to Communism, she never makes an analogous argument to distinguish her liberalism from the nineteenth- century liberalism supported by those who in the American context are labeled conservatives. In place of a boundary based on differences in principles or philosophy, there appears to be only a distinction based on the putative moral superiority of liberalism to conservatism.

The notion that conservatism is necessarily linked with a mean-spirited acquiescence in the status quo seems the most plausible explanation for her rejection of the label of "neoconservatism" for the political views of both herself and Lionel Trilling; no other difference seems available. In *The Beginning of the Journey* Diana Trilling emphasizes that any criticisms Lionel Trilling made of liberalism were made "from within the ranks of liberalism"; it was "criticism from within the family." She makes this comment to affirm her "firmest belief" that her husband "would never have become a neoconservative." Diana Trilling goes on to clinch her characterization of her husband as a liberal *tout court* by distinguishing between the leftism corrupted by Stalinism and the true liberalism of both her husband and, apparently, herself. Lionel Trilling was a "traditional liberal until his death," and his politics took their "stand in the traditional liberalism of the nineteenth century" (404). But this is a distinction without a difference, since neoconservatives and even simple conservatives, in the United States if not elsewhere, also take their "stand in the traditional liberalism of the nineteenth century." American neoconservatives differ from "paleos" mainly in their acceptance of social reforms from the New Deal through the civil rights legislation of Lyndon Johnson, an acceptance that they share with both Lionel and Diana Trilling. Neoconservatives, even more clearly than other American conservatives, are also liberals. Their criticism of mainstream liberalism is also "criticism from within the family."

Philosophically and politically, then, the differences between the neoconservatives and either Lionel or Diana Trilling are minuscule and perhaps nonexistent. For Diana Trilling that putative agreement is unimportant, because a most important difference between conservatives and liberals remains. A conservative of any variety has made a mean-spirited bargain with things as they are, probably in the hope of personal gain. Writing of her and Lionel Trilling's long friendship with Irving Kristol and Gertrude Himmelfarb (Bea Kristol), Diana Trilling comments that she had no way of predicting "the course of the Kristols' politics," but she has no trouble summing up at least Irving Kristol's neoconservatism as simply the "politics of self-interest" (405).

Even if Diana Trilling is on weak philosophical and political grounds in distinguishing the politics of herself and her husband from contemporary neo-conservatism, the case that either one could be claimed by the neoconservative camp is still not completed. She is surely right that Lionel Trilling's work is antipathetic to any "sectarianism," any attempt at "rule by doctrine" (404). It is reasonable to assume that neither Lionel nor Diana Trilling would join a neoconservatism in which adherence to a doctrine took precedence over independent thinking. On the other hand, recent nonpolemical but convincing testimony supporting the notion that strong affinities exist between Lionel Trilling and at least some varieties of neoconservatism may be found in Gertrude Himmelfarb's 1994 *On Looking into the Abyss*, especially the eloquent first chapter, inspired by Lionel Trilling's essay "On the Teaching of Modern Literature." The book itself is dedicated "To the Memory of Lionel Trilling." In the preface to *The Liberal Imagination* Lionel Trilling famously observed that liberalism was "the sole intellectual tradition," adding that the "conservative impulse" expressed itself not in ideas but "in irritable mental gestures which seek to resemble ideas." He went on to say that it was not a good but a bad thing for liberalism that it lacked an articulate opposition. Absent that opposition, it was up to liberals like himself to take up the task that otherwise, conservatives would undertake, to put "under some degree of pressure the liberal ideas and assumptions of the present time" (Preface, n.p.). Whether neoconservatism is a movement that enforces "rule by doctrine," as Diana Trilling claims, whether Lionel Trilling would have regarded it as the intelligent opposition he wished for, or whether he would have opposed it at all are questions that cannot be answered in this discussion.

Diana Trilling is not the only one, of course, who has had trouble drawing a clear line between American liberals and American conservatives; the difficulty is that she does seem to think that the attempt is worth making—and her own characterization of liberalism is thus left incomplete. She clarifies the line between liberalism and Communism, but she fails to distinguish her own liberalism from the most obvious domestic alternatives. One hopes that she may still be stirred to make the attempt, not so much because she might enlighten a future biographer or for the sake of intellectual history but, rather, because her stubborn integrity and its corollary, her insistence on finding a "third way" between absolute commitment to either revolution or reaction, remains exemplary in the era of culture wars as much as in the days of World War II or the cold war.

Fifty years after World War II the commemorations of the great events of that war induce us to look back to that era with a kind of nostalgia. It was a time of horrors, but it was at least a simple time, a time when it was easy to distinguish right from wrong. Fascism and Nazism were the enemy, and anything that contributed to their defeat was right. The task of intellectuals was reduced to cheerleading. With a good conscience one could stop bothering to make distinctions between politics and culture, between, for example, enlightened attitudes and literary merit. The refusal of such distinctions has consequences that, in the long run, are certainly troubling: if literature, for example, can be judged by political standards alone, then there seems to be no particular reason for paying any special attention to novels or plays or poems. In the short run, however, a world war was going on; critical judgment could be suspended for the duration.

Today the culture wars seem to demand an equivalent suspension of judgment. To continue to respect the disparate claims of morality, art, and politics while also recognizing the connections between each is not easy. The attempt to subsume the traditional disciplines of the humanities into the superdiscipline of cultural studies increases the pressure to reduce literary questions, for example, to moral issues and then to offer political solutions to moral questions. Those who feel threatened by the demand for "political correctness" might well draw inspiration from the example offered by Diana Trilling's literary criticism during and after World War II. Although she believed in the justice of a war against Hitler when most of her radical colleagues joined the Right in opposing involvement, she refused to allow her opposition to Nazism to control her literary judgment. *Reviewing the Forties*, a collection of her book reviews for *The Nation* from 1942 to 1949, provides an example of independence of judgment exercised at a time when the temptations and the pressures to relax the effort must have surely exceeded any that we confront today, just as shooting wars are worse than culture wars.

Diana Trilling herself emphasized the difference between actual physical combat and intellectual debate. Though she shared Arthur Koestler's disillusionment with Communism, though she was sympathetic to the difficulties facing Jews in an Israel controlled by Great Britain, she was ready to raise questions about Koestler's portrayal of Jewish terrorism in his novel describing Palestine in 1937–39, *Thieves in the Night*. What bothers her is that Koestler's novel not only sympathizes with the dilemmas facing the Jewish settlers but goes on to make a case for "the principle of terror" itself. Trilling notes that the war years have taught the lesson that "there are times in which immediate extreme action is demanded and when to stop to scruple is to be destroyed." Writing a novel, however, Trilling suggests, is not one of those times, nor is writing a review. There are those who insist that the distinction between life and literature, between thought and action, should be ignored. Trilling's seemingly obvious reminder, offered about a writer she admired defending a cause with which she sympathized, remains pertinent:

> It is surely not the same moral thing to be a Jew confronted by an Arab with a gun in his hand, or an anti-Nazi confronted by a Nazi with a gun in his, or a Negro confronted by a white lyncher, and to be a writer with a pen in his hand. (190)

Trilling draws a distinction between sympathetic understanding and the commitment that rejects all qualifications, that insists on glorifying not only a noble end but also all the means to that end. The writer goes further than the combatant, the former romanticizing what the latter is forced to confront. Koestler, argues Trilling, shirks "the duty of the novelist" because his work fails "to remind us of the moral consequences of exigent conduct upon the individual who is forced to it" (190). Those who possess "even the illusion of safety," those who are free to think and write, need to remember that "moral reflection is still our everlasting duty" (191).

It might be argued that Trilling's criticism emphasizes one distinction while collapsing another. Stressing the difference between life and literature, does she go on to discount the difference between a novel and a work of moral philosophy? One response would be that Arthur Koestler was a "philosophical novelist" who wrote his fiction to raise large moral, political, and philosophical questions. More important, Trilling does not debate Koestler's case for "the principle of terror" on philosophical grounds. She argues that he fails as a novelist, even one concerned with ideas, because he gives short shrift to what should be "the main concern of a philosophical novelist: the vital difference between passionately meeting the demands of a particular time and place and the promulgation of a 'rational' program of passion" (190). The philosophical novel, as distinct from a philosophical treatise, deals not only with ideas but with the human consequences of those ideas. For Trilling the "duty of the novelist" includes the obligation not merely to distinguish between actions forced upon one by circumstances and those that one chooses freely but also, more subtly, "also to remind us of the moral consequences of exigent conduct upon the individual who is forced to it." Trilling finds Koestler's novel "morally irresponsible," in the same way that the "this-is-the-way-to-kill-Nazis novels produced at a several-thousand-miles remove from the Nazi horror" are irresponsible. The issue is literary as well as moral. Trilling has no doubt that a philosophical and political case can and should be made for the war against the

Nazis, but she argues that novels depicting the war tell only half the story when they fail to reveal "the *tragedy* of necessary violence" (191).

Repeatedly, Diana Trilling demonstrates the confusions that arise when a wholehearted commitment to a cause, even a truly good cause such as opposition to Nazism, is allowed to excuse literary weaknesses. Frederick Hazlitt Brennan's *Memo to a Firing Squad* is not just a thriller but an anti-Nazi thriller. The novel attempts to "warn us against a negotiated peace" with Hitler (16), no doubt a praiseworthy goal. As a novelist, however, Brennan cannot simply make an unexceptionable political point and stop; whether he wants to or not, he conveys also a view of the world. Brennan is so anxious to avoid appeasement that he romanticizes murder—"in Mr. Brennan's world murder becomes a fine art" (17). The result, Trilling argues persuasively, is to present a view of life uncomfortably similar to that of the Nazis themselves:

> One had thought that a reason we are at war is that the Nazis find slaughter so heart-warming. How ironic it is, then, that at the same time that we are fighting to outlaw the violence of Nazism, we are this busy creating a literature that glorifies it. (18)

In *The Beginning of the Journey* Diana Trilling emphasizes the ways in which her anticommunism set her off from others on the Left. Noting that throughout the 1940s the *Nation*, under the leadership of Freda Kirchwey, was committed to viewing the Soviet Union in the best light possible, she comments that her book reviews took a very different line: "my anti-Communism was seldom far from the surface of my reviews" (342). Fifty years later, however, what strikes a reader is not so much Trilling's "anti-Communism" as her continuing battle with the temptation to judge novels by their political commitments.

Trilling demolishes the pretensions of many anti-Nazi novels but explicitly disputes the pro-communist sympathies of only three: Ruth McKenney's *Jake Home* (21–23), Michael Blankfort's *A Time to Live* (26–28), and Anna Seghers's *Transit* (95–98). Even in these reviews her objections are nuanced. Trilling points out that, while the plot of *Jake Home* adheres to the "wavy line" of Communist dogmas (21), its stylistic affinities are all with capitalism:

> As frank fiction . . . Miss McKenney's story . . . is basically such fourteen-carat goldwyn that you need only soft pedal the cops and occasionally turn the camera on a kindly capitalist to wind up with one of those movies in

which idealism triumphs over low sexual-commercial temptation and Hollywood saves its soul. (22)

While the "core guilt" of the protagonist of *A Time to Live* is that he has "never had the courage or faith to join the Party" (27), Trilling's conclusion emphasizes the guilt itself rather than its particular source: "If there is little fictional good to be got from a writer's hatred of others, there is even less to be got from hatred of himself" (28). There is only one occasion when a reference to Communism seems far-fetched. Anna Seghers's *Transit* treats refugees seeking escape from Vichy France with "something between ironic superiority and sneer," while the protagonist's readiness to stay in France is "a kind of affirmation of life." Trilling makes no attempt to connect this "new and thoroughly unpleasant slant on a tragic situation" with communist doctrines, but she does speculate that the author's apparent approval of the amorality of the protagonist "is rooted in the Communist belief that means are justified by the ends they serve" (97). Even here it is worth noting that Trilling considers Seghers's previous novel, *The Seventh Cross*, "a better book" than *Transit* (95), although it is in the former that "the author makes frank confession of her Communist preference," while the latter "has no expressed political bias" (97). Meanwhile, Trilling praises Eleanor Clark's disillusioned novel *The Bitter Box* as "a serious, funny, and truthful picture of Communist doings in this country, and therefore a work of courage," but again politics does not have the last word. Trilling objects to Clark's "semi-symbolical method" (162), suggesting that "there is still very much to be written out of the traditional powers of observation and insight" (164).

Any claim for the independence of Trilling's literary judgment is likely to be met with the response that this praise of Trilling is just another way of saying that one agrees with Trilling's own politics. In the middle of World War II, however, Diana Trilling was able to judge novels proclaiming their anti-Nazism by reference to their literary achievement and their moral and cultural implications as novels. Doing so was an act of faith. The war would eventually be over, and society would continue. We would again need to be able to turn to literature not simply as an instrument for advancing a particular agenda but also as a source of independent insight, an occasion for self-reflection. Diana Trilling's ability to maintain her integrity of judgment throughout the war years and beyond remains a valuable rejoinder to those who urge that such integrity is impossible in theory and unknown in practice.

Diana Trilling's continuing refusal to lower her literary and political standards for any cause, even anti-Nazism, insures that her work will continue to affront all those who desire exemption from criticism for a particular trend or movement. In 1959 Josephine Herbst attacked what she took to be Trilling's dismissal of Allen Ginsberg and other Beat poets, in "The Other Night at Columbia: A Report," as an example of "the academic powerhouse mind" (qtd. in *The Beginning of the Journey*, 363). The essay, perhaps the best known of those collected in *Claremont Essays*, describes a reading by Allen Ginsberg, Gregory Corso, and Peter Orlovsky at the McMillin Theater on the Columbia campus at a time when the Beats were at the height of their notoriety. The essay, Lionel Trilling's favorite "of anything I wrote," according to Diana Trilling in *Beginning* (364), does not, indeed, endorse the Beats' own claims to artistic and cultural significance. Yet the essay also refuses to draw a boundary between academic respectability and the Beats—despite Morris Dickstein's use of "Diana Trilling's condescending essay" (11) in *Gates of Eden* (1977) as a key instance for his thesis that the great weakness of the 1950s was "its weakness for hard-and-fast cultural distinctions, exclusions, hierarchies" (4). Against Dickstein it is important to note that Trilling criticizes Ginsberg and his followers most sharply for a stance that, she insists, they share with "liberal intellectuals" and a good part of the nation. The Beats proclaim that they are "out of their minds, not responsible" (161), but that gesture, Trilling argues, is only more theatrical and more extreme than the analogous effort of the "respectable liberal intellectual" to "divest oneself of responsibility." The common assumption of powerlessness and thus of innocence is one that connects "any number of the disparate elements of our present culture—from the liberal intellectual journals to Luce to the Harvard Law School, from Ginsberg to the suburban matron" (162). There is certainly a difference of "taste or style" between "the 'beats' and those intellectuals who most overtly scorn them" (163), but they share the same "acceptance of defeat" (164). The essay ends with Trilling's admission that she "had been moved" by the evening, especially by Ginsberg's "passionate love-poem" addressed to Lionel Trilling (170). There may be an "unfathomable gap" between the atmosphere of the poetry reading and her own living room (173), but it is one she attempts to bridge rather than to widen.

Trilling later speculated that the opposition that the essay aroused derived from her "refusal to grant Ginsberg and his friends any special privilege because they were poets." She "robbed them of their role as victims," thereby irritating the poets and robbing their sympathizers "of their virtuous role as defenders of the victimized" (*Beginning*, 363). In the 1960s the student radicals were even more insistent than the Beats about their status as victims, and their defenders were likewise more strident. Diana Trilling's "On the Steps of Low Library," a report on the 1968 student rebellion at Columbia, was condemned more harshly, but for much the same reasons, as her essay on the Beats. Trilling characteristically included Robert Lowell's harsh comments with her own replies when she reprinted the essay in *We Must March My Darlings*. Lowell claimed that she was evidently "more preoccupied with the little violence of the unarmed student uprisings than with the great violence of the nation at war," more worried about "the piss on President Kirk's carpet" than "horrified by napalm on human flesh." Lowell could only explain Trilling's essay by the speculation that she carried around "a picture of herself as some housekeeping goddess of reason" (148). What strikes a reader of the essay twenty-five or so years after the events it describes is not Trilling's opposition to the rebels but, rather, the extent to which she feels implicated in their actions. The students, she suspects, are acting out ideas they have learned in the classroom, ideas that she herself shares. It is the "revolutionary content of the contemporary literary works" that the Columbia students are taking as their starting point (94). The rebellion is, finally, a cultural rather than a political phenomenon; it represented "indeed the triumph of culture over politics." And it is important to note, especially in an era of culture wars, that the culture with which Trilling connects the rebellion is her own; it is not youth culture or pop culture that can be blamed; the students are acting out "the moral substance of contemporary art" (95).

Trilling's "On The Steps of Low Library" counterposes Norman Mailer's *Armies of the Night*, an account of the protest at the Pentagon in October 1967, with her own account of the student rebellion at Columbia. The title of her essay is borrowed from "On the Steps of the Pentagon," the first section of Mailer's book. Trilling makes use of Mailer's book to gain a larger perspective on events so close to home that a balanced perspective would be a difficult accomplishment. In key ways the march on the Pentagon and the Columbia rebellion are similar events; they have the same "cultural and political message" (78). Both intended to force bystanders like Trilling into a new awareness of "the discrepancy between democratic theory and practice," and both revealed "the capacity for hatred and violence which many of the educationally privileged left-wing youth share with those they most condemn on the score of their hatred and violence" (79).

Norman Mailer, of course, wrote about the Pentagon march as a participant, one determined to distinguish his own protest from "merely dull liberal opposition to the war" (109), as Trilling puts it—in other words, her sort of opposition, which refuses to join "marches or demonstrations" because it is unwilling to "march under the flag of the Viet Cong," unwilling to suggest that America is "uniquely greedy and rapacious among nations" (152). These considerations do not deter Norman Mailer, and in *The Armies of the Night* he describes how his willingness to outrage bourgeois proprieties discomfits even his friends Robert Lowell and Dwight Macdonald, who both supported the student rebellion at Columbia and the march on the Pentagon. Mailer himself clearly believes that his outrageous behavior provides evidence that he "stands an important few paces forward" of not only Diana Trilling but even Dwight Macdonald and Robert Lowell in "the march toward freedom." Surprisingly, Trilling asks: "Is [Mailer's own belief] "not ours as well? Is it not the belief of all of us whose advanced politics are indissolubly joined to the advanced culture of our time?" (111)

It is the sort of question that Diana Trilling has raised before in similarly inconvenient settings. In analyzing a British sexual-political scandal in "After the Profumo Case," she argued that the osteopath-procurer Stephen Ward would have been justified in wondering why society was so outraged:

> But was not enlightenment—sexual enlightenment no less than political or cultural enlightenment—the very cornerstone of modernity? And what did enlightenment consist in if not the ability to accommodate values different from your own: the values of our political enemies, of different races and ethnic groups, the values of the emotionally ill and the sexually deviant? (3)

On what grounds, then, could anyone, at least anyone who claimed to be enlightened, condemn the "sadomasochistic, orgiastic indulgences which Ward provided for his clients" (7)? Diana Trilling provides no simple answer; as in "On the Steps," her purpose in "After the Profumo Case" is not to rally believers but, rather, to explore the complications of contemporary political and cultural life.

"On the Steps of Low Library" makes no attempt to demonize the students, no attempt to identify the author with simple righteousness. The kind of "centrist moderation" that she would like to oppose to the extremes of revolution and reaction now seems inadequate. She can no longer share "the comfortable assumption that liberalism has only to shine up its old medals and resurrect its old rhetoric of responsibility" (133). She asks herself an uncomfortable question about whether the "useful changes" at Columbia after the rebellion would have taken place anyway. No, she must answer, not at least so soon, because "there wasn't that much quiet will for change." The liberalism with which she identifies herself contributed to the uprising "by confusing quiet with quietism, by buttressing legality with inertia" (134). Her strongest criticism of both Norman Mailer and the student rebels is their common "stance of blamelessness" (84).

Robert Lowell's criticism of Diana Trilling as a "housekeeping goddess of reason"—after earlier referring to her as "a respected, not too much on target, though a great lady, controversialist" (144)—was unfair because it took unprincipled polemical advantage of Trilling's status as a woman and, perhaps more subtly, at her status as a married woman not working at a full-time job outside the home, whatever the extent of her publications as a free-lance writer. Diana Trilling rarely, if ever, sought to exploit her status for polemical gain. It would probably be futile to attempt to consider to what extent her perspective was either cramped or enriched from her situation as a married woman with no full-time job outside the house. When, for example, she comments in 1967 that Joe McCarthy was aided in his "reactionary and demagogic anti-Communism" by the failure of liberal intellectuals to carry out "their own principled job of intellectual housecleaning" ("Two Symposiums," 57), one should not read too much into the choice of "housecleaning" as a metaphor for the task of cultural-political self-criticism, which liberal intellectuals, in her view, managed so often to avoid.

In *The Beginning of the Journey* Diana Trilling comments on her recognition that there was something about her writing, some aspect of tone or style, that irritated many beyond any disagreement with her ideas. Reflecting on Lowell's charge, she speculates that she has been "too much burdened by superego and by the need to keep a firm rein on instinct" (374). She notes that her writing resonates with an "implicit if not expressed moral judgment" that inevitably seems "severe, adverse" to those who might conceivably be indicted by her judgments. Today a comment such as Robert Lowell's would arouse, rightly, a storm of protest. Those who would protest most loudly might, however, share Lowell's exasperation, though their objections would be voiced quite differently.

Elaine Showalter, a prominent academic feminist, speaks for an influential trend when she advocates criticism that "makes itself definitely vulnerable, virtually bares its throat to the knife." Showalter is not content, however, simply to affirm a preference for a particular rhetorical mode. She argues that the existence of such criticism "is an implicit rebuke to women critics" who adopt a different approach, who, for example, exhibit a "tight-lipped Olympian intelligence." She agrees with Adrienne Rich that such women write "from somewhere outside their female bodies."[1] Showalter, it is worth noticing, presents herself as an opponent of sectarian judgments; she distances herself from those feminists who make "cruelly prescriptive" denunciations of female writers who avoid the confessional mode (58). On this occasion Elizabeth Hardwick in *Seduction and Betrayal* and Susan Sontag in *Illness as Metaphor* provide the examples of writers to be "rebuked" if not proscribed, but, undoubtedly, *Claremont*

Essays or *We Must March My Darlings* would serve just as well. It would be just as easy (and just as mistaken) to criticize Diana Trilling's essays for their "tight-lipped Olympian intelligence" as to condemn them as expressions of either "the academic powerhouse mind" or a "housekeeping goddess of reason."

In the light of such criticisms it is especially striking to observe that the way of thinking most distinctive to Diana Trilling parallels the habit of mind commended by a very different personality, one whom nobody ever accused of being a "tight-lipped Olympian" or an "academic powerhouse." In "The Crack-Up" F. Scott Fitzgerald offers the "general observation" that "the test of a first-rate intelligence is the ability to hold two opposed ideas in the mind at the same time, and still retain the ability to function" (69). For Fitzgerald this ability was surely a version of the "negative capability" that Keats connected with poetic achievement, the ability to remain "in uncertainties, Mysteries, doubts, without any irritable reaching after fact and reason" (193).[2] If the ability noted by Fitzgerald has affinities with poetic creation on the one hand, however, it also has affinities with Diana Trilling's "housekeeping" reason.

Robert Lowell's incredulity that Diana Trilling could possibly, in good faith, oppose both the Vietnam War and the tactics of the students at Columbia provides an example of the continuing power of the either-or logic so compelling during the McCarthy period. The vehemence of the Columbia uprising aimed at forcing an either-or choice on the faculty, on students and on all involved: "The uprising demanded that one choose, simply, between conservatism and revolution" ("On the Steps of Low Library" 127). The pressure to make an absolute choice was intensified and broadened at the Democratic convention in August. One was either with the hippies, with Jerry Rubin and Abby Hoffman, or with Mayor Daley and the "pigs." It was difficult for anybody to keep his or her head and retain the ability to hold opposing ideas in one's mind and still function. Trilling points out that Eugene McCarthy, for example, could not do it:

> He failed to hold two ideas in his mind simultaneously and with equal force—in his public statements he condemned only Daley and the Chicago police, and failed to name the provocateurs of violence who had deliberately invited retaliation. (128)

But opposition to both protestor tactics and government strategy is indeed the stance that Diana Trilling assumes, the one that Robert Lowell asserts could only be assumed by someone who has "a picture of herself as some housekeeping goddess of reason" (148).

Repeatedly, Diana Trilling argues that a truly complex view requires holding onto "two opposed ideas." In confronting D. H. Lawrence, a writer access to whom would seem difficult to one who relied solely on a "tight-lipped Olympian intelligence," Trilling grounds her stance in the "double judgments" against which she encounters such resistance:

> For the current of modern feeling is peculiarly against the making of double judgments. We want both our literature and our politics to deal in absolutes. We want truth all in one piece. . . . We resent . . . being compelled to admit that a subtle truth can inhere in what has all the appearance of falsehood. (*Portable D. H. Lawrence*, 10)

Her awareness of opposed truths and the consequent necessity for making double judgments is the key to her stance as a liberal anticommunist. In characterizing her own politics in contrast to those of Lillian Hellman, she stresses her own opposition to a kind of thinking she calls "either/or-ism": "left-wing intellectuals, in an orgy of either/or-ism, split on the question of which was the enemy of democratic safety and decency, Communism or McCarthyism" ("Two Symposiums," 50). In *The Beginning of the Journey* she recalls that her opposition to "both Communism and McCarthyism" gained little favor since "it appears to be too much to ask of us that we hold two opposing ideas in our minds at the same time" (345). Nor was the recognition of "opposing ideas" a motif devised solely for its political usefulness. Trilling made use of it in her literary criticism in regard to D. H. Lawrence and elsewhere and also in everyday life. In *Mrs. Harris* Trilling notes that the "errors of the Harrison police" may be real enough, but they nevertheless did not provide "proof of Mrs. Harris's innocence." It was possible to believe both that the police had bungled and that Jean Harris had killed Herman Tarnower with malice aforethought. Most of us, however, do not welcome such disparate possibilities, since to do so

> requires that we hold two negative judgments in mind at the same time and nothing in our culture prepares us for so difficult a feat. Wherever there's wrongdoing on one side, we're accustomed to take it as proof that the opposite side is virtue incarnate. (118).

Diana Trilling's own ability to hold onto opposing truths, to make double judgments, remains exemplary. It is an ability that is at least as rare and certainly as valuable in the era of culture wars as it was during the cold war or World War II.

Chapter 6

A Masterpiece of Cultural
Self-Criticism: Edmund Wilson's
Patriotic Gore

Patriotic Gore (1962) is Edmund Wilson's masterpiece, a great work of criticism and of literature.[1] With its "excellencies," however, it "has likewise faults, and faults sufficient to obscure and overwhelm any other merit," as Samuel Johnson said of Shakespeare's plays ("Preface, 1765," 18). These faults are apparent to even casual readers, while the work's excellencies are more difficult to explicate. The former may be divided for convenience into intellectual, moral, and structural faults, though each is linked to the others. Intellectually, the zoological reductionism of the introduction provides a theoretical framework so impoverished that one need only read the rest of the book to find a refutation. Morally, Wilson's failure to consider any African-American writings beside Charlotte Forten's diary raises the suspicion that he failed at some level to recognize that the dilemmas of African Americans might be as complicated and worthy of discussion as those of whites. The suspicion is increased by Wilson's apparent preference for the "cause of the South," which seems to imply a lack of concern, to put it mildly, about the evil of slavery. Structurally, the book seems to lack unity; *Patriotic Gore* brilliantly displays Wilson's ability to discover and illuminate obscure texts and marginal lives, but it is difficult to see how the individual portraits add up to any overall perspective.

Patriotic Gore often seems to point opposed morals in politics and culture. The introduction's rejection of the cold war was a left-wing gesture in 1962, yet the major themes that emerge from *Patriotic Gore* as a whole could scarcely appeal to any proponent of revolution, left-wing or otherwise; Wilson suggests that messianic crusades, despite or because of the idealistic slogans with which they begin, almost inevitably deteriorate into mere power grabs. In academic terms *Patriotic Gore*, in retrospect, may be seen as a prominent contribution to

"American Studies" and thus another indication that the United States was developing a cultural identity to match its emergence as a world superpower— yet the work criticizes and debunks the moral center of the American tradition, the "rebirth of freedom" affirmed by Lincoln.

Besides its critique of the self-congratulatory motifs in American culture, *Patriotic Gore* offers an implicit critique of Edmund Wilson's own earlier enthusiasm for the remaking of the world by intellectuals. In *To the Finland Station* (1940) Wilson was willing to criticize the excesses of revolutionaries, but his prose emphasized the overwhelming appeal of the revolutionary project itself. Wilson presents the French Revolution through a sympathetic recreation of Michelet's narrative of French history. In Wilson's retelling even the Terror seems to be justified as the working out of Vico's notion of "humanity creating itself." The only political actor of the Revolutionary period whose story is told is "Gracchus" Babeuf, whose call for a "Republic of Equals" is presented as the essence of selfless revolutionary idealism. In explaining why Babeuf's plan failed to gain mass support, Wilson refers to a "period of frivolity," which caused the people to connect "uncompromising principles and the guillotine" (87–88). Yet Wilson's own brief description of the "mechanics of a planned society" Babeuf envisioned refers to both the forced removal of populations ("The cities were to be deflated and the population distributed in villages") and the replacement of private life and the family with the state ("the people were to eat at communal tables") [86]. For Wilson "Babeuf was like a last convulsive effort of the principles of the great French Revolution to work themselves out to their logical ends" (94), and readers caught up in the book cannot help but feel that Babeuf's failure is tragic indeed.

Later Wilson proposes that the key notion of Marxism "is the idea that the human spirit will be able to master its animal nature through reason," though he admits that the usual version of Marxism asserted exactly the opposite—"that mankind was hopelessly the victim of its appetites" (213). Wilson criticizes Marx and Engels for "an element of mysticism" (189) involved in "the myth of the Dialectic" (231), but he never questions the aspiration to organize human life through reason. Wilson characterizes Lenin at the Finland Station in St. Petersburg as a figure who "stood on the eve of the moment when for the first time in the human exploit the key of a philosophy of history was to fit an historical lock" (546). Even though Wilson acknowledges that the revolution that Lenin made did not live up to expectations, he regards this failure as unimportant from the viewpoint of history: "The point is that Western man at this moment can be seen to have made some definite progress in mastering the greeds and the fears, the bewilderments, in which he has lived" (547). In his

"Summary as of 1940" (omitted from the 1972 edition) Wilson notes that "Marxism is in relative eclipse" (475) and asks, "Is there nothing left of Marxism, then?" (483). What he finds still living is the vision of "a society which will be homogeneous and cooperative as our commercial society is not, and directed, to the best of their ability, by the conscious creative minds of its members" (484). Today the notion that homogeneity is to be desired will, rightly, draw instant criticism; it is worth noting as well that Wilson in 1940 still held to the notion that "conscious creative minds" ought to direct society, though he no longer believed in the dictatorship of the proletariat.

In *Patriotic Gore* this faith that society can and should be restructured by conscious creative minds has disappeared. Wilson compares Lincoln to Lenin only to link both with Bismarck, as figures who "presided over the unifications of the three great new modern powers" (xvi). Wilson praises the obscure Francis Grierson for recognizing that "Lincoln, Napoleon and Bismarck" were not merely statesmen but "creative forces" (75)—but the very juxtaposition of Lincoln with two such enemies of radical idealism inevitably has a debunking effect. Later Wilson reports on a conversation between Bismarck and Grant in which Lincoln is compared to Wilhelm I—both personally kind, both targets of assassination. Grant's emphasis on the importance of opposition to slavery is interpreted by Wilson as proof that slavery was merely a pretext for the war: "The General [Grant] is quite unaware that, by putting things in this way, he has indicated that slavery, on the part of the Unionists, has at the last moment been recruited to justify their action in the struggle for power" (171). Wilson pays eloquent tribute to the *Memoirs* for their clarity and force, but Grant's military triumph becomes morally equivocal for the American reader when Wilson insists on presenting Grant as "the equal, the sympathetic colleague, of the master of that other great new state which had consolidated the German principalities" (173). The revolutionary force of Lincoln's call for "a new birth of freedom" in the Gettysburg Address has no resonance for Wilson in *Patriotic Gore*. His admiration goes to those figures such as Oliver Wendell Holmes Jr. who manage to fight holding actions, who stick it out with integrity and stubbornness in a world ruled by agglomerations of power. The duty of intellectuals now, it seems, is to debunk rather than lead such power units.

One way of reconciling admiration for *Patriotic Gore* as a text while rejecting many of its ideas is to view it as a work of art, not a book of criticism. To defend *Patriotic Gore* by considering Wilson's ideas as merely instrumental motifs void of any meaningful reference outside the text would, however, result in an interpretation that would salvage the text by robbing the work of its seriousness. *Patriotic Gore* is best understood as a great work of cultural self-criticism, a work that illuminates the hidden links between ourselves and our history and between our ideas and our emotions. In *Patriotic Gore* Edmund Wilson dramatizes the tension of contrary ideas, coming to no explicit resolution but providing the clarification that the sympathetic presentation of opposing values can accomplish. At first Wilson develops the theme of self-assertion, which he identifies with the cause of the South; he then turns in the second half to present the seemingly opposed notion of responsibility, which he connects with the cause of the Union. *Patriotic Gore* thus achieves something of the disinterestedness that great fiction or drama attains when characters affirming opposing values confront one another, and the author grants to each his or her full humanity.

After discussing Wilson's introduction, with its seemingly nihilistic pessimism, the movement of the first four hundred–plus pages, ending with the long chapter on Alexander Stephens, will be compared to the countermovement that runs through the rest of the book, ending only with the summarizing portrait of Justice Holmes. The chapter concludes with a consideration of the book's meaning for us now, more than thirty years after publication.

The introduction of *Patriotic Gore* is notorious for its blunt refusal to see anything in the causes of the Civil War more complicated or more edifying than a collision of instinctual drives. For Wilson the essence of all human wars can be summed up in an image from a Walt Disney film on life at the bottom of the sea:

A primitive organism called a sea slug is seen gobbling up small organisms through a large orifice at one end of its body; confronted with another sea slug of an only slightly lesser size, it ingurgitates that, too. Now, the wars fought by human beings are stimulated as a rule primarily by the same instincts as the voracity of the sea slug. (xi)

The force of Wilson's zoological language, so startling in the introduction, is not blunted by Wilson's decision to present the Civil War through the narration of individual lives. Instead, it is precisely Wilson's presentation of the diversity of individual destinies that serves to intensify the reader's sense of the blindly zoological irrationality of a force that can cause such a "fissure" in so many varied individual lives (435). Yet in the body of *Patriotic Gore* the zoological emphasis does not have the reductive effect that appears in the introduction. The unpredictable and often delayed effect of the war on individuals is conveyed not so much by the portraits of major personalities, such as Harriet Beecher Stowe or Lincoln, as by Wilson's investigations of its impact on figures such as Francis

Grierson, who moved from an Illinois boyhood memorialized in his book *Valley of the Shadows*—a forgotten minor classic rescued by Wilson—to become a Parisian dandy sought after for his piano improvisations who died in obscurity in Los Angeles, and General Sherman's son, Tom Sherman, whose Catholic priesthood and final delusions were somehow connected to—perhaps an expiation for—his father's "reckless elation" on the March to the Sea through Georgia (210).

Wilson's narratives of diverse individual lives, all somehow broken or twisted by the cataclysm of the war, reach a conclusion in the long chapter on Alexander Stephens, the vice president of the Confederacy. In the last pages of that chapter, which marks the conclusion of the first half of the book dealing with the war itself—the second half will deal primarily with the poetry and fiction rising out of the war—Wilson raises the question "whether it may not be true, as Stephens said, that the cause of the South is the cause of us all." The question, startling as it appears out of context, has come to seem plausible, even inevitable, because of Wilson's presentation of the victory of the North as simply the victory of more efficiently organized, more highly centralized power over a less organized, less powerful grouping. Wilson views the Civil War not so much as an event that resolved the great national issue of slavery but as a national consolidation that raised for the United States a question that "presses hard on our time," the "question of the exercise of power, of the backing up of power by force, the issue of the government, the organization, as against the individual, the family group—for the South that fought the war was a family group" (434). But Wilson brings the meaning of the conflict even closer to home. He argues that "we can most of us find a key in ourselves" to the real issue of the Civil War:

> There is in most of us an unreconstructed Southerner who will not accept domination as well as a benevolent despot who wants to mold others for their own good, to assemble them in such a way as to produce a comprehensive unit which will satisfy our own ambition by realizing some vision of our own.(435)

The chapter on Alexander Stephens is an appropriate place for these reflections, since Wilson presents Stephens as Lincoln's opposite, the embodiment of "the Southern cause" as Lincoln is of the cause of the North:

> Abraham Lincoln and Alexander Stephens, who commanded one another's respect and who in intellect and character were peers, have come

by this time to stand, in the crisis of the Civil War, at two opposite moral-political poles. They, in fact, now inhabit two quite different spheres, and their minds are more or less incommensurable. For Lincoln is the "man of destiny" who is also the self-appointed leader; who must decide and discriminate in practical affairs, who must discipline and calculate in action, yet who draws his conviction from non-rational impulse, who responds to popular stresses, who hunts as one of a pack. Stephens, too, of course, belongs to his people, and his convictions—as in the case of slavery—have ultimately non-rational sources; but he differs essentially from Lincoln in being usually at odds with the pack. (432–33)

Lincoln opposes slavery; Stephens supports it. But for Wilson here it is not moral or political categories that are decisive but, rather, zoological ones. Lincoln "hunts as one of a pack," while Stephens is "usually at odds with the pack"; that is enough for Wilson to place his sympathies with Stephens rather than with Lincoln and for him to suggest that "the cause of the South" may today be "the cause of us all."

Wilson's arresting formulations about the cause of the South are never withdrawn. Nevertheless, the last four hundred pages of *Patriotic Gore*, dealing with the literature arising from the war, subtly qualifies, transmutes, and finally virtually reverses the emphases of the first four hundred pages. First, Wilson's study of postwar Southern literature changes one's sense of what the cause of the South entails; then, "responsibility" as a counter-concept to the idea of the cause of the South emerges through a consideration of the literature of the North.

Before the transformations of the cause of the South in the last half of *Patriotic Gore*, already in the discussion of Alexander Stephens there are suggestions that the concept involves more than a simple "refusal to accept domination." Stephens is, in Wilson's phrase, "an impossibilist" (434), who has for us "such a value as the impossibilist may sometimes have: that, by carrying an ideal to extremes, he may raise certain fundamental issues in a way that the more practical and prudent man could never allow himself to do" (434). And the fundamental issue for Wilson, the issue that for him is the core of the cause of the South, is that of the freedom of the individual.

The cause of individual freedom seems noble, yet Wilson's statement of its consequences in Stephen's career raises certain doubts. Wilson says of Stephens that,

though an accomplished parliamentarian, though skilful as a politician, the purity and logic of his principles, the resolve to be himself and nothing but himself, will never, in the long run, allow him to be respectful to contingencies or particularly serious about results. (433)

If one is not "particularly serious about results," then that would seem to mean that one would not be particularly serious even about such a result as the victory of the Confederacy. That is to say, Stephens was apparently capable of encouraging men to fight and die for a cause about whose achievement he was not, in the long run, "particularly serious." How noble is that? Isn't it, to say the least, irresponsible?

And, if one can wonder about the consequences of Stephens's commitment to an absolute individualism, one can also raise questions about the origins of his single-minded devotion to principle, no matter what the situation. Wilson tells us that,like Lincoln's beliefs, Stephens's convictions "have ultimately non-rational sources" (433). Since, however, Lincoln is depicted as one who hunts as one of a pack, whereas Stephens is usually at odds with the pack, it appears that Lincoln's ideas draw their emotional power from aggressive impulses, whereas the emotional sources of Stephens's ideas seem innocuously pacific. Yet Wilson himself provides evidence that suggests Stephens's intransigence, his determination to "be himself and nothing but himself," has its own links to destructive or violent impulses.

Wilson quotes a letter from Stephens to his half-brother Linton in which Stephens reveals:

the secret of my life has been revenge. Not revenge in the usual acceptation of that term—but a determination to war over against fate—To meet the world in all its forces, to master evil with good . . . I have often had my whole soul instantly aroused with the fury of a lion and the ambition of a Caesar by . . . as slight a thing as a look! Oh what have I suffered from a look! What have I suffered from the tone of a remark . . . from a supposed injury? an intended injury? But each . . . such pang was the friction that brought out the latent fires. (389–90)

Here Stephens's attempt to rationalize his struggle as a battle "to master evil with good" is betrayed by the much stronger language suggesting personal animosities. In Wilson's words "Stephens, in order to prove his strength, must always pit it against that of others; he must cut a diagonal line, establish a separate axis . . . that will cause the whole globe to wobble" (433).

In Wilson's characterization, for Stephens the result that matters is causing "the whole globe to wobble," a pseudo-result that is entirely destructive. On the basis of Wilson's own presentation of Stephens's life, then, the cause of the South, which Stephens is supposed to embody in its purest form, seems much less innocuous and much more complicated than his summary formulation of the issue as one between the isolated individual and big government, between one "who will not accept domination" and a "benevolent despot" seems to suggest.

The second half of *Patriotic Gore* slowly brings out these complications. One learns, for example, that, against the Northern myth of the war as a crusade for freedom, "the South had a reciprocal myth . . . a hallowed ideal of gallantry, aristocratic freedom, fine manners and luxurious living." Despite Wilson's reference to the "equal fanaticism" of the South, this passage suggests that there remains a qualitative difference between the myth of the North and the myth of the South. An attempt to hold onto "a hallowed ideal of gallantry, aristocratic freedom, fine manners and luxurious living" would seem to offer far less license for any departure from traditional moral restraints than would the "Armageddonlike vision" of the North (438). However wrongheaded or factually inaccurate it may have been, the "myth of the South" seems less dangerous than the North's belief in a holy crusade. Today it is surely versions of the Northern myth that excuse violence and aggression throughout the world. No contemporary nation calls its troops to battle or builds its nuclear armory on behalf of "a hallowed ideal of . . . fine manners and luxurious living."

Yet Wilson's study of postwar Southern literature reveals that the myth of the South carries its own emotional dynamite. Sidney Lanier's poem "The Revenge of Hamish" provides striking evidence for his argument. Hamish, a servant of a Scottish Highland laird, gains revenge for a whipping by leaping off a cliff with the laird's son in his arms, after he has already forced the laird himself to endure a whipping in the hope of saving his child—after, that is, it would appear that Hamish has gained compensation for his own injury. Wilson comments that "the fierce pride of the Scottish henchman, his instant retaliation, at whatever cost to himself, when beaten by his choleric master, really figure the revolt of the South and make one of its most tragic expressions in literature" (522).

The spirit of Lanier's South is now characterized by Wilson as "self-annihilating fury" (522). But the danger of the impulse that animated the South is not characterized fully by even such a phrase as "self-annihilating fury," suggestive though that is. Hamish kills not only himself but the laird's child as well. Wilson is ready to incorporate this motif also into his view of the historical significance of the poem:

The arrogant suicide of Hamish, leaping with the child in his arms, is a parable of the action of the South in recklessly destroying the Union. Tall Hamish the henchman dies poisoned—by hatred, by the lust for revenge. (528)

On the basis of Wilson's interpretation of this poem the "unreconstructed Southerner" in all of us seems at least as dangerous to ourselves and others as his opponent, the "benevolent despot."

Wilson drives the point home in his consideration of George Washington Cable's *Gideon's Band*, a novel whose main characters are a "courteous old fraud of a Southern senator and an insufferable young pair of Southern twins" (600). The conclusion parallels "The Revenge of Hamish," as the twins finally commit suicide in a scene that Wilson describes as a "a parable for the suicide of secession, the self-doomed demise of the Confederacy through truculent honor and pride of race" (601).

The South is not only self-destructive but also despotic, the quality once identified only with the North. Wilson notes the unanimity with which the official and literary South condemned Cable for his evenhanded treatment of racial issues; he shows how Cable was virulently attacked in public even by those who privately commended his work, and he draws a parallel with far-reaching implications: "The fierce patriotism and pride of defeat override all mercy and reason. We have seen it in Hitler's Germany" (576). The South is identified with Hitler's Germany because of the development of what one might call a "culture of defeat" in both. Victimization, apparently, does not render one innocent; if the Northern myth is associated with benevolent despotism, the cause of the South is now associated with a despotism that is anything but benevolent.

Earlier in *Patriotic Gore* the stubbornness of the South was associated with the simple assertion of individual selfhood, but now the impulse seems less simple and more problematic. Reflecting on those Southerners who applauded Cable in private but excoriated him in public, Wilson comments:

There was evidently in this stubbornness of the Southerner in sticking to an official position when it must lead to conscious falsity an element of the strategy for which George Orwell, in writing of the modern dictatorships, has coined the word "doublethink." (575–76)

The cause of the South thus lends itself, Wilson reveals, not to the defense of individual freedom but, rather, to the kind of self-induced brainwashing portrayed in the most powerful literary picture of modern tyranny.

By this time, without explicitly retracting or even modifying his original formulation of "the Southern cause," Wilson has nevertheless greatly altered the reader's sense of what that cause entails. This qualification or transmutation is made through the devices of art rather than by straightforward argumentation. The same motif arises in a series of different contexts, is seen from a number of different perspectives; no one perspective is simply wrong, but any one is inadequate to the overall perspective afforded the reader.

If the discussion of Southern poets and novelists alters our view of the cause of the South by allowing us to see the elements of sheer destructiveness inherent in the revolt of the South, Wilson's study of Northern writers encourages us to see the cause of the North in a more complex and sympathetic way, so that finally the concept associated most closely with that cause is not "despotism" but, instead, a concept virtually its opposite in its moral implications: "responsibility."

The literary movement that corresponds to the acceptance of responsibility Wilson calls the "Chastening of American Prose Style." Wilson argues that American prose before the Civil War was characterized, for better and for worse, by a style that reflected the lack of pressure exerted by society on its writers. Under the pressure of events the older American prose style came to seem "grandiose and imprecise" (638). Likewise, the "florid American rhetoric" ((639) could not answer the demands of the war years, as Edward Everett's speech at Gettysburg demonstrates. Lincoln's Gettysburg Address, on the other hand, is the outstanding example of a "terser, less pretentious style" (640). In part, Wilson speculates, the style of the Address derives from "the language of the West, the simple and forceful speech that Lincoln had been hearing from his boyhood" (646–47).

But the Gettysburg Address is unique only in its greatness; the movement toward a chaster, less pretentious prose was a general one. One reason for the tendency to speak the language of ordinary life was politicians' desire to reach a wider public. "But were there no other reasons . . . ?" Wilson asks. He notes that the development of that very mechanical age that crushed the spontaneity of poetic utterance also promoted "the ideal of neat contrivance," thereby, paradoxically, leading to more intense artistic expression. The observation is convincing and important. But Wilson is searching for something more, some quality in the new prose that is not merely a reflection of the times but, instead, a response to its demands. Wilson finds this response in the "lucidity, precision, terseness" of Lincoln and Grant. And Wilson asks again the question that he had posed in a general way before: "What was it they had in common that gave them the same traits of style?" (649). Wilson notes their common Western background but rejects that as a sufficient cause. He then asks, "What was it, then, that led Grant and Lincoln to express themselves with equal concision?" (650).

Wilson has now posed the same question three times. Clearly the answer is very important to him, and, indeed, the answer is surely one of the key passages of the entire book—as important in its own way as the more striking passage in which Wilson announces that "the cause of the South is the cause of us all" (434). The passage is not only an answer to the immediate question but also a response, long-delayed but nevertheless direct, to the earlier passage:

> What was it, then, that led Grant and Lincoln to express themselves with equal concision? It was undoubtedly the decisiveness with which they had to speak. They had not time in which to waste words. To temporize or deceive was too dangerous. They are obliged to issue orders and to lay down lines of policy that will immediately be understood. Their role is to convince and direct. This is the language of responsibility. (650)

In the context of the Stephens chapter Lincoln's practicality seemed merely a kind of mean craftiness, while "impossibilism" signified a romantic affirmation of human freedom. Now, however, Wilson presents the commitment to practical results of a Lincoln or a Grant as an acceptance of moral responsibility whose aesthetic results are prose works of honesty and directness. This turn in Edmund Wilson's long book is very impressive and even moving. Perhaps it was this passage that Alfred Kazin had most in mind when he said that *Patriotic Gore* "contains, almost incidentally, the most profound considerations on literature in this country that I have ever seen" (44).

Yet something is left out; something is missing. It seems odd to attribute the literary impact of the Gettysburg Address entirely to the need "to issue orders and to lay down lines of policy" (650). Lincoln did neither on the battlefield at Gettysburg. Instead, Lincoln played a role on a ceremonial occasion, attempting to find meaning and offer consolation in the face of death. Lincoln met the occasion with a speech which, although brief—"terse," to use Wilson's word—possesses, nevertheless, the evocative and intellectual power of great literature. Wilson recognizes the power of the Gettyburg Address but finally cannot account for it.

Why is Wilson unable to come to terms with the greatness of the Address? To do so would be to admit that "Lincoln's epic" is something more than the rationalization of "benevolent despotism" and even something more than the assumption of responsibility. It would suggest that perhaps the Civil War was a war for human freedom, after all. And this Wilson cannot admit. To discover some moral basis in all the carnage of the Civil War would lead to another admission: that the modern United States, superpower though it may be, is not utterly remote from the traditions of the old Republic. And to go so far might seem to suggest that his anger at the preparations for biological and nuclear warfare, at the lies of the cold war, has somehow been soothed.

Nevertheless, obliquely, Wilson makes that admission in the last sentences of *Patriotic Gore*. In the closing chapter, on Justice Oliver Wendell Holmes Jr., Wilson has emphasized Holmes's skepticism, his doubts about democracy, his attempt to achieve intellectual integrity by becoming a "jobbist," by "touching the superlative" in his own field and refusing to care about the rest of humanity. But Wilson also suggests that, despite his skepticism and despite his commitment to personal integrity, Holmes throughout his life maintained the "conviction that the United States had a special meaning and mission to devote one's whole life to which was a sufficient dedication for the highest gifts" (796). And in the last sentence of the work he interprets Justice Holmes's decision to leave his estate to the United States government in words that suggest that Wilson is also articulating his own feelings about his own relation to U. S. society:

> The American Constitution was, as he came to declare, an "experiment"—what was to come of our democratic society it was impossible for a philosopher to tell—but he had taken responsibility for its working, he had subsisted and achieved his fame through his tenure of the place it had given him; and he returned to the treasury of the Union the little that he had to leave. (796)

In thus interpreting the significance of Justice Holmes's will, Edmund Wilson achieves a final artistic balance. The conclusion of the first half of *Patriotic Gore* is the suspicion that "the cause of the South is the cause of us all," while the book as a whole ends with an affirmation, however oblique and qualified, of the cause of the Union. The urge to unrestrained freedom has been balanced against the claims of society, of responsibility to others. The universal reductionism of the introduction has been countered by the depiction of individual lives in the full particularity of their circumstances. *Patriotic Gore* has achieved a complex unity that is based on the dramatic presentation of unresolved oppositions, reconciled only by the achievement of dramatic balance.

Wilson's work is finally a work of cultural self-criticism, a working through of American myths that ends with no consolations except the dignity of truth and the unity of literature. The "unrepentant Southerner" and the "benevolent despot" in ourselves and in our history have not been harmonized. The contemporary discomfort with *Patriotic Gore* is in large part a token of the achievement of Edmund Wilson's masterpiece as cultural self-criticism. *Patriotic Gore* continues to judge and trouble us today and thus to demonstrate, still, its greatness.

Chapter 7

The Example of Ralph Ellison

In the essays that make up *Shadow and Act* (1964) and *Going to the Territory* (1986) Ralph Ellison demonstrates that a commitment to democracy and equality does not require a rejection of standards in art, music, and literature. Ellison argues persuasively that the democratizing of culture demands that even works arising outside the conventional venues of high culture—for example, the music of Duke Ellington, Charlie Christian, and Charlie Parker—be judged by the highest relevant standards. Ellison's essays are particularly important today because they provide exemplary instances of the ways in which an insistence on aesthetic excellence can be united with a flexible awareness of the multiple, often unexpected routes by which excellence may be achieved. Repeatedly connecting art and politics without reducing one to the other, Ellison's essays demonstrate the possibilities of sensibility and imagination when these are freed from the obstructions of methodology and system and illuminated by critical intelligence. "The Little Man at Chehaw Station," an essay from *Going to the Territory*, exemplifies both Ellison's central themes and the novelistic flair with which he explores them.

Ellison tells us that he first heard about the "little man behind the stove" at Chehaw Station as a student at Tuskegee Institute during the mid-1930s. His informant was Hazel Harrison, "a highly respected concert pianist and teacher" (3), whose talents had been recognized in Europe by composers such as Sergei Prokofiev but whose race had prevented such recognition in the United States. She tells the incredulous Ellison that, while it is always important to play one's best, "in this country, there's something more involved." Here, she says,

> you must *always* play your best, even if it's only in the waiting room at Chehaw Station, because in this country there'll always be a little man hidden behind the stove. . . . There'll always be the little man whom you

don't expect, and he'll know the *music,* and the *tradition,* and the standards of *musicianship* required for whatever you set out to perform! (4)

Chehaw Station itself "was a lonely whistle-stop," which, the young Ellison pondered, "was the last place in the area where I would expect to encounter a connoisseur lying in wait to pounce upon some rash, unsuspecting musician" (4–5).

As the narrator of *Invisible Man* broods over his grandfather's injunction to "overcome 'em with yeses" (16), so Ellison ponders the meaning of Hazel Harrison's "little man at Chehaw Station." The figure comes to have several meanings for him. He associates the little man "with the metamorphic character of the general American audience . . . that unknown quality which renders the American audience far more than a receptive instrument that may be dominated" (6–7). The little man has strong likes and dislikes: "Being quintessentially American, he enjoys the joke, the confounding of hierarchical expectations" (11). On the other hand, "he is repelled by works of art that would strip human experience—especially American experience—of its wonder and stubborn complexity" (13).

The cultural effect of democracy is not to depress tastes to the same low level but, rather, to free taste and artistic ability from dependence on social class or status. No human being anywhere can be explained entirely by environment and heredity, but Ellison suggests that "America's social mobility, its universal education, and its relative freedom of cultural information" brings such unpredictability to the fore (8). Given such uncertainty, "the chances are that any American audience will conceal at least *one* individual whose knowledge and taste will complement, or surpass" the artist's own (9). Ellison suggests that "the man behind Chehaw's stove" might serve "as a metaphor for those individuals we sometimes meet whose refinement of sensibility is inadequately explained by family background, formal education, or social status" (8).

Ellison makes his case by recourse to experience rather than statistics, depicting scenes he takes to be representative, in their very uniqueness, of a culture peculiarly American. On a "sunny Sunday afternoon on New York's Riverside Drive" Ellison runs across

a light-skinned, blue-eyed, Afro-American-featured individual [who] . . . disrupted the visual peace of the promenading throng by racing up in a shiny new blue Volkswagen Beetle decked out with a gleaming Rolls-Royce radiator . . .

Clad in handsome black riding boots and fawn-colored riding breeches of English tailoring, he took the curb wielding—with an ultra-pukkasahib haughtiness—a leather riding crop. A dashy dashiki . . . flowed from his broad shoulders down to the arrogant, military flare of his breeches-tops, while six feet six inches or so above his heels, a black Homburg hat, tilted at a jaunty angle, floated majestically on the crest of his huge Afro-coiffed head. (22)

Who was this individual? The very difficulty of classifying him according to some "rigid ethno-cultural perspective" (23) suggests to Ellison that he is quintessentially American:

Whatever his politics, sources of income, hierarchical status, and such, he revealed his essential "Americanness" in his freewheeling assault upon traditional forms of the Western aesthetic. Whatever the identity he presumed to project, he was exercising an American freedom and was a product of the melting pot and the conscious or unconscious comedy it brews. Culturally, he was an American joker. (24)

Whatever the artistic or literary tastes of this "American joker" might be, they could be as little predicted by his social class or income as his personal appearance.

Ellison tells another story that makes his point even more emphatically. In the late 1930s he found himself in the basement of a tenement in Harlem, where he heard "male Afro-American voices, raised in violent argument. The language was profane, the style of speech a Southern idiomatic vernacular such as was spoken by formally uneducated Afro-American workingmen." As the young Ellison listened to the voices and gradually became aware of what the argument was about, he began to feel that "a bizarre practical joke had been staged" (33);

The subject of their contention confounded all my assumptions regarding the correlation between educational levels, class, race, and the possession of conscious culture. Impossible as it seemed, these foul-mouthed black workingmen were locked in verbal combat over which of two celebrated Metropolitan Opera divas was the superior soprano! (34)

When Ellison discovered that the four had been appearing in operas at the Metropolitan as "the finest damn bunch of Egyptians you ever seen" he began to laugh "in appreciation of the hilarious American joke that centered on the incongruities of race, economic status, and culture" (37).

The joke is on him, as much as anybody—it is Ellison's own assumptions that have been "confounded." As an earnest young radical, he has been gathering signatures for a petition on behalf of the oppressed. He is an enlightened individual, superior to those he believes he is assisting both in his ability to appreciate high culture and in his understanding of radical theory. Yet both his sources of pride play him false. It turns out that one does not have to attend college to be an opera buff, and the sociological categories he has learned "cast less illumination than an inert lump of coal." Discomfited but not defeated, Ellison recognizes the furnace tenders as incarnations of the little man behind the stove at Chehaw Station about whom Hazel Harrison had warned him. Their individuality is invisible or at least unimportant for sociology, but that individuality becomes something to cherish and celebrate when seen with the aid of "the clear, pluralistic, melting-pot light of American cultural possibility" (38).

Ellison finds a basis for critique not only in the abstract principles of democracy and equality but also in the incidents of his own experience, which fail so dramatically to fit the patterns of anybody's theory. Just as the narrator of *Invisible Man* is repeatedly confounded when his expectations collide with events, so throughout his essays Ellison himself is recurrently forced to acknowledge the force of experience over fixed ideas. It is not theories but plays and novels, music and art, that respond most adequately to the tensions and complexities of experience. Watching a stage performance of Erskine Caldwell's *Tobacco Road* in 1937, Ellison is "reduced to . . . helpless laughter." Despite appearances, his out-of-control laughter is no simple response to the play's stunning ability to fasten the most virulent "anti-Negro stereotypes" suddenly "upon the necks of whites" ("An Extravagance of Laughter," 186). If *Tobacco Road* debunks the pretensions of whites, it also threatens Ellison's own pretensions to sophistication and maturity. The young Ellison had protected himself by thinking of his way of life as "segregated but in many ways superior" to that of the poor whites of *Tobacco Road* (197), but the sexual comedy of Caldwell's play turns out to be "embarrassingly symbolic of my own frustration as a healthy young man whose sexual outlet was limited" (196). Ellison's laughter signifies his ability to move from the "embarrassment, self-anger, ethnic scorn" that the play first aroused in him to a rueful recognition of "certain absurd aspects of our common humanity" (193).

Throughout his essays Ellison insists upon a truth that his own experience will not let him deny, whatever sociologists or even radical theorists may assert—the specific richness and integrity of the African American experience, despite slavery, discrimination, and prejudice. Ellison's criticism of U. S. society for its failure to live up to "the sacred principles of the Constitution and the Bill of Rights" ("Brave Words for a Startling Occasion," 104) would seem to echo the thesis of Gunnar Myrdal's book *An American Dilemma*, which contrasts the American Creed of equality with the reality of segregation and bigotry. In 1944, however, Ellison criticized Myrdal for failing to recognize the vitality of the life created by "American Negroes," despite all the obstacles put in their path:

> Are American Negroes simply the creation of white men, or have they at least helped to create themselves out of what they found around them? Men have made a way of life in caves and upon cliffs, why cannot Negroes have made a life upon the horns of the white man's dilemma? (*"An American Dilemma*: A Review," 315–16)

When Irving Howe in 1963 argued that Richard Wright's angry novels were more authentic and truer to the black experience than the fiction of James Baldwin and Ralph Ellison, Ellison replied with anger of his own. In "The World and the Jug" he questions Howe's apparent willingness to reduce African-American experience to nothing except "unrelieved suffering" (111). He notes that Howe's desire to maintain a "revolutionary posture" prevents him from noticing the individuality of particular African Americans, since for Howe each is simply "an abstract embodiment of living hell" (112). The young Ellison was not willing merely to enjoy the reversal of stereotypes employed in *Tobacco Road*; he could not help connecting Erskine Caldwell's depiction of poor whites with the most vulnerable aspects of his own identity. Radical theorizing and sloganeering seems, however, to provide a means of working out personal conflicts while escaping self-examination; harmless enough, perhaps, except that the humanity of the "oppressed" about whom one theorizes gets lost in the process. What begins as an innocent, indeed meritorious, impulse turns into a kind of cultural crime:

> One of the most insidious crimes occurring in this democracy is that of designating another, politically weaker, less socially acceptable, people as the receptacle for one's own self-disgust, for one's own infantile rebellions, for one's own fears of, and retreats from, reality. It is the crime of reducing the humanity of others to that of a mere convenience, a counter in a banal game which involves no apparent risk to ourselves. (124)

Ellison's argument should not be caricatured as a refusal to allow whites to comment on African-American culture. In the same essay, "The World and the Jug," in which he points out the limitations of Howe's "sociological vision of society" (116), Ellison also points out how Richard Wright's eagerness to use art as a weapon led to Wright's own failure to present a portrait of African-American life that would leave room for the possibility of an African American "as intelligent, as creative or as dedicated as himself [Richard Wright]" (120). In other words, "Wright could imagine Bigger, but Bigger could not possibly imagine Richard Wright" (114). Ellison honors Richard Wright as a friend and "perhaps a great man" (141), but he is as ready to challenge Wright's apparent endorsement of the view that "Negroes" lack "high humanity" (120) as he is Howe's assertions about what constitutes "the authentic Negro writer" (118).

Highlighting "the sheer unexpectedness of life in these United States" ("Going to the Territory," 120), Ellison deflates both the old racist myths and well-meaning patronizing, both the white refusal to recognize any independent black culture and the black impulse toward separatism. In "The Myth of the Flawed White Southerner" Ellison analyzes his differences with a group of liberal white intellectuals who in 1965 boycotted a presidential ceremony, a National Festival for the Arts, on the grounds of their opposition to the Vietnam War. Ellison reflects that, although he has much in common with "my fellow intellectuals," his perspective is inevitably different from theirs. His liberal friends, it seems to Ellison, had supposed that "I and those of my background possess no interest that they, my friends and colleagues, had any need to understand or respect" (77). Ellison also calls upon that very "background" to question the proponents of cultural separatism. Himself a great exploiter of the possibilities of vernacular speech, Ellison takes issue with all those, black or white, who think that standard English is "beyond" African Americans. Recalling Dr. Inman Page, the principal of Ellison's Douglass High School in Oklahoma City and the first African American graduate of Brown University, Ellison knows better:

> Today we hear much discussion of what is termed "Black English," a concept unheard of during my school days. And yet we were all the grandchildren of slaves and most of us spoke in the idioms that were native to the regions from which our families had migrated. Still, no one, much less our teachers, suggested that Standard English was beyond us; how could they with such examples as Dr. Page before us? He could make the language of Shakespeare and the King James version of the Bible resound within us in such ways that its majesty and beauty seemed as natural and as normal coming from one of our own as an inspired jazz improvisation or an eloquently sung spiritual. ("Going to the Territory," 137)

Noting that few African American musicians have received the respect due them from the society at large, Ellison celebrates the music of Duke Ellington,

Charlie Christian, Charlie Parker, Jimmy Rushing and Mahalia Jackson, among others. A truly democratic culture, he suggests, will appreciate the excellence of vernacular styles as well as "the styles associated with aristocracy," but Ellison refuses to concede that the very demand for excellence is somehow antidemocratic. Hazel Harrison taught him a quite different lesson: democracy requires the highest standards from both creator and performer, since the citizens of a democratic polity refuse to limit themselves to the roles that class or status seem to assign them. Although Ellison argues for a cultural pluralism that recognizes vernacular styles as well as genteel, he points out that those theorists who reject all value judgments find themselves in disagreement with the very artists whom they claim to be defending:

> Although jazz musicians are practitioners of a vernacular style, they are also unreconstructed elitists when it comes to maintaining the highest standards of the music which expresses their sense of the American experience. ("Going to the Territory," 140)

Ralph Ellison's delight in variety, his exploration of what democracy means for culture, and his insistence on the particular richness of African American culture all link him to the valid concerns of the proponents of "political correctness." The tone and spirit of his writings, however, move beyond the self-righteousness and the aesthetic nihilism that so often attend the moral claims of the cultural Left. In contrast, throughout his career Ellison has refused to exploit the sufferings of himself or his ancestors for rhetorical purposes; against Irving Howe's declaration that the only authentic black posture is protest, he declares proudly: "There is also an American Negro tradition which teaches one to deflect racial provocation and to master and contain pain. It is a tradition which abhors as obscene any trading on one's own anguish for gain or sympathy"("The World and the Jug," 111).

Ellison's novel and his essays frequently move into the comic mode, not as a means of avoiding the truth but because comedy sometimes allows one to confront harsh or unexpected truths that would otherwise be ignored. Ellison explores the ramifications of the "American joke" to which Henry James referred when, in a famous passage of his book *Hawthorne*, James listed all the ways in which the United States differed from the older, hierarchical societies of Europe and thereby made things so difficult for the novelist, concluding that "the American knows that a good deal remains; what it is that remains—that is his secret, his joke, as one may say" (352). For Ellison, if not for James, the "joke" is inextricably connected with the disjunction between the official national commitment to human equality and the realities of race. Those who consider Ellison's "joking" about racial matters a sign of his lack of concern would do well to ponder his exploration of humor as a response to lynching:

> For the ultimate goal of lynchers is that of achieving racial purification through destroying the lynchers' identification with the basic *humanity* of their victims. Hence their deafness to cries of pain, their stoniness before the sight and stench of burning flesh, their exhilarated and grotesque self-righteousness. . . . Yes, but for the group thus victimized, such sacrifices are the source of emotions that move far beyond the tragic conception of pity and terror and down into the abysmal levels of conflict and folly from which arise our famous American humor. Brother, the blackness of *Afro-American* "black humor" is not black, it is tragically human and finds its source and object in the notion of "whiteness." ("An Extravagance of Laughter," 178)

Ellison's willingness to explore the roots of the "American joke" to such "abysmal levels" enables him to move in *Shadow and Act* and *Going to the Territory* from considerations of the tall tale as folk art to celebrations of Charlie Christian and Duke Ellington to appreciations of more canonical figures such as Hemingway and Faulkner, always without the crutch of categorization but with a readiness to be surprised by the unexpected in both art and life.

In *Blues People* Imamu Amiri Baraka, then writing as LeRoi Jones, seems, according to Ellison, to interpret the blues as politics and sociology but rarely "as lyric, as a form of poetry" ("Blues People" 248). It is enough, Ellison comments, "to give even the blues the blues" (249). Although Jones's book is undoubtedly written in order to aid the black struggle for freedom, Ellison in "Blues People" notes that Jones's refusal to take the blues seriously as art has the effect of reducing the humanity of African Americans themselves. Quoting Jones's assertion that "a slave cannot be a man," Ellison retorts that such a dictum fails to do justice to the stubborn insistence with which African Americans asserted their humanity, through music and in multiple other ways, even during slavery:

> "A slave" writes Jones, "cannot be a man." But what, one might ask, of those moments when he feels his metabolism aroused by the rising of the sap in spring? What of his identity among other slaves? With his wife? And isn't it closer to the truth that far from considering themselves only in terms of that abstraction, "a slave," the enslaved really thought of them-

selves as *men* who had been unjustly enslaved?...A slave was, to the extent that he was a *musician*, one who expressed himself in the world of sound. Thus . . . he would never feel awed before the music which the technique of the white musician made available. (254)

Despite Ellison's use of the inclusive masculine, his argument anticipates a contemporary contretemps over language. It has been argued that the use of "slaves" rather than, say, "enslaved human beings" is a kind of implicit racism, since the terminology suggests that slavery was at the core of being rather than a product of specific historical and social conditions. Unlike some present controversialists, Ellison has no interest in impugning the good faith of his adversary, nor, given his delight in vernacular forms of expression, could Ellison endorse programs to purify language of all expressions that might be offensive sometime to somebody. In reviewing *Blues People,* Ralph Ellison does succeed in demonstrating how political zeal, even on behalf of the oppressed, can lead to an inadvertent negating of the humanity of those on whose behalf one is supposedly struggling.

In *Invisible Man* Ellison demonstrates how the drive for revolutionary purity, when unleavened by the self-knowledge that humor can provide, perverts the noblest aspirations. The strangely familiar language in which the heartfelt speech of the narrator is denounced by a member of The Brotherhood offers prima facie evidence that the fall of Communism has not left this section of the novel outdated: "'In my opinion the speech was wild, hysterical, politically irresponsible and dangerous,' he snapped. 'And worse than that, it was *incorrect*! He pronounced 'incorrect' as though the term described the most heinous crime imaginable'"(341). The members of The Brotherhood see themselves as saviors, an elite vanguard with history on their side. The narrator is drawn to them because of his own fear of getting "lost in the backwash of history" (366). His break with The Brotherhood is not occasioned by a sudden faith in capitalism or even in electoral politics but, instead, by an epiphany in which he recognizes the human reality of those whom Brother Jack dismisses as "only our raw materials, *one* of the raw materials to be shaped to our program" (461). Perhaps, the narrator muses, perhaps it's at least as possible that the "true leaders" will emerge from the politically incorrect and illiterate as from the vanguard. Looking at the crowd emerging from a Harlem subway stop, he sees African Americans "such as I had been before I found Brotherhood" (429), people whose political ignorance renders them expendable, mere "raw material" for the political elite:

What about those three boys, coming now along the platform, tall and slender, walking stiffly with swinging shoulders in their well-pressed too-hot-for-summer suits, their collars high and tight about their necks, their identical hats of black cheap felt set upon the crowns of their heads with a severe formality above their hard conked hair? It was as though I'd never seen their like before . . . who knew but that they were the saviors, the true leaders, the bearers of something precious? The stewards of something uncomfortable, burdensome. (429–431)

Neither Ellison nor the narrator of *Invisible Man* are interested in romanticizing the poor or the oppressed; the insight at which the narrator finally arrives is the sheer impossibility of summing up even one individual, let alone an entire group, in the language of political slogans. The way in which the narrator defends the dead Clifton against Brother Jack's willingness to define him simply as "a traitor" makes a general statement about the complexity of human beings:

"He was a man and a Negro; a man and a brother; a man and a traitor, as you say; then he was a dead man, and alive or dead he was jam-full of contradictions." (456)

Against this hard-won insight any attempt to condemn an entire sex, race, people, or epoch by reference to the allegedly higher standards of a contemporary moral elite seems irremediably frivolous. Throughout his career Ralph Ellison was periodically denounced as an out-of-date Uncle Tom by figures attempting to certify their own membership in the moral avant-garde. Yet in the last decade of the twentieth century both his novel and his essays seem more important than ever, his stature only enhanced by the years.[1]

Part 3

Criticism and Cultural Radicalism

Chapter 8

Innocence Regained: The Career of Leslie Fiedler

Leslie Fiedler's influence on contemporary programs in American literature is twofold. The Leslie Fiedler who wrote *Love and Death in the American Novel* (1960) helped shape yesterday's critical consensus on nineteenth-century American fiction. Fiedler's work is one of the reasons why the American novels of that century are no longer seen as stages on the road to the "triumph of realism." If many students first encounter Leslie Fiedler on the reading list for Ph.D. exams in American literature, Fiedler is also an important author for those who wish to do away with such lists. He is one of the founding fathers of the popular culture movement, and in *What Was Literature?* (1982) he forcefully argues that cultural studies should be viewed not merely as another academic specialty but as a fundamental challenge to traditional academic categories. It is a striking example of the—often unacknowledged—influence of Fiedler that he is both a shaper of one consensus and a source for its challenger, the new orthodoxy of "cultural studies." Ironically, Fiedler's long pursuit of the outrageous has ended in the fostering of two (contending) academic orthodoxies.

But there is yet another Fiedler, one whose work retains its capacity to outrage academics. Few of those required to read *Love and Death in the American Novel*, and even fewer of those influenced by Fiedler the cultural radical, are likely to have read Fiedler the spokesman for liberal anticommunism, a view he defended in controversial essays on the Hiss case, on the trial and execution of Ethel and Julius Rosenberg, and on Joseph McCarthy. When these essays are mentioned it is usually to dismiss them as particularly egregious examples of cold war rhetoric. In *The New York Intellectuals* (1987) Alan Wald characterizes them as "virulent anticommunist essays . . . full of dubious psychologizing and calls for atonement by the entire left" (279). Ten years earlier Morris Dickstein had asserted, "It would be hard to find more vicious examples of serious political writing than the first three essays in Leslie Fiedler's *An End to Innocence*"

(41).[1] In contrast, this chapter argues that these essays, and particularly the essays on "Hiss, Chambers, and the Age of Innocence" and "Afterthoughts on the Rosenbergs," present examples of cultural-political criticism superior to Fiedler's later, emphatically antiestablishment writings. The cultural criticism that these essays exemplify remains important, even after the end of the cold war, while books such as *Being Busted* (1969) and *What Was Literature?* seem dated already.

In *What Was Literature?* Fiedler offers his own interpretation of the movement of his career. Repeatedly, Fiedler insists that the movement of his thought can be seen as a turn from hypocrisy to honesty, from shame-faced moralizing to open expression of his inmost feelings. Whereas sentimentality was once the key curse word of his criticism, now "hypocrisy" seems virtually the only sin that is really sinful—against which "sado-masochistic voyeurism," for example, seems downright healthy (49). Repeatedly, *What Was Literature?* tells us how its author's onetime commitment to elitist standards forced him to deny his own literary experience and his own emotions. Now, however, he has come out of the closet, not only admitting but reveling in his willingness to be moved by schlock movies such as *Beyond the Valley of the Dolls* and, conversely, his boredom with much high culture (21).

In an introduction to *Inadvertent Epic*, a 1979 work incorporated into *What Was Literature?* Barrie Hayne sums up Fiedler's work with the assertion that "the whole direction of his career is toward affirmation" and asserts that "health and self-understanding lie in the direction Fiedler is pointing" (xi). "Affirmation" is indeed the dominant mood of Fiedler's later work, but whether the personal and cultural affirmations of *What Was Literature?* lead to self-understanding is another question.

Fiedler himself seems to believe that he has moved to an advocacy of cultural and political radicalism from an earlier anticommunist liberalism and cultural elitism; though there is some truth in this, a more significant reversal is Fiedler's move away from any acknowledgment of responsibility for the culture and, especially, for the politics of his time—a move that ends with an implicit assertion of simple innocence. The later Fiedler—roughly, that work including and after *Being Busted*—is vulnerable to the critique of political and cultural innocence that the early Fiedler articulated in *An End to Innocence* (1955) and *Love and Death in the American Novel.*

A consideration of the essays in *An End to Innocence* reveals an author quite different from the portrayal in *What Was Literature?* of a snobbish elitist, secure in his insider position within the bastions of high culture and academic respectability. Instead, one sees an author engaging in the most difficult form of analysis, criticism from within, criticism of social and political tendencies with which one shares the most. Fiedler's essays collected in 1955 as *An End to Innocence* criticize intellectuals, especially liberal intellectuals and, even more specifically, liberal intellectuals of his own generation. Not that Fiedler is interested in presenting himself as one somehow beyond such labels; instead, he asserts proudly:

> I have, as a matter of fact, been pleased to discover how often I have managed to tell what still seems to me the truth about my world and myself as a liberal, intellectual, writer, American, and Jew. I do not mind, as some people apparently do, thinking of myself in such categorical terms; being representative of a class, a generation, a certain temper seems to me not at all a threat to my individuality. (xiii)

For this discussion the most important essays in *An End to Innocence* are those dealing with the Hiss case and with the Rosenbergs. Although Hiss was convicted of perjury rather than espionage, his trial convinced many that liberal intellectuals, even those who appeared most respectable, were capable of treason and were inclined to lie about it when caught. The trial and execution of the Rosenbergs smeared left-wing Jewish intellectuals in particular with the charge of treasonous disloyalty. Both cases remain controversial today, more than thirty-five years later. Fiedler's essays assume the guilt of both Hiss and the Rosenbergs, and so far his assumption has not been disproven. But the essays do not depend for their significance on whatever the facts of the cases finally turn out to be. Fiedler is primarily concerned with analyzing the political-cultural significance of the trials for American liberals, especially those, like himself, who had moved to liberalism from an earlier Communism or sympathy with Communism.

Fiedler argues that the willingness of many liberals to defend both Hiss and the Rosenbergs was not based on a reasoned analysis of the evidence in either case. The liberal defenders of both held to a sentimental belief that people of goodwill—meaning people on the Left, like themselves—could not possibly commit the crimes of which they were accused. More desperately, some believed that even if Hiss or the Rosenbergs were factually guilty, such guilt was merely a kind of technical detail. Perhaps they had made errors, but their hearts were in the right place, and their accusers were right-wingers, whose accidental factual justification mattered little compared to the evil of their ideology.

For Fiedler, on the other hand, the guilt of Hiss and the Rosenbergs is an ugly but unavoidable reality. Fiedler notes that Hiss was tried for perjury rather than treason, since the statute of limitations prevented prosecution for his possibly treasonous actions in 1936–37. Why, then, did Hiss not tell the truth and thus avoid indictment for perjury? For Fiedler, in "Hiss, Chambers, and the Age of Innocence," Hiss's unwillingness to admit and take responsibility for his past actions exemplifies the moral failure of Fiedler's own generation of liberal intellectuals. It is a generation that has refused to grow up, since "the qualifying act of moral adulthood is precisely this admission of responsibility for the past and its consequences, however undesired or unforeseen" (4). Fiedler finds the statement of Henry Julian Wadleigh, a minor figure in the Hiss case, symptomatic; Wadleigh's "confession" was really "a disguise for self-congratulation, a device for clinging to the dream of innocence. He cannot, even in the dock, believe that a man of liberal persuasion is capable of wrong." It is the perpetuation of this myth of innocence that, Fiedler argues, connects American liberalism with Hiss and Wadleigh, and it is the collapse of this myth that is one of the inadvertent, even illogical, but nonetheless most important results of the Hiss trial:

> It was this belief that was the implicit dogma of American liberalism during the past decades, piling up a terrible burden of self-righteousness and self-deceit to be paid for on the day when it would become impossible any longer to believe that the man of good will is identical with the righteous man, and that the liberal is *per se* the hero. That day came at different times to different people . . . for a good many . . . it came on August 17, 1948, when Hiss and Chambers were brought face to face before the House Committee on Un-American Activities. (8)

What makes Fiedler's analysis still exemplary is his inclusion of himself in the criticism he offers against his own generation and—equally important—his refusal to use the case and his critique as a basis for rejecting politics or disowning liberalism itself. The indictment Fiedler draws up is sweeping but carefully drawn:

> Certainly a generation was on trial with Hiss—on trial, not, it must be noted, for having struggled toward a better world, but for having substituted sentimentality for intelligence in that struggle, for having failed to understand the moral conditions that must determine its outcome. (21)

The character witnesses for Hiss included many respected liberal figures, whose trust in Hiss proved them to be, according to Fiedler, "in some sense, fools" (20). But for Fiedler this is a judgment on himself as well as others: "It is not an easy admission, certainly not for them, but not even for those (among whom I include myself) who have admired in them a vision of national life that still appears worth striving for" (21).

Thus, Fiedler does not use the Hiss case to make a simple about-face to the Right or to withdraw from politics, saying "a plague on both your houses." The hard-won knowledge that "there is no magic in the words 'left' or 'progressive' or 'socialist' that can prevent deceit and the abuse of power" (24) would mean little if the political aspirations summed up in those words were simply abandoned. Rejection of politics, after all, would mean merely the attempt to protest one's innocence by renouncing complicity. Instead, Fiedler issues a call to "move forward from a liberalism of innocence to a liberalism of responsibility" (24). Out of context the phrases seem like typical political slogans. As the conclusion to "Hiss, Chambers, and the Age of Innocence," they take on meaning, since they reveal Fiedler's refusal to distance himself from the political tradition that he has criticized so harshly. Disillusionment is an experience that affects every generation; a characteristic American response is simply to give up politics altogether. It is Fiedler's willingness to identify himself with liberalism even as he criticizes liberal culture that infuses the essay with real moral weight and makes it relevant decades later, even for those who might quarrel with its factual assumptions.

"Afterthoughts on the Rosenbergs," first published a little over two years later, in 1953, raises some of the same issues as the Hiss essay. The emotional intensity of "Afterthoughts" is even greater, however, because Julius and Ethel Rosenberg were tried for espionage rather than perjury, because they were not merely imprisoned but executed, and because they were linked to Fiedler not only as leftists but also as Jews. As in the Hiss essay, Fiedler takes issue with those leftists who affirm the innocence of the accused in order to assert their own innocence. In contrast to the Hiss essay, however, Fiedler does not criticize liberals alone. Instead, he finds that both political officials and ordinary citizens have betrayed a "lack of moral imagination," which has left them with "a certain incapacity to really believe in Communists as people" (34). Both leftists and rightists, argues Fiedler, have been eager to see the Rosenbergs merely as symbols, to see the case as a mythical confrontation between good and evil.

Although Fiedler believes that the Rosenbergs' "legal guilt . . . was clearly established at their trial" (37), he argues against their execution on two grounds. One involves a humane use of political symbolism: "The world has turned to us . . . for a symbolic demonstration that somewhere a government existed willing to risk the loss of political face for the sake of establishing an unequivocal moral position" (34). But Fiedler's more important point is that the case against the

execution of the Rosenbergs rests ultimately on a realization that they themselves, Julius and Ethel Rosenberg, are not simply mythic figures but actual
human beings:

> Under their legendary role, there were, after all, *real* Rosenbergs, unat-
> tractive and vindictive but human; fond of each other and of their two
> children; concerned with operations for tonsillitis and family wrangles; iso-
> lated from each other during three years of not-quite-hope and deferred
> despair; at the end, prepared scientifically for the execution; Julius' mous-
> tache shaved off and the patch of hair from Ethel's dowdy head . . . finally
> capable of dying. . . . This we had forgotten . . . thinking of the Rosen-
> bergs as merely typical. (32–33)

The passage seems tasteless—why call the Rosenbergs "unattractive" and talk
about "Ethel's dowdy head"?—but its recognition of the limits of myth, of the
importance of an unpleasant, grubby reality, remains impressive. Here Fiedler
makes no attempt to inflate what he later called the *"mythic* resonance" (*No!*
152) but, instead, explores the relation between myth and reality and the moral
consequences of that relation. Ronald Radosh and Joyce Milton later concluded their study of the trial by making much the same point: "But if the
Rosenberg case has an ultimate moral, it is precisely to point up the dangers of
adhering to an unexamined political myth" (453).

   No! in Thunder and *Love and Death in the American Novel*, both published in
1960, are transitional works. Their criticism of self and society is blunted by an
attempt to find a position beyond criticism—a position of innocence. The
introduction to *No! in Thunder* and Fiedler's discussion of *Adventures of Huckleberry Finn* in *Love and Death in the American Novel* reveals the ambiguities of the
new stance.

   Although *No! in Thunder* is not concerned with politics, the introduction
stresses Fiedler's continued unwillingness to look at literature as a merely academic subject. If politics may be momentarily ignored, moral principles cannot.
For Fiedler "the practice of any art at any time is essentially a moral activity."
As he puts it, "I do not know how to begin a book or talk about one without
moral commitment" (1). And Fiedler defines the moral greatness of literature in
terms that correspond to the kind of self-criticism he had undertaken in his
essays on Hiss and the Rosenbergs:

> When the writer says of precisely the cause that is dearest to him what is
> always and everywhere the truth about all causes—that it has been imper-

fectly conceived and inadequately represented, and that it is bound to be betrayed, consciously or unconsciously, by its leading spokesmen—we know that he is approaching an art of real seriousness if not of actual greatness. The thrill we all sense but hesitate to define for ourselves—the thrill of confronting a commitment to truth which transcends all partial allegiances—comes when Dante turns on Florence, Molière on the moderate man, de Sade on reason, Shaw on the socialists, Tolstoy on the reformers, Joyce on Ireland, Faulkner on the South, Graham Green on the Catholics, Pasternak on the Russians and Abraham Cahan or Nathanael West on the Jews. (7)

Yet, in the same introduction in which Fiedler makes this eloquent statement, he seems to disengage himself from that tradition. He himself says "No! in Thunder" to "the last widely held *Weltanschauung* of the West: the progressive and optimistic, rational and kindly dogma of liberal humanism" (10). Yet, Fiedler does not here identify himself in any way with the liberal view of the world, as in *An End to Innocence* he did identify with liberal politics even while critiquing liberal attitudes. Now his formulation of the "liberal view of man" contains no acknowledgment of shared assumptions:

This view sees man as the product of a perhaps unplanned but rationally ordered and rationally explicable universe, a product which science can explain, even as it can explain the world which conditions him. (11)

Since Fiedler no longer identifies himself with liberalism but with "the truly contemporary writer" for whom the world is "not only absurd but also chaotic and fragmentary" (17), his critique of the "liberal view of man" now costs him nothing.

Fiedler asserts that the "No! in Thunder,' -with which he does identify himself, "is never partisan; it infuriates Our Side as well as Theirs, reveals that all Sides are one, insofar as they are all yea-sayers and hence all liars" (7). Thus, Fiedler, as a proponent of the "No! in Thunder" stance, takes a position that avowedly transcends all "partisan" wrangling. He himself, therefore, remains above the battle, innocent of partisan or political involvement. Fiedler's presentation of the "No! in Thunder!" seems finally vacuous for the very reasons presented in his evocation of the "commitment to truth" in great literature—which comes when a writer judges not merely others but himself or herself as well.

Fiedler's most famous, most ambitious, and longest book, *Love and Death in the American Novel*, reveals similar ambiguities. To most readers the book lives as a celebration of the peculiarly American romance between two males of different races, both escaping the chains of society as personified in women. And it is true that Fiedler finds in such romances the "No! in Thunder" that is now for him the mark of great literature. The difference between Tom Sawyer and Huckleberry Finn lies in the depth of their respective renunciations:

> Huck ends with a total renunciation, not only of Aunt Sally but implicitly of Tom, too; for he learns at last the world of boys sustains the world of mothers, privileged make-believe understraps "sivilization" . . . he rejects not only the claims which sanctify slavery (that was easy enough in 1884), but also those which sanctify work, duty, home, cleanliness, marriage, chivalry—even motherhood! (587)

Nevertheless, Fiedler throughout this study argues that the evocation of male comradeship—whether in Cooper, Melville, or Twain—begins with an imaginative failure to grow up. The failure to grow up means the failure to accomplish the "qualifying act of moral adulthood," the acknowledgment of one's involvement in society's ills, the same failure for which Fiedler had earlier criticized both Alger Hiss and his own generation of liberal intellectuals. Likewise, Fiedler's eagerness to reveal the "dirty," hidden significance of books apparently dealing with asexual innocence is comparable to his earlier attempt to criticize the political versions of the myth of innocence. Fiedler's emphasis on the "duplicity" of the classic American novel points to his own concern for the truth and his belief that it is his task as critic to reveal the hidden, sometimes unpleasant or unsavory truths of his own tradition. His references to Marxism and psychoanalysis suggest that his treatment of the mythology of American literature is critical, an unmasking of the duplicity of myth in the name of truth and reason.

     Yet the overall mood of the book is one of celebration. After all, the "total renunciation" that Huck achieves is, in Fiedler's reading, not without its rewards for him and for us. It makes possible the affirmation of innocence offered by the black victim to the white offender. In Fiedler's words,

> Certainly, our classic writers assure us that when we have been cut off or have cut ourselves off from the sources of life, he ["our dark-skinned beloved"] will receive us without rancor or the insult of forgiveness. (368)

This is too good to be true, and thus it is sentimental, but it is also too good to reject either in the name of reason or heterosexual maturity. Instead, Fiedler rejects the critical task of analysis. He refuses to make use of either Marxism or psychoanalysis to analyze the "archetypes" he discovers. Instead, he simply celebrates their raw emotional power.

In *Love and Death* Fiedler seemed to have trouble making up his mind about whether he wished to finally celebrate innocence or the achievement of maturity. The 1960s in general and his own arrest in particular helped him decide that innocence—legal, moral and political—would be the more attractive stance. Perhaps if Fiedler had not been "busted" on a charge of "maintaining a premise" where marijuana was consumed (*Being Busted* 159), he might have viewed his life differently; perhaps he would have written an autobiographical work dealing with the ambiguities of middle age. Fiedler was busted, however, and his autobiographical statement, *Being Busted,* presents his life as a series of struggles between himself and one or another establishment.

Fiedler compares the Rosenbergs unfavorably to "the old-style radical, who rises up in court to declare that he has acted in the teeth of accepted morality and law for the sake of certain higher principles" ("Afterthoughts on the Rosenbergs" 44). But Fiedler himself, suddenly put in the position that Alger Hiss and the Rosenbergs claimed for themselves—a defendant framed by the establishment for political reasons—does not rise to the occasion. One might argue that such a comparison is not really fair, since, in fact, Fiedler was really innocent of the legal charges against him, while Hiss and the Rosenbergs were really guilty. Fiedler, however, himself admits that his account has been tailored to fit the difficulties of his legal situation—the truth has had to come second to what is expedient:

> And, indeed, though what I wrote is nothing but the truth, it is not quite the whole truth—not even in the approximate sense in which that phrase is used in courtrooms. It is, however, as much of the truth as I could then and can now tell without endangering other people whose lives and fates are inextricably bound up with my own. I might have said a little more without my lawyer looking over my shoulder; but I am not finally unhappy that the account I give is incomplete and must remain so forever. (128)

If one were to indulge in the same kind of analysis that Fiedler does in his essays on Hiss and the Rosenbergs, one might argue that this passage constitutes a kind of "code" statement, implying without explicitly admitting legal guilt. After all, if Fiedler can't tell all the truth because to do so would cause him to endanger "other people whose lives and fates are inextricably bound up with my own," isn't it reasonable to assume that what he is saying is that he can't tell the reader that members of his own family used illegal substances, because to do so would "endanger them"? And, of course, it would endanger Fiedler himself as well. He was charged, after all, not with personal consumption of marijuana but simply with "maintaining a premise" where it was used by others, a charge that he explicitly denies throughout *Being Busted*. So, was he, after all, guilty as charged? Here is the seemingly unqualified "judgment" that Fiedler asserts he and his wife have made of themselves:

> That judgment was and remains "innocent": collectively and individually innocent, not only of the absurd police charges (about which there was never any real doubt), but also of having in any essential way failed our own personal codes.
>
> To make this clear to everyone, my wife and I intend to keep on insisting not just that we are "not guilty," which is a legal formula only, but that we are "innocent," in the full sense of the word. We will make this assertion in conversation, bugged or not bugged, in writing public and private, as well as before any judge and jury we may eventually have to face. (249)

But such protestations of total innocence were exactly what troubled Fiedler about Hiss and the Rosenbergs. The issue here is not whether anybody at Fiedler's house ever smoked grass. The issue is to what extent Fiedler regained the pose of innocence that in *An End to Innocence* he had ascribed to his own generation. In *Being Busted* and in later works Fiedler indeed assumes a pose of political innocence, of one unimplicated in the complexities of political life, the pose of a permanent outsider. In the preface to *Being Busted* Fiedler describes the "true subject" of the book as "the endless war, sometimes cold, sometimes hot, between the dissenter and his imperfect society" (7). The qualifying adjective for society and the lack of one for dissenter is symptomatic of the pose of innocence. The Fiedler of *Being Busted* tells us that he has achieved the moral purity of a stance beyond politics: "I am, in fact, adverse to politics as ordinarily defined . . . only saying with Bartleby the Scrivener, 'I would prefer not to,' which is good unmelodramatic American for the satanic Latin of 'Non serviam'" (234).

The stance of *Being Busted* is twofold: on the one hand, Fiedler is a cultural rebel, a "spokesman for an adversary culture more progressive, more revolutionary" than the traditional high culture (234). On the other hand, he rejects the political involvements that led him first to radical Marxism, then to Trotskyism, then to anticommunist liberalism. He will no longer commit himself to a specific political program, to any political identity more specific than that of "dissenter."

What Was Literature? reveals the consequences of this split between culture and politics. The essays that make up *What Was Literature?* argue for a divorce between emotion and reason in order to liberate the passions. The implicit stance is that of the self-marginalized individual, the clown, whose ideas can never be cause for guilt because they are not meant to be taken seriously. The voice of the dissenter is the voice of the innocent, whatever the personal idiosyncrasies of the dissident. And, because Fiedler is a political innocent, he is free to confess to bad taste or bad manners without really risking anything, without accepting responsibility.

In the foreword to *No! in Thunder* Fiedler insisted, "I am not, let it be clear, for all my occasional hamminess, an entertainer." (x). In *What Was Literature?* Fiedler is "bugged" to realize that most readers of *Love and Death in the American Novel* "are likely to encounter it on assignment and in a classroom," when after all he is not an intellectual engaged in the search for truth but, rather, an entertainer "paid to allay boredom" (34). Earlier he had declared that "the practice of art at any time is essentially a moral activity" and that writer and critic share a common commitment to truth; now he argues that the critic, like the artist, should seek not truth but ecstasy:

> The only critical works which long survive . . . are those which attempt not to prove or disprove, construct or deconstruct anything, but to compel an assent scarcely distinguishable from wonder, like the songs or stories which are their immediate occasion. (131)

Although Fiedler insists that he is "not suggesting that the search for standards be abandoned completely and that evaluation be confined to noises of admiration or distaste" (126), he specifically rejects the traditional belief that literary myth criticism of the sort that he himself has practiced "represents an attempt to speak logically, rationally, objectively about the *mythoi* which lie at the heart of all works which please many and please long" (37).

If criticism should eschew logic and reason, it is not surprising that the primary task of literature itself seems to be to induce the momentary triumph of passion over reason in the reader:

> It is indeed an essential function of literature to release in us unnatural impulses—including the need from time to time to go out of our heads—

which we otherwise repress or sublimate for the sake of law and order, civilization, sweet reason itself. (136)

Art moves us "viscerally rather than cerebrally" (133), and "the most honest
name for what we seek in mythic art" is "privileged insanity" (137).

The critical position at which Fiedler has arrived is at odds with his stance
in *An End to Innocence* in many ways, of which the least important is his new
interest in popular culture. In *An End to Innocence* he criticized the disjunction
between feeling and reason that vitiated liberalism's view of the world. Liberals,
he argued, were all too ready to reject reasoned analysis that conflicted with
cherished emotions. Both *An End to Innocence* and *No! in Thunder* argued that a
commitment to truth, especially unpleasant truths, was the most important
requirement for meaningful literary and cultural criticism. And, especially in *An
End to Innocence*, Fiedler insisted that he remained part of the political tradition
that he was criticizing, so that his cultural criticism was essentially self-criticism.

In *What Was Literature?* all these values have been reversed. A disjunction
between reason and emotion is held to be proper and necessary, and it is the
function of literature and literary criticism to further this disjunction. Truth,
whether unpleasant or otherwise, is no longer an important issue for either literature or criticism. And Fiedler himself, despite his self-dramatizing confessions, quite different from the reflective activity of self-criticism, presents himself as entirely on the side of the angels. He is a radical who takes on the
establishment, and the very extremism of his views insures that he will remain
"innocent"—without complicity, not responsible, for whatever happens in our
society in either culture or politics.

For the later Fiedler elitism in culture and authoritarianism in politics are
the great sins. He sees himself as an anti-elitist in culture, one whose program
calls for "Opening up the Canon," as part 2 of *What Was Literature?* is entitled.
Politically he is antiestablishment, libertarian, but also democratic and populist
(129, 140). But the implications of his position are not necessarily as unambiguous as he now believes.

Fiedler intends his emphasis on the mythic power of art to widen the realm
of what is considered true art. His definition becomes enormously restrictive,
however, if one takes seriously his declaration that the sign of real art is its ability to induce us "to go out of our heads." It seems to rule out some of the most
popular classics, such as the works of Jane Austen or Anthony Trollope or, in
popular culture, the songs of Cole Porter or the music of Sy Oliver. If "privileged insanity" is the state of mind that true mythic art arouses, then not much
true art is around—unless privileged insanity means nothing more than the old

formula of "suspension of disbelief." In the name of "opening up the canon" Fiedler has formulated a criterion at least as restrictive as Matthew Arnold's "high seriousness."

Likewise, although Fiedler presents the movement "From Ethics and Aesthetics to Ecstatics" (126) as an aspect of his conversion to an anti-elitist, radically democratic, populist stance, his cultural position has no necessary connection with such antiestablishment rhetoric. Indeed, the closest analogue to Fiedler's position is to be found in the writings of a highbrow of the high-brows—Thomas Mann, during Mann's most reactionary, most antidemocratic phase. Mann wrote *Reflections of a Nonpolitical Man* during World War I to defend Germany on the basis of the superiority of its authoritarian, hierarchical culture. In making this argument, Mann stresses as strongly as does the later Fiedler the necessarily amoral, irrational, even primitive quality of authentic art. While Fiedler, however, makes his argument in the name of a populist justification of popular and mass culture, Mann offers the same theory on behalf of a German high *Kultur* that he opposes to the shallow, "enlightenment" literature of democratic France and England. And if the cultural implications of Mann's argument are precisely the opposite of Fiedler's, the political implications of the thesis point in the opposite direction as well. Furthermore, Mann's political position seems to flow much more directly from his aesthetics than does Fiedler's.

A few quotations from Mann's *Reflections* suffice to indicate the similarity—and suggest the danger for those who, like Fiedler, attempt to link a renunciation of reason to an antiestablishment position:

> Art will never be moral in the political sense, never virtuous. . . . It has a basically undependable, treacherous tendency; its joy in scandalous anti-reason, its tendency to beauty-creating "barbarism," cannot be rooted out, yes, even if one calls this tendency hysterical, anti-intellectual, and immoral to the point of being a danger to the world. (289)

> It [art] will speak of passion and unreason; it will present, cultivate and celebrate passion and unreason, hold primordial thoughts and instincts in honor, keep them *awake* or reawaken them with great force, the thought and instinct of war, for example. (291)

> In short, then: war, heroism of a reactionary type, all the mischief of unreason, will be thinkable and therefore possible so long as art exists. (291)

For Mann the glorification of war is an important, inevitable aspect of his aesthetics. War, he declares, "has nothing at all to do with brutalization, it would signify much more an elevation, intensification and ennoblement of human life" (339)—at least it would so signify once the viewpoint of mere "civilization," with its privileging of reason, is replaced by the perspective of German high culture, with its emphasis on passion. And, for the Mann of *Reflections*, that is what World War I is all about and why a German victory is essential.

Thomas Mann's speculations of the World War I years reveal the inner significance of the positions at which Fiedler has finally arrived—and how far their implications are from the innocence of the simple dissenter. But there is a difference between Mann and Fiedler that is also relevant. After World War I Mann rethought the ideas that he had worked out with such intensity during the war. If *Reflections of a Nonpolitical Man* in retrospect seems to have at least the seeds of a cultural Nazism embedded in it, Mann's later works, such as *The Magic Mountain* and especially *Doctor Faustus*, embody an impressive and thorough critique of those aspects of German high culture that had some affinity with Nazism. Mann moved from the irresponsibility of the "nonpolitical man" to an acceptance of the burden of political responsibility unique among the modern masters—a burden in which self-criticism was the central task.

Fiedler, on the other hand, has moved from requiring both himself and his generation to accept responsibility for their cultural and political past through self-critical analysis to the celebration of emotion for its own sake, detached from reason and immune to self-criticism. Fiedler himself sees his career as a movement from intellectual elitism to cultural populism, from hypocrisy to honesty. Those who oppose elitism and admire honesty need to study that career closely rather than accept Fiedler's description at face value. The early Fiedler rejected the pose of innocence, particularly political innocence. The later Fiedler has regained his lost innocence by refusing to adopt a specific political position. Instead, he has assumed the pose of the outsider, the clown, the antiestablishment radical. The very fact of having been "busted" becomes, paradoxically, a certification of "innocence," since it certifies his position as an antiestablishment figure. And the more "confessions" he makes about his "pop" tastes, the more his stance as an anti-elitist is guaranteed.

The early Leslie Fiedler knew that the cultural critic must begin by acknowledging his or her own complicity with the culture that is criticized. Even cultural analysis is vitiated when politics is ignored; the attempt to connect culture to politics is an inescapable aspect of the more general attempt to reconcile reason and emotion, a central task of the cultural critic. Leslie Fiedler remains one of the few critics who continues to raise large questions without retreating into a special jargon. This critique of his career is premised on a recognition of the importance and significance of the task that he has taken up, the work of cultural criticism.

Chapter 9

Susan Sontag and the Possibility of Humanism

Susan Sontag gained her reputation as an exponent of the most radical trends in contemporary art and culture in a decade in which extremity had many adherents. *Against Interpretation* (1966) and *Styles of Radical Will* (1969) distinguished their author from other adherents of the "new sensibility" affirmed in the closing chapter of *Against Interpretation* by the cool brilliance with which the most shocking ideas were discussed. Today Susan Sontag is best known as the author of *Illness as Metaphor* and *AIDS and Its Metaphors*, two books in which her talents as a literary and cultural critic are applied "to the real world this time," as she puts it in *AIDS and Its Metaphors* (102). In some ways the later books continue themes that Sontag first took up in the 1960s; this continuity is stressed by Sontag herself. In other ways, however, the later books reveal a significant, though largely implicit, reconsideration of the ideas with which Sontag was once most closely associated. A study of Sontag's more recent work reveals both a new maturity of insight—with no loss of her original rhetorical power—along with a curious refusal to explore the implications of those insights. A look at Sontag's career as a whole demonstrates both a consistent stylistic brilliance and a series of conflicting affirmations whose divergent assumptions reveal a good deal not only about Sontag but about the confusions of her, and our, times.[1]

Against Interpretation is permeated by an explicit animus against traditional humanism, especially the version associated with Matthew Arnold. When Sontag wants to disparage an emphasis on content in art, she pairs "tired ideologies like humanism or socialist realism" as equivalent enemies of culture ("On Style," 31). When she criticizes "neo-Marxist critics" such as Georg Lukàcs, Walter Benjamin, and Theodor Adorno for their willingness "to perpetuate an ideology," the ideology she has in mind is "humanism" ("Literary Criticism of Georg Lukàcs" 90). Sontag admires Peter Weiss's *Marat/Sade* all the more because "art like Marat/Sade entails a rejection of 'humanism' " ("Marat/Sade/ Artaud," 171). The book closes with an affirmation of a "new sensibility" offered as a replacement for "the Matthew Arnold notion of culture." Instead of "art as the criticism of life," the new sensibility championed by Sontag "understands art as the extension of life" ("One Culture," 299–300). Arnold's traditional conception is not only misguided, it has become "historically and humanly obsolescent" (299). Contemporary artists are "engaged in programming sensations"; "uninterested in art as a species of moral journalism," they no longer need the old "Matthew Arnold apparatus" (302), which attempted to distinguish between high and low.

And yet some of Susan Sontag's own most highly charged terms of praise and condemnation are derived from the vocabulary of Matthew Arnold, especially from his critique of philistinism but also from his emphasis on "high seriousness." Throughout *Against Interpretation* philistinism is the ultimate sin, whether the topic is art, art criticism, Marxism, or even science. Clearing the ground for a critique of interpretation, she denounces the "very idea of content itself" as "a subtle or not so subtle philistinism" ("Against Interpretation," 5). It is not, however, interpretation itself that she opposes; she is against only the "philistinism of interpretation" that results from "the philistine refusal to leave the work of art alone" (8). In the arts it is literature, and especially the novel, that is most susceptible to the threat; the twentieth-century novel, Sontag fears, has been "deeply, if not irrevocably, compromised by philistinism" ("Nathalie Sarraute," 102). Eugene O'Neill's *Marco Millions* fails as an attack on "the philistine values of American business civilization" because the play itself "reeks of philistinism" ("Going to Theater," 144). Disagreeing with the "liberal intellectuals" (148), who notice only the overt politics of *Doctor Strangelove*, Sontag argues that the film's governing philosophy is not only nihilism but, much worse, "philistine nihilism" (149). (On the other hand, the Oedipus plays of Sophocles provide an example of nihilism that is "heroic or ennobling" ["Death of Tragedy," 136].) Even the inclusive camp sensibility cannot abide sincerity when it is tainted with "simple philistinism" ("Notes on 'Camp,' " 288). It is important to Sontag to emphasize that the new critical interest in popular culture, which she applauds, is *not* "a new philistinism" ("One Culture, " 303). Georg Lukàcs earns grudging praise as a Marxist who carries "the burden of ideology" but also "assist[s] in the taming of its philistinism" ("Literary Criticism of Georg Lukàcs," 89). Claude Lévi-Strauss, on the other hand, deserves criticism because his ingenuity as a structuralist does not save him from accepting "the philistine formulas of modern scientific 'value neutrality' " (Anthropologist as

Hero," 74). Adherence to such formulas probably does not entirely explain the general "philistinism of scientists," a syndrome apparently shared by C. P. Snow, whose celebrated lecture on "The Two Cultures" is dismissed as a "crude and philistine statement" ("One Culture," 294).

For Susan Sontag in *Against Interpretation* "seriousness" is a key criterion for distinguishing the most significant art and thought (including criticism) from work of the second rank. Sontag is writing for, and arguing with, "people who take any of the arts seriously" ("Against Interpretation," 5), "people with serious and sophisticated taste" ("Nathalie Sarraute," 111). This is the audience that is attracted to modern art, even though "the seriousness of modern art precludes pleasure in the familiar sense" ("One Culture," 302). The new sensibility she proclaims has "an excruciating seriousness" (304). Sontag and the contemporaries for whom she speaks are attracted most deeply to writers—few of whom write novels—whose works are expressions of "acute personal and intellectual extremity" ("Simone Weil," 49) because "we love seriousness . . . we are moved by it, nourished by it" (51). Simone Weil provides an example of those saints of modern culture who achieve their eminence by "the example of their seriousness" (50–51).

Simone Weil's example does not, it should be emphasized, lead Sontag to stress any necessary connection between seriousness and religion. Quite the opposite. Marx and Freud, for example, provide incontrovertible proof that an "entirely secular attitude" is quite compatible with "immense moral seriousness" ("Piety without Content," 255). Sontag has a proprietary interest in opposing the attempt to conflate religion with "*seriousness*, seriousness about the important human and moral issues," since she identifies her own project with the "modern seriousness" which is attempting "to work out the serious consequences of atheism for reflective thought and personal morality" (254–55). Herbert Marcuse and Norman O. Brown, both of whom she names as contributors to that project, are praised for the "new seriousness about Freudian ideas" offered by *Eros and Civilization* and *Life Against Death* ("Psychoanalysis," 256). Heretofore, Sontag confesses, "We have not been serious or honest enough about sexuality" (258).

Sontag laments the novel's superficiality as opposed to "serious contemporary poetry, painting, sculpture, and music"; she hopes for a "serious 'modern' tradition of the novel" ("Nathalie Sarraute," 103). Only when that occurs will the novel become an art form one "can take seriously" (111). The highest praise for the films of Robert Bresson is that they are "about the most serious way of being human" ("Spiritual Style," 195). Likewise, Sontag emphasizes that Jean-

Luc Godard's *Vivre Sa Vie* "is about seriousness" ("Godard's *Vivre Sa Vie*" 203). *Vivre Sa Vie*, indeed, seems to Sontag "a perfect film" because the director sets out "to do something that is both noble and intricate," and he "wholly succeeds in doing it" (207). In contrast, Sontag judges Arthur Miller's *After the Fall* "on the authenticity of its moral seriousness" ("Going to Theater," 140) and finds it "sadly wanting, in both intelligence and moral honesty" (144).

If one considers the essays that make up *Against Interpretation* together, Susan Sontag's attitude toward traditional "high seriousness" seems at least as ambivalent as her feelings about camp; she is both "strongly drawn" to it and "strongly offended" ("Notes on 'Camp,'" 276). Despite her explicit disclaimers, in practice Sontag remains at least intermittently committed to a traditional, even an Arnoldian, respect for high seriousness. Her praise for Robert Bresson and Jean-Luc Godard, for example, is in an Arnoldian vein, as is her disparagement of Arthur Miller. When she praises Marx and Freud for their "immense moral seriousness" ("Piety without content," 255), she is not praising Marx and Freud as exponents of the kind of seriousness "whose trademark is anguish, cruelty, derangement" ("Notes on 'Camp,'" 287) and whose philosophers include Sade and Artaud. Instead, she is claiming that Marx and Freud are among the liberators and heros of humanity, that they have a stature equivalent to that of the great religious figures. Sontag, that is, makes a case for Marx and Freud on grounds to which a follower of Matthew Arnold would be bound to assent, even though he or she might disagree with Sontag's own favorable estimate of Marx and Freud themselves.

Matthew Arnold believed in ranking writers as a means to achieve "the benefit of clearly feeling and of deeply enjoying the really excellent" ("Study of Poetry," 166). In "The Study of Poetry" he offered his technique of employing "touchstones" as a device for distinguishing between the first and second ranks. Like Matthew Arnold, Susan Sontag often ranks writers, carefully distinguishing between the merely very good and the truly great. Sontag, however, prefaces *Against Interpretation* with the comment, "I should perhaps explain that the assessment of this or that novel, film, play, or whatever, does not greatly interest me: I don't ultimately, care about handing out grades to works of art." ("A Note," vii–viii). The underlying unity of *Against Interpretation*, she asserts, lies in her effort to "expose and clarify the assumptions underlying certain judgments and tastes"; the essays together contribute to the "task of theoretical clarification" (viii). The preface, like other self-descriptions in *Against Interpretation*, does not prepare the reader for the ways in which Sontag's criticism carries on the tradition of Arnold, albeit without explicit acknowledgment.

Arnold admired *The Canterbury Tales* but, notoriously, declared, "Yet Chaucer is not one of the great classics" ("Study of Poetry," 176). Praising Chaucer's sanity, his "large, free, simple, clear yet kindly view of human life" (174), Arnold denies Chaucer the very highest status because Chaucer lacks what his contemporary Dante possesses so completely: high seriousness. Susan Sontag admires Albert Camus for his "reliability, intelligibility, generosity, decency," for his willingness to assume "the responsibilities of sanity" ("Camus' *Notebooks*" 52–53). Nevertheless, Sontag feels that it is her responsibility as a critic to inform the reader that Camus is not "a truly great writer"; he is "just a very good one" (54). His novels and his essays provide evidence of "neither art nor thought of the highest quality" (55), according to Sontag's exacting standards. In contrast, Jean-Paul Sartre, despite his political errors, has the kind of "powerful and original mind" next to which Camus reveals himself as merely "an extraordinarily talented and literate epigone" (54). Again, Eugène Ionesco has done some good work but judged "by the most exacting standards" ("Ionesco," 118)—compared, that is, to "Brecht, Genet, and Beckett, Ionesco is a minor writer." The grounds of comparison are not "high seriousness," but the terms are parallel; Ionesco, when compared to the masters, "does not have the same weight, the same full-bloodedness, the same grandeur and relevance" (121). Sontag's sympathies for the "stylized art" that appeals to camp taste are curbed by her awareness that such art "can never be of the very greatest kind" ("On Style," 20).

Susan Sontag does not seem to recognize and certainly does not discuss the conflict between her explicit rejection of Arnoldian humanism and her continuing resort to Arnold's critical vocabulary and devices. In one of the few passages in which the issue is acknowledged even obliquely, Sontag adopts the effective rhetorical technique of defining seriousness in such a way that the Arnoldian aura of the term vanishes, thus obviating the recognition that Sontag's relation to Arnold is a good deal more complex than her explicit attacks would suggest. The technique is all the more effective because the new definition is simply asserted, without any prefatory argument or explanation. The passage occurs within a parenthesis in note 51 of the "Notes on 'Camp'"; in this particular note the main topic is the controversial question of "the peculiar relation between Camp taste and homosexuality." Sontag draws upon the situation of Jews in modern culture in order to clarify the position of homosexuals: although not all liberals are Jews, it remains true that Jews have "a peculiar affinity for liberal and reformist causes." Likewise, although "not all homosexuals have Camp taste," Sontag argues that there is "a peculiar affinity" between homosexuality and camp. She then goes on to offer a parenthetical defense of the comparison between Jews and homosexuals and incidentally offers a new characterization of "seriousness" as well:

> Jews and homosexuals are the outstanding creative minorities in contemporary urban culture. Creative, that is, in the truest sense: they are creators of sensibilities. The two pioneering forces of modern sensibility are Jewish moral seriousness and homosexual aestheticism and irony. (290)

Although the placement of this characterization of seriousness discourages analysis—the focus of note 51 and of the "jottings" (276) as a whole is on homosexuality and camp rather than on Jewishness or moral seriousness—the implications of the passage deserve close consideration. Most strikingly, Sontag asserts a special, causal connection between "moral seriousness" and Jewishness (not Judaism). The Jews are the "creators" of moral seriousness. At first, the implications seem startling. Not only Matthew Arnold but no Gentile of any time or place is capable of moral seriousness. A reading of the passage that draws this broad implication must be mistaken; perhaps Sontag is making a much narrower claim. She must be arguing that the special kind of seriousness that acts as a "pioneering force" on the "modern sensibility" derives from Jewish culture but not religion, from Jews who left Judaism to create modern culture— Jews such as Marx and Freud, Simone Weil and Herbert Marcuse. The implication, then, would not be that only Jews have moral seriousness but, rather, that it is "Jewish moral seriousness" in particular that has influenced the modern sensibility. Other varieties of moral seriousness, presumably including the Arnoldian high seriousness, may exist, but they simply have not been determinative forces in modern culture.

The latter reading seems much more plausible than the former, yet it raises its own problems. Most obviously, Susan Sontag often praises the seriousness of writers and artists who are certainly contributors and even creators of the modern sensibility but who are not Jewish. In *Against Interpretation* alone, the list would include, for example, Norman O. Brown, Jean-Luc Godard, and Robert Bresson, not all of whom, presumably, are Jewish. This objection could be met, perhaps, by arguing that such figures have derived their seriousness from Jewish sources. On the other hand, one could argue that the Jewish moral seriousness of Marx and Freud is itself no different in kind from the seriousness of other, non-Jewish figures, such as Voltaire or Kant, for example. But the attempt to pair off Jews against Gentiles quickly becomes unrewarding. What is surely required is an attempt to explore whether there are indeed qualities that set apart the Jewish moral seriousness which is held to be so determinative for modern culture from other, garden varieties of seriousness. No such exploration occurs in *Against Interpretation*.

In note 34, however, Sontag does distinguish between two kinds of seriousness, the kind associated with Arnoldian conceptions of high culture and the other peculiarly connected with modern culture. There is "the pantheon of high culture: truth, beauty and seriousness" (286), and then there is "the kind of seriousness whose trademark is anguish, cruelty, derangement." Sontag advises the reader to "think of Bosch, Sade, Rimbaud, Jarry, Kafka, Artaud, [to] think of most of the important works of art of the 20th century," in order to grasp what this second kind of seriousness is all about. In this section, note 34, Camp is characterized as "third among the great creative sensibilities" (287)—third, that is, after both traditional high seriousness and the second kind of seriousness, "whose trademark is anguish, cruelty, derangement." If Sontag's notes are to add up to a consistent point of view, then this second version of seriousness must be the equivalent of the Jewish moral seriousness that in note 51 is paired with "homosexual aestheticism and irony" (290), as one of the "two pioneering forces of modern sensibility." The trouble is that the concept of Jewish moral seriousness doesn't explain much about Hieronymous Bosch, the Marquis de Sade, Rimbaud, Jarry, Artaud, or anybody on Sontag's own list except, arguably, Kafka.

Indeed, both the concept of Jewish moral seriousness and the seriousness trademarked "anguish, cruelty, derangement" seem mere improvisations, rhetorical constructs scarcely intended to be taken seriously. One the one hand, the two concepts are at odds with each other; on the other, neither can be finally distinguished from Arnold's high seriousness. In "One Culture and the New Sensibility," Sontag's closing manifesto on behalf of the "new sensibility," neither of her conceptions of seriousness is even mentioned. The new sensibility, it turns out, is not much concerned with morality at all, whether Jewish or the upside-down morality of cruelty. The "most interesting works of contemporary art" provide "adventures in sensation" ("One Culture," 300), while neglecting moral or intellectual questions. If the new sensibility indeed has an "excruciating seriousness" (304), as Sontag claims that it does, it is a seriousness without content. But then, the absence of content, defined as a concern with morality and metaphysics, is virtually the defining quality of the art of the new sensibility. According to Sontag, the new art is "notably apolitical and undidactic" (300), uninterested in the moral and social questions that have been the traditional province of literature. Indeed, the "primary feature of the new sensibility" is the negative fact that "its model product is not the literary work, above

all, the novel" (298). The "model arts of our time" are those that eschew morality or at least adopt "a much cooler mode of moral judgment" than the novel,
arts such as "music, films, dance, architecture, painting, sculpture" (298–99).
Although the proclamation of the new sensibility in the closing essay simply drops the two versions of modern seriousness proffered in the "Notes on
'Camp,'" it does take up a theme adumbrated elsewhere in *Against Interpretation*,
most notably in the title essay and in "On Style." For Sontag the key problem
to be addressed by contemporary critics is neither intellectual nor moral, except
by indirection; it is the "steady loss of sharpness in our sensory experience." In
a world in which "all the conditions of modern life . . . conjoin to dull our sensory faculties" ("Against Interpretation," 13), the task of the critic is not to clarify or to enlighten but, rather, to point. The sophisticated audience does not go
to art for moral guidance but for sensory replenishment. Sontag speaks on behalf
of the new sensibility when she declares: "What is important now is to recover
our senses. We must learn to *see* more, to *hear* more, to *feel* more" (14). Ordinary people bring moral concerns to art because for them "aesthetic pleasure is
a state of mind essentially indistinguishable from their ordinary responses" ("On
Style," 23). When, on the other hand, "a person possessing some training and
aesthetic sensibility looks at a work of art appropriately," he or she does so
knowing that "a work of art is an experience, not a statement or an answer to a
question" (21). (Presented as a manifesto of ultra-contemporary trends, Sontag's
view of art echoes Archibald MacLeish's 1920s pronouncement that "A poem
should not mean/But be" [107].) For Sontag "cinema is the most alive, the
most exciting, the most important of all art forms right now" ("Against Interpretation," 11), because it is not depth but "*transparence*" that, she proclaims, "is
the highest, most liberating value in art—and in criticism—today" (13). Literature and fiction are suspect because of their unregenerate insistence on ideas and
morality.

Laypeople may find this attitude confusing because the world is likely to
present itself to them as an arena in which moral and practical issues are urgent
and unavoidable, while aesthetic questions are secondary. Sontag suggests,
however, that ordinary people have their priorities confused. One of the virtues
of the camp sensibility is that it provides at least "*one* way of seeing the world as
an aesthetic phenomenon" ("Notes on 'Camp,'" 277). There may be other,
possibly better ways of seeing, but Sontag agrees with the fundamental intuition
of camp since, in her view, "the world *is*, ultimately, an aesthetic phenomenon"
("On Style," 28). It is morality, not aesthetics, that should be relegated to secondary importance; while art is valuable in and of itself, "morality, unlike art, *is*
ultimately justified by its utility" (29).

Here is the true contrast between the tradition of Arnoldian humanism and

Sontag's "new sensibility." The forms of seriousness commended by Sontag, despite her attempts to distance them by characterizing one as peculiarly "Jewish" and the other as downright immoral (glorifying "anguish, cruelty, derangement"), in practice cannot be clearly distinguished from the high seriousness that Arnold admired. Sontag's treatment of Simone Weil, a key figure for Sontag, and not merely because she seems to embody both versions of modern seriousness, makes this point clear. Susan Sontag's own belief that "the sane view of the world is the true one" makes it impossible for her to share Simone Weil's key ideas ("Simone Weil," 50). Simone Weil's life was "absurd in its exaggerations and degree of self-mutilation"; it was filled with "fanatical asceticism" and a "tireless courting of affliction." Although Sontag herself has no interest in imitating Weil's actions, she takes Weil's "dedication to martyrdom" as evidence of her ability to reach "a level of spiritual reality" that certifies Weil as a saint of modern culture (51). Sontag and those who share her tastes reserve their deepest respect for those artists and writers who forsake sanity in favor of a deeper, more intense seriousness. Sontag speculates that in the contemporary world "sanity becomes compromise, evasion, a lie" (49). In this era only those numbered among the "bigots, the hysterics, the destroyers of the self" are candidates for sainthood (48). The avant-garde sensibility earns its standing from its willingness to confront the paradoxes with which Sontag concludes her essay on Simone Weil: "some (but not all) distortions of the truth, some (but not all) unhealthiness, some (but not all) denials of life are truth-giving, sanity-producing, health-creating, and life-enhancing" (51). As the four final hyphenated phrases suggest, the modern "seriousness" endorsed by Sontag is, ultimately, only a variation of Matthew Arnold's high seriousness. The means may differ, but the ends are parallel.

Arnold's theses on culture attempt to connect and balance the claims of truth, beauty, and morality. Sontag's desire to distance herself from Arnoldian humanism often takes precedence over her own need to balance the same, sometimes conflicting claims. Thus, she neglects the difficult task of sorting out what is valuable and what is merely extreme in Simone Weil, what is sane and what is hysterical, in favor of an aesthetic response for which "sanity" is irrelevant and all extremes are fine, as long as they are aesthetically interesting. Sontag recognizes conflicting qualities in Weil but then neglects these difficulties to focus on the aesthetic unity of an "exemplary" life, the life of a modern saint of culture:

Some lives are exemplary, others not; and of exemplary lives, there are those which invite us to imitate them, and those which we regard from a distance with a mixture of revulsion, pity, and reverence. It is, roughly, the distance between the hero and the saint (if one may use the latter term in an aesthetic, rather than a religious sense). Such a life . . . was Simone Weil's. ("Simone Weil," 51)

Sontag's use of Arnoldian terminology persists after *Against Interpretation*, though she does not again rely on it so extensively. "The Aesthetics of Silence," a 1967 essay included in *Styles of Radical Will*, asserts that artistic silence may provide "a certificate of unchallengeable seriousness" (6), while pointing out that there is also such a thing as "philistine silence" (21). Another essay in the same collection, "The Pornographic Imagination," argues that pornography may be art according to grounds familiar to readers of note 34 of the "Notes on 'Camp' ": "What makes a work of pornography part of the history of art rather than of trash . . . is the originality, thoroughness, authenticity, and power of that deranged consciousness itself, as incarnated in a work" (47). In "The *Salmagundi* Interview" (1975) Sontag finds the danger of philistinism lurking on both cultural Left and Right. Feminists are criticized for their tendency to "perpetuate these philistine characterizations of hierarchy, theory, and intellect" (333), while her own attraction to the canon is qualified by her awareness that "consensus about 'great' books and 'perennial' problems, once stabilized, tend[s] to deteriorate eventually into something philistine" (344).

If Sontag's terminology becomes less recognizably Arnoldian, it is not because she is moving toward a conception of human beings and culture that is more fluid, more resistant to block categories, than Arnold's opposition between philistinism and high seriousness. Indeed, Susan Sontag moves in 1966 to a radical division of human beings into categories more absolute by far than any that could be derived from Matthew Arnold's old conception of the English middle class as "philistine." Arnold, after all, thought there was hope for the middle class. His own criticism was designed to guide the philistines toward the "sweetness and light" of culture. He never claimed that the middle class could not be redeemed; to do so would have been to declare his life's work a failure.

In her response to a *Partisan Review* symposium included in *Styles of Radical Will* under the title "What's Happening in America (1966)," Sontag declares that American culture was stunted because, following the closing of the frontier, the United States had been "created mainly by the surplus poor of Europe." Whereas others believe that the immigrants enriched American culture by bringing a variety of national and ethnic traditions with them, Sontag characterizes them all as "culturally deprived, uprooted people." Despite their material poverty, the sheer number of the immigrants and their descendants unfortunately insured that America would not be "built up" according to the standards afforded by a high culture; instead, a "tawdry fantasy of the good life" would provide the only basis for American civilization (195). And, if the aesthetic failings of the immigrants and their descendants are a misfortune for the United States, their moral flaws are a disaster for the world.

According to Sontag in "What's Happening in America (1966)," the United States remains "a passionately racist country" and would "continue to be so in the foreseeable future," despite the landmark civil rights legislation of 1964 and 1965. No legislation could make any real difference, since the basic problem is not the political or even the cultural limitations of the immigrants and their descendants. The former could be alleviated, and the latter could be at least ameliorated. The problem is their race. The immigrants, like the original colonists, were "white Europeans" (195), and, according to Sontag, "the white race *is* the cancer of human history" (203). And "if America *is* the culmination of Western white civilization," then the "painful truth" is that America "is a doomed country" and deserves to be (202); Sontag "only pray[s] that, when America founders, it doesn't drag the rest of the planet down, too" (204). The rest of the planet is endangered not just by our leaders but by the population at large. Getting their politics as well as their culture from the movies, "not just *some* Americans but virtually all Americans" believe that "the only good Red is a dead Red" (196). In other words, "Most of the people in this country believe what Goldwater believes, and always have" (198).

Sontag is a long way from her emphasis, only a year earlier, on the new sensibility, which was "less snobbish, less moralistic" ("One Culture," 303), which favored "a much cooler mode of moral judgment" (298–99). Then the big problem about contemporary society was not moral or political at all, and it called for sympathy rather than condemnation; "Western man," it seemed, had been undergoing "massive sensory anesthesia . . . since the Industrial Revolution," and it was the task of modern art to provide "a kind of shock therapy" so that the patient could enjoy life again (302). Sontag's emphases are so different in "One Culture and the New Sensibility," written in 1965, and "What's Happening in America (1966)" that the two essays almost appear to be written by two different people. Some concerns do overlap, however. The new sensibility championed in the 1965 essay reappears in 1966 in Sontag's affirmation of the young, "the way they dance, dress, wear their hair, riot, make love." She even approves of "their interest in taking drugs" ("What's Happening," 199), though here an Arnoldian reservation and term appears. As sometimes occurs in Sontag's prose, the key point occurs in a parenthesis. Sontag approves of "taking certain drugs (in a fully serious spirit: as a technique for exploring one's consciousness, not as an anodyne or a crutch)" (202). The awkward phrase "fully

serious spirit" used to affirm drug taking reminds one of Sontag's attempts in
Against Interpretation to characterize a particularly modern form of seriousness, a
form that might seem immoral but whose intensity and spiritual depth could be
equivalent to the high seriousness of the past.

The more important link between *Against Interpretation* and "What's Happening in America (1966)" is not between the explicit advocacy of a new sensibility common to both but in the latter's embodiment of a kind of seriousness
that is only described and admired in the first. In the first volume Sontag
explains why she admires Simone Weil and her peers; in the latter essay she
becomes Simone Weil, at least for a moment. The parallels between the aspects
of Simone Weil's life and work noted by Sontag and Sontag's own later essay
are striking. Although Simone Weil was of Jewish ancestry, she had a "violently
unfair hatred" of the Jews ("Simone Weil," 50). To characterize Sontag's feelings about immigrants, Americans, and whites in "What's Happening" as "violently unfair hatred" might be an understatement. Although an American and a
child of immigrants, of white European immigrants at that, Sontag both implies
and states explicitly that such people should be destroyed, along with all their
works. In search of a higher "level of spiritual reality," Weil indulged in "noble
and ridiculous political gestures" (51). Insofar as Sontag's essay is motivated by,
as she explained years later, "despair over America's war on Vietnam" (*Illness as
Metaphor*, 84), her aspiration is undoubtedly "noble"; as a demonstration of
political insight, it is arguably "ridiculous." Sontag emphasized that Simone
Weil's "dedication to martyrdom" commands respect, insofar "as we love seriousness." Susan Sontag demonstrates her own seriousness about the war in
Vietnam, her own "dedication to martyrdom" ("Simone Weil," 51) by calling
for the destruction of her own ancestors (immigrants), her own country (United
States), her own race (white), and even her own culture ("The truth is that
Mozart, Pascal, Boolean algebra, Shakespeare, parliamentary government,
baroque churches, Newton, the emancipation of women, Kant, Marx, and Bal-
anchine ballets don't redeem what this particular civilization has wrought upon
the world" [203]). Sontag herself offers an analogy between the Jews, "a people
doomed to disappear," and the United States, "a doomed country" (203, 204);
in this passage, the difference between the two fates is left implicit. Susan Sontag accepts both as inevitable; the difference, presumably, is that the United
States deserves its fate, while the Jews do not.

Sontag's essay surely fails as moral and political commentary, but it succeeds by the standards set in "Simone Weil." By those standards it makes no difference that one disagrees with Sontag's ideas, nor even that they appear bigoted
or mad. What is important is that a "sense of acute personal and intellectual

extremity" is conveyed ("Simone Weil" 49). When Susan Sontag writes that "the white race *is* the cancer of human history," the sophisticated reader knows that she is not arguing that there is a biological or genetic difference that sets Caucasians apart from other races. Of course, such arguments (sometimes claiming superiority, sometimes inherent inferiority) have been made. Theories alleging absolute moral and even metaphysical differences between races have been influential in the past, and even today they continue to exert a malign appeal. The milieu in which Sontag writes, however, has not been friendly to such ideas. It is most unlikely that she intended to make a case for the importance of race and on behalf of racism in the *Partisan Review* symposium in which "What's Happening" first appeared. Presumably, Susan Sontag, like her audience, not only rejects theories that assert the reality of racial characteristics but also condemns "racism" as an immoral attitude—in fact, one of the worst sins of the civilization she is condemning. If the sophistication Sontag shares with her readers insures hostility to theories of racial difference, the same sophistication encourages readers to judge her comments not "by the standard of an objective truth" but, instead, by the "level of spiritual reality" intimated by their intensity and extremity (50, 51). By such standards Sontag's welcoming of a doom of which she herself would be among the victims is a formidable achievement. Sontag's embrace of catastrophe for herself and her country might lead others to canonize Susan Sontag as a saint of culture, just as Sontag celebrated Simone Weil for her "dedication to martyrdom" (51). Sontag doesn't expect the young radicals to succeed politically, but she thinks that "a few of them may save their own souls" ("What's Happening," 203). A reader of "What's Happening" might well conclude that Susan Sontag has saved her own soul amid the general collapse.

Although Susan Sontag has often changed her emphases and her approaches, she has not published any extended reflection on the ideas she has discarded. A consideration of Susan Sontag's earlier work in the light of her later career, especially *Illness as Metaphor* and *AIDS and Its Metaphors*, is well worth undertaking for reasons beyond Sontag's own case. Despite the stylistic brilliance of her prose, she has always spoken for many besides herself, and her intellectual career forms an important part of the cultural history of the last few decades. Her career only gains in importance when one comes to see to what an extent her work since *Styles of Radical Will* has been an often brilliant, usually tacit, exercise of cultural self-criticism.

Against Interpretation drew attention in large part because it made a radical case against traditional humanism. With stylistic aplomb Sontag brushed aside as "obsolescent" the humanistic project of linking aesthetics with morality and truth. In the essays of *Against Interpretation* one discovered that modernist culture had left ordinary morality behind in favor of sheer extremity, any extremity as long as it was antibourgeois. Jean Genet, for example, was a culture hero for both Sontag and Jean-Paul Sartre, even though, or because, he gloried in "crime, sexual and social degradation, above all murder" ("Sartre's *Saint Genet,*" 95). Sontag's book left the impression that the contemporary seriousness that honored Genet marked a radical break with Arnoldian humanism. Such an impression had its utility, since its seeming radicalism contributed to the shock value and thus to the success of the book. A rereading of Arnold's "Study of Poetry," however, would have revealed that the gap between Sontag's modern seriousness, with its focus on intensity and its rejection of bourgeois morality, and Arnold's high seriousness was not as wide as Sontag's rhetoric suggested. If Sontag could admire Jean Genet, Matthew Arnold had held up François Villon, that "voice from the slums of Paris," with his "life of riot and crime," over Geoffrey Chaucer (177).

The real difference between the older humanism and Sontag's new sensibility derived not from a putatively broader version of seriousness but from the contemporary surrender of the Arnoldian effort to balance morality and truth against aesthetics. From the viewpoint of the new sensibility, the moral differences between, for example, Simone Weil and Jean Genet became unimportant. The lives and work of both were considered important only as aesthetic constructs. The critic relieved the audience from the trouble of discriminating between truth and falsity, between extremes deriving from mystical insights and extremes of self-indulgence. The only important questions now were: Is it interesting? Is it aesthetically compelling?

Susan Sontag came to reject the affirmation of aesthetics over both morality and truth that provided the basis for her earlier eagerness to reject traditional humanism and embrace extremity. Already sympathetic to camp's readiness to see "the world as an aesthetic phenomenon" ("Notes on 'Camp,'" 277), in "On Style" Sontag had straightforwardly affirmed the notion that "the world *is*, ultimately, an aesthetic phenomenon" ("On Style," 28). The rehabilitation of Leni Riefenstahl and her films, however, occasioned a rethinking. The separation and exultation of aesthetics over truth or morality seemed innocent enough when the topic was Simone Weil, a passionate enemy of fascism, but it seemed more questionable when the topic was Leni Riefenstahl, Nazism's most famous filmmaker. The "ideal of life as art," it turned out, was one of the characteristic ideals of fascism. Sontag now warns that the new respectability of Leni Riefenstahl "does not auger well for the keenness of current abilities to detect the fascist longings in our midst" ("Fascinating Fascism," 320), though she does not add that her own writings might have contributed to this dullness. In an interview published in *Salmagundi* in 1975, Sontag blames the influence of Friedrich Nietzsche and Oscar Wilde, among other nineteenth-century figures, for the notion that there was something intrinsically "generous and large-spirited" about viewing the world under the aspect of aesthetics. It was "the evolution of fascism in the twentieth century" that "taught us that they were wrong" (331). She does not mention that she was advocating the same view in the 1960s, two decades after the close of World War II.

When Susan Sontag does make an explicit reference to her past ideas, the passage deserves consideration for what it reveals about both the strengths and the limitations of her reconsideration. *Illness as Metaphor* emphasizes no thesis more strongly than the danger of using cancer as a metaphor for social, cultural, or political issues. Sontag notes that the Nazis described "the Jewish problem" as a cancer, for which radical surgery was the only solution (83). Noting that the metaphor has been used by many political persuasions, from totalitarian to liberal, she nevertheless cautions that the use of such metaphors is "never innocent," since an analogy between cancer and any human group carries a suggestion that is "implicitly genocidal." Having pointed out all this, it is much to Sontag's credit that she goes on to recall her own most striking use of the metaphor: "The cancer metaphor seems hard to resist for those who wish to register indignation. . . . I once wrote, in the heat of despair over America's war on Vietnam, that 'the white race is the cancer of human history'" (84). Attempting to "register indignation" over a society that, she had insisted, had been "founded on a genocide," ("What's Happening," 195), she made use of language that, on reflection a decade later, she finds "implicitly genocidal." Such an observation demands a good deal of moral courage and registers an important deepening of insight.

Having made such a significant criticism, it seems unfortunate that Sontag goes no further down this path. She does not, for instance, take the occasion to comment on the substance of the passage after she criticizes the metaphor. Does she still believe that "the white race" is a uniquely destructive force in human history? Does she still believe that it serves enlightenment to divide up humanity by color—black, white, yellow—for the purpose of assessing blame according to race? Does she still believe, as she did in 1966, that America, and the Jews, are indeed doomed? Sontag does not tell us. The most troubling implication of these omissions is not what they might suggest about Sontag herself. What disturbs most about Sontag's truncated reflection is the impression it leaves that these other matters are not terribly important, not important enough, at any rate, to require breaking the flow of her argument—which is, of course, about illness and metaphors.

Her own use of cancer as a metaphor is left as an isolated instance, comparable to its appearance in another passage that she does not bother to mention, a passage in "Sartre's *Saint Genet*" in which Sontag uses the cancer metaphor to describe a manuscript that has expanded beyond its planned length: "*Saint Genet* is a cancer of a book, grotesquely verbose. . . . One knows that the book began as an introductory essay . . . and grew to its present length" (93).

Since Susan Sontag does not follow up her specific admission with any further discussion, a reader of *Illness and Metaphor* and *AIDS and Its Metaphors* is likely to get the impression that the two long essays simply continue the themes of *Against Interpretation* into new areas. *Illness as Metaphor*, in fact, should be seen as a further application of "that quixotic, highly polemical strategy, 'against interpretation,' to the real world this time," declares Susan Sontag at the beginning of *AIDS and its Metaphors*. Once again she was attempting "to deprive something of meaning," not, this time, works of art, but, instead, the body and its diseases. Her goal was to encourage patients and society as a whole "to regard cancer as if it were just a disease—a very serious one, but just a disease. Not a curse, not a punishment, not an embarrassment. Without 'meaning'" (*AIDS and its Metaphors,* 102).

The calm dignity that suffuses *Illness as Metaphor* arguably derives, nevertheless, from Susan Sontag's tacit willingness to rethink key ideas and assumptions. Having already broken with the notion that viewing the world from an aesthetic vantage constituted an advance on traditional culture, Sontag in *Illness as Metaphor* questions the other alternative to humanism offered in *Against Interpretation*, the notion of a radical seriousness "whose trademark is anguish, cruelty, derangement" ("Notes on 'Camp,'" 287). Sontag's description of the qualities allegedly shared by the victim of tuberculosis (earlier in the century) and insanity (now) sounds very much like one of the saints of culture championed in *Against Interpretation*: "the sufferer as a hectic, reckless creature of passionate extremes, someone too sensitive to bear the horrors of the vulgar, everyday world" (*Illness as Metaphor,* 36). The sufferer resembles the Simone Weil whose saintly attributes included, according to Sontag in 1963, "her migraines, her tuberculosis" ("Simone Weil," 51). Among those who, like Susan Sontag in the 1960s, accept the romantic mythology according to which extreme states of feeling provide evidence of spiritual depth, insanity provides "the index of a superior sensitivity" (*Illness as Metaphor,* 35) as "the current vehicle of our secular myth of self-transcendence" (36). Susan Sontag's careful debunking of the putative connections between art and illness succeeds admirably in depriving such ideas of the standing they once enjoyed and to which her own earlier writings contributed.

If *Illness as Metaphor* demonstrates a rethinking of the notion of extremity as a source of cultural prestige, it also reveals a reconsideration of the counter-image to the mad saint of culture, the stereotype of the philistine. According to the mythology that Sontag now debunks, the typical cancer patient resembles the philistine personality Sontag formerly decried. Cancer strikes "those who are sexually repressed, inhibited, unspontaneous, incapable of expressing anger" (21). The disease marks the patient as "one of life's losers" (49), a bourgeois robot victimized by his or her own "repression of emotion," by a "failure of expressiveness" (48). Intellectuals who die of cancer are paying "the gruesome penalty exacted for a lifetime of instinctual renunciation" (49). Both tuberculosis and cancer are thought to spring from the "repression" of "passionateness" (36). Sontag notes that the psychoanalyst Wilhelm Reich is the "source for much of the current fancy that associated cancer with the repression of emotion" (23). In *Illness as Metaphor* Reich appears as something of a crank, writing with an "inimitable coherence" as he worries about something he calls "deadly orgone energy" in the atmosphere (67). One might well wonder why anybody would pay attention to his ideas about cancer. In *Against Interpretation*, however, Reich was treated with respect. He was linked with Herbert Marcuse and Norman O. Brown as one of the "dissidents" of the Freudian tradition attempting to work out "the serious consequences of atheism" ("Piety without content," 255) and praised as one of the few followers who "grasped the critical implications of the Freudian ideas" and were thus "far truer to Freud than the orthodox psychoanalysts" (Psychoanalysis," 259).

In *Illness as Metaphor* and *AIDS and Its Metaphors* Sontag tacitly retrieves much of the old humanism. The old standard of objective truth, so outdated in *Against Interpretation* ("We measure truth in terms of the cost to the writer in suffering—rather than by the standard of an objective truth" ["Simone Weil," 49-50]), once again becomes important. If a theorist such as Wilhelm Reich conveys false theories, he can no longer be justified simply because he attacks bourgeois morality. Truth matters, and morality matters as well. Her aim now is "to alleviate suffering," a project that suggests complicity with traditional moral and religious values, though Sontag finds a quotation demonstrating that Nietzsche would have approved also (*AIDS and Its Metaphors*, 101–2). The notion, which once seemed so modern, that "cruelty" and "derangement" were to be accepted and even celebrated because aesthetics was paramount over morality, now seems out-of-date, inoperative, obsolescent.

Because Sontag's rethinking is carried out tacitly, she does not consider the possibility that her latest books seem to raise. If extremity is not always to be praised as seriousness, if adherence to the bourgeois virtues is not always to be stigmatized as philistine, if advanced thought and culture could be so unenlightened as to produce what now seems so wrongheaded a mythology of diseases, is it possible that the entire attempt to advance "beyond" humanism needs to be reconsidered? This question does not receive explicit formulation in Susan Sontag's writings, earlier or later. It is all the greater a tribute, then, to both the power of her earlier writings and the depth of her reconsiderations that her work as a whole forces one to confront such an unthinkable possibility.

Part 4

Cultural Studies

Chapter 10

Fredric Jameson: Marxism without Difficulty

In *The Political Unconscious* (1981) Fredric Jameson consolidated his position as not only the most important Marxist literary critic in the United States but as one of the most important cultural critics of any school. In *Marxism and Form* Jameson argued for the literary and cultural relevance of European Marxists who could not be subsumed under the Stalinist label of dialectical materialism. *The Political Unconscious*, however, presents Jameson's own version of Marxism. In *Marxism and Form* Jameson argued that Marxism could actually encourage rather than inhibit a full response to the form of a literary work. In *The Political Unconscious* he moved beyond commentary to present a Marxist theory that assigns a central role to the concept of "modes of production" but also is at home among the theoretical debates of French poststructuralism. *The Political Unconscious* announces a Marxism committed to revolutionary change that is also able to treat cultural phenomena in a nonreductive way. A decade later *Postmodernism, or, The Cultural Logic of Late Capitalism* responds to the developments of the 1980s with an attempt "to project some conception of a new systematic cultural norm and its reproduction in order to reflect more adequately on the most effective forms of any radical cultural politics today" (6). Although Jameson formulates new conceptions to deal with different times, he also aims to keep faith with the revolutionary commitments of *The Political Unconscious*, telling readers that "the analysis of postmodernism is not alien to my earlier work but rather a logical consequence of it" (399). It may be that *Postmodernism* represents a contemporary example of that "cultural self-criticism" that this book identifies, perhaps too exclusively, with an earlier tradition. Considerations of *The Political Unconscious* and *Postmodernism* in turn may suggest to what extent academic Marxism is capable of self-reflection; history has rarely given would-be revolutionaries so much food for thought as in the second half of the decade between 1981 and 1991. In the concluding chapter of *Postmodernism*

Jameson offers a rationale for his own version of cultural studies, asserting its superiority to the "cultural journalism" of an earlier time; a consideration of his argument will serve to clarify some central themes of this book.

The critical response to *The Political Unconscious* revealed Jameson's ability to formulate an explicitly Marxist argument that compels the attention of both opponents and defenders of revolution. Hayden White is "against revolutions, whether launched from 'above' or 'below'" (125). Nevertheless, he is quoted on the back cover of the paperback edition of *The Political Unconscious* describing the text as a "major work" and endorsing Jameson's mode of argument in the strongest terms: "It seems impossible for him to write anything that is not illuminating in an original way. There is no cant, no cliché, no jargon in his work, only sustained *dialectical* reflection." In the same symposium Edward Said, a supporter of at least one revolution, the Palestinian, finds "a number of nagging difficulties" but stresses his fundamental admiration for the work:

> Fredric Jameson has recently produced what is by any standard a major work of intellectual criticism, *The Political Unconscious*. What it discusses it discusses with a rare brilliance and learning: I have no reservations at all about that. . . . It cannot be emphasized too strongly that Jameson's book presents a remarkably complex and deeply attractive argument to which I cannot do justice here. This argument reaches its climax in Jameson's conclusion, in which the utopian element in all cultural production is shown to play an underanalyzed and liberating role in human society. (19)

Despite the eminence of Jameson's supporters, a consideration of *The Political Unconscious* through analyses of Jameson's style, his use of Marxism, and finally his employment of ideology and utopia as polar terms reveals certain difficulties. The easy brilliance of Jameson's style, which in *Marxism and Form* appeared so original, now seems an instrument for evading pertinent objections, nowhere more so than in Jameson's explicitly Marxist formulations. Meanwhile, the virtues of Jameson's proposed division of cultural phenomena into utopian desire and ideology seem questionable at best.

Jameson, *The Political Unconscious* makes clear, is committed not only to political revolution but to a cultural radicalism that he presents as a necessary component of political radicalism. Jameson's work, however, inadvertently strengthens the suspicion that to base one's criticism of society entirely on a vision of the future is inevitably to capitulate to the dominant currents of the society one intends to criticize. The future is conjectural, while an independent scheme of values cannot be worked out without reference to some realm other than the present—which can only be the past. Christopher Lasch, Philip Rieff, and the Gerald Graff of *Literature against Itself,* among others, have pointed out that contemporary capitalism has robbed the concept of a cultural avant-garde of its original critical significance. In Graff's words, "the real 'avant-garde'" is advanced capitalism, with its built-in need to destroy all vestiges of tradition, all orthodox ideologies, all continuous and stable forms of reality in order to stimulate higher levels of consumption" (8). Graff himself may no longer endorse this view; both *The Political Unconscious* and *Postmodernism* provide evidence for its continuing validity.[1]

Jameson's style is often stunning in its easy movement from one theoretical position to another. Although much of *The Political Unconscious* deals with abstract issues, Jameson's approach is nevertheless impressionistic; he works by letting the reader know how it feels to hold a particular position. He evokes, conjures up, and then dismisses concepts rather than presenting arguments and answering them with opposing arguments. The reader, swept along by the style, assents to the "transcending" of particular views without stopping to consider possible objections to Jameson's "sublations."

When Jameson builds on Lévi-Strauss's idea of literature as symbolic resolution to his own thesis about the form these symbolic resolutions take, a Marxist might well want to object:

> With political allegory, then, a sometimes repressed ur-narrative or master fantasy about the interaction of collective subjects, we have moved to the very borders of our second horizon in which what we formerly regarded as individual texts are grasped as "utterances" in an essentially collective or class discourse. (80)

The idea of an "ur-narrative," or "master fantasy," is plausible if one thinks of literature as occurring at a simultaneous moment in a dimension in which history is irrelevant. If history happens all at once, as Jameson's passage intimates, it is reasonable to posit a constant, ahistorical dimension in which the aspirations and drives of a particular period can be interpreted as "Desire as such"—as Jameson does in his dehistoricizing interpretation of Balzac: "the desire for a particular object is at one and the same time allegorical of all desire in general and of Desire as such" (156). And, once specific, historically conditioned desires are understood as Desire as such, it is plausible to interpret Balzac's work, or that of any author, in terms of a "Utopian impulse" (157), which is itself unvarying, since it refers to a static future.

What, after all, is the concept of history formulated by this author, who urges us to "Always historicise!"? Would it be possible to translate this slogan into rather less aphoristic language such as "Always put your ideas into an historical context"? Apparently, it would not be possible, since Jameson rejects the idea of history as a context, ground, or referent, insisting that history can only be understood as an "absent cause" (35). If Jameson's point is simply that we never directly apprehend History or the Real, both capitalized, as essences in their naked purity, then its sense is unexceptionable if trivial. Throughout *The Political Unconscious*, however, Jameson has no compunctions about referring to Desire as such, so that, although History as "an absent ground" is treated with respect, history in any recognizable sense is simply absent from Jameson's discussion of cultural phenomena in terms of utopian desire and ideology.

These topics raise questions about Jameson's Marxism rather than his style. Key aspects of that Marxism include Jameson's conception of history as that which "refuses desire" (102), his view of history "in its vastest sense as a sequence of modes of production" (75), and the implications of his ideas for the relation between theory and practice.

In closing his theoretical introduction, "On Interpretation," Jameson offers a definition of history that responds to the attacks made on Marxism when the priority of "modes of production" is taken to imply "a form of technological or 'productionist' determinism" (101). What matters here for Jameson is not so much that technological determinism is in fact a false interpretation of history as that the putting forth of any such specific theory—one interpretation among others—is a false step in a poststructuralist culture, since other critics will pounce on such a definition as an inadmissible move, an attempt to refer directly to the "Real" without acknowledging the fictional, symbolic quality of all language and all conceptions. (It is hard to resist a sneaking sympathy for those backward technological determinists for having the courage to offer a definite concept that is open to criticism and which frankly presents itself as one possible theory among others.)

Jameson, on the other hand, feels that he must come up with a concept of history that is not a concept at all, which does not contain a reference, however disguised, to "reality." Therefore, he argues that instead of defending a particular interpretation of history in terms of a concept of modes of production,

> it would seem therefore more useful to ask ourselves, in conclusion, how History as a ground and as an absent cause can be conceived in such a way as to resist such thematization or reification, such transformation back into one optional code among others. (101)

History is therefore defined negatively as "the experience of Necessity." "Conceived in this sense," says Jameson, "History is what hurts, it is what refuses desire and sets inexorable limits to individual as well as collective praxis" (102).

The passage and the definition are effective as rhetoric. The reader sees the author brooding soberly over historical disasters and human suffering, proposing a view of historical experience that is both invulnerable to the kind of objections offered by deconstructionists yet takes account of the harsh realities of the modern world. When one pauses to consider the implications of such a definition, however, problems arise. At first glance it is odd for a Marxist to identify History with "the experience of Necessity," with "what sets inexorable limits to praxis" in the light of Marx's own view that the life of his own times could only be considered "prehistory" since real history would begin only when the "inexorable limits" Jameson mentions would be removed.[2]

The issue is not simply one of terminology. Jameson's definition reveals a view of history that is radically at odds with that of classical Marxism and Hegel as well. For Hegel (as for Marx) history is, so far from being the opposing term to desire, a product of desire:

> The first glance at history convinces us that the actions of men spring from the needs, passions, from their interests, their characters and their talents. Indeed, it appears as if in this drama of activities these needs, passions and interests are the sole springs of action and the main efficient cause. (26)

Marx and Engels rejected Hegel's view that the "Absolute" is the hidden power behind the course of world history but shared his view—in contrast to the Enlightenment belief in human reason as the agency of change—that human needs and interests, only partially understood by the individuals themselves, moved human beings to act and to fight. For Marx these conflicts could never be settled through mere intellectual debate, since they were expressions of class struggle and thus not amenable to settlement by discussion.

Marx and Georg Lukàcs both have pointed out that the achievement of Balzac is to reveal the real movement of human history. Surely, the greatness of Balzac as a historical novelist lies in his ability to demonstrate how history is generated precisely from human desires, desires often utterly personal and without overt political content. The reader of Balzac learns, along with Mme Vauquer of *Père Goriot*, that history is not simply the result of decisions taken by prime ministers and generals but is also generated by the conflicting desires of the tenants of middle-class boardinghouses, individuals whose desires are shaped by history but who also, through their own drives and aspirations, themselves shape history so that even Mme Vauquer is affected:

> To think that all these things should happen in my house, in a district where there's never a cat stirring! Upon my word as an honest woman I must be dreaming! For it's true we've seen Louis XVI have his accident, we've seen the Emperor fall, we've seen him come back and fall again, but that's all in the natural order of things, those are things that can easily happen, you see, whereas middle class boarding houses are firmly settled, unchanging things, they don't have upsets like that: You can do without a king but you can't do without your dinner. (238)

Political allegory seems a weak word to describe what Balzac is accomplishing here—in fact, the wrong word—and, indeed, Jameson makes no attempt to discuss *Père Goriot*.

For him Balzac's novels reveal an opposition between history and Desire, as his comment on Lukàcs's interpretation of Balzac demonstrates:

> This is the sense in which Lukàcs is right about Balzac, but for the wrong reasons: not Balzac's deeper sense of political and historical realities, but rather his incorrigible fantasy demands ultimately raise History itself over against him, an absent cause, as that on which desire must come to grief. . . . The Real is thus—virtually by definition in the fallen world of capitalism—that which resists desire. (183–84).

For Jameson desire's relation to history is reduced to an epistemological rather than creative function: "this Real—this absent cause . . . can be disclosed only by Desire itself" (184). Given such an impoverished conception of the relation between desire and history, it is understandable that for Jameson desire is only worth thinking about as utopian desire, and therefore as always the same (capitalized) Desire, referring to what is apparently the only permissible referent, a Utopian future of libidinal gratification. The cultural implications of such a perspective will be considered later.

Jameson's notion of modes of production provides the basis for his concept of "history now conceived in its vastest sense of the sequence of modes of production" (75). What is the sense of this "vastest sense"? It would seem that one committed, as Jameson is, to conceiving of History as an "absent cause" could scarcely also be able to identify it as "the sequence of modes of production" without self-contradiction. Jameson's tactic is simply to void the concept of mode of production of any determinate content. The phrase itself sounds reassuring, as though in the middle of arcane literary and academic debates Jameson is willing to grapple with the fundamental realities confronted by traditional Marxism. His is not merely a literary Marxism related only to the realm of culture but one that bases itself on the unliterary conception of modes of production. Jameson repeatedly refers to mode of production as the key concept of his Marxism and, indeed, of any Marxism: "Marxism is, however, not a mechanical but a historical materialism: it does not assert the primacy of matter so much as it insists on an ultimate determination by the mode of production" (45). Yet the reader looks in vain for an example or explanation of such "determination." Attempting to avoid the vulgar errors of traditional Marxism in identifying the mode of production with the "narrowly 'economic'" (36), Jameson wholeheartedly accepts the theories of Louis Althusser, whose ideas once seemed to mark an epoch in Marxist dialectics, in identifying "this concept with the structure as a whole" (36).[3]

> From this point of view, the mode of production is identical with the synchronic system of social relations as a whole . . . it is nowhere empirically present as an element, it is not a part of the whole or one of the levels, but rather the entire system of relationships among those levels (36).

Once one identifies the mode of production with society as a whole, one has certainly avoided vulgar Marxism and the charge of economic or technological determinism, but one has also avoided any determinate meaning at all. Without any specific analysis—lacking in *The Political Unconscious*—it seems hard to see what difference it would make if one spoke of the "mode of thought" or any other "mode" as a shorthand term for the relationships of society as a whole. Matters are not improved when Jameson offers the idea that any particular society includes not one but "several modes of production all at once." If a given mode of production is indeed to be identified with society as a whole, it is difficult to see how there is any room for other modes of production to enter the conceptual scheme, but Jameson does not pause to consider such objections. For him the concept of competing modes of production is a theoretical breakthrough: "But if this suggestion is valid, then the problems of the 'synchronic' system and of the typological temptation are both solved at one stroke" (95).

The conception is so powerful that it can resolve practical dilemmas, such as those confronted in the debate between Marxists and feminists about the most urgent goals for cultural and political struggle:

The notion of overlapping modes of production outlined above has indeed
the advantage of allowing us to short-circuit the false problem of the priority of the economic over the sexual, or of sexual oppression over that of
social class. . . . The affirmation of radical feminism, therefore, that to
annul the patriarchal is the most radical political act—insofar as it includes
and subsumes more partial demands, such as the liberation from the com-
modity form—is thus perfectly consistent with an expanded Marxian
framework, for which the transformation of our own dominant mode of
production must be accomplished and completed by an equally radical
restructuration of all the more archaic modes of production with which it
structurally exists. (100)

Ignoring the question of what meaning one can give to the assertion that patri-
archy in late capitalism is a mode of production—as opposed to a cultural and
social phenomenon—one wonders how Jameson's formulation will "short-circuit" such immediate dilemmas as the question of whether women should fight
the injustices of contemporary capitalism as they affect all persons or rather fight
to enter the marketplace on equal terms with men.

Such belief in the efficacy of concepts to solve political problems suggests
an affiliation with Hegel rather than with Marx. George Lichtheim sardonically
entitled a collection of his essays *From Marx to Hegel* to suggest that, when intellectuals have no clear relation to the course of events, their perspective, whatever their intentions and personal militancy, becomes Hegelian rather than
Marxist.[4] Marx believed that he voiced the demands of an incipiently revolutionary class, the proletariat, and emphasized that only on such a basis could his
thought be distinguished from that of academic philosophers. Georg Lukàcs
argued in 1922 that a Communist Party organized on Leninist principles could
adopt the viewpoint that the proletariat, if it were truly revolutionary, would
hold and thereby grasp the totality.[5] Later Western Marxists have been forced to
admit that the proletariat is not revolutionary and that the attempt to adopt the
viewpoint that the proletariat would hold if it were revolutionary is futile.

It is instructive to compare the response to this problem by two theorists
of the Frankfurt School, Theodor Adorno and Herbert Marcuse, both discussed
by Jameson in *Marxism and Form*, to that taken by Jameson himself. Adorno
argued in *Negative Dialectics* that the traditional Marxian belief in the unity of
theory and practice could no longer be maintained: "Philosophy, which once
seemed obsolete, lives on because the moment to realize it was missed" (3). In
One-Dimensional Man Marcuse acknowledged that his critique of contemporary
society differed from that of traditional Marxism. Marx and Engels had no

doubts about "the presence of real forces (objective and subjective) in the established society which moved (or could be guided to move) toward more rational and freer institutions" (254). Marcuse admits that the situation has changed:
"The critical theory of society possesses no concepts which could bridge the gap
between the present and its future; holding no promise and showing no success,
it remains negative" (257).

In thus acknowledging the difference between their theoretical position
and traditional Marxism, Adorno and Marcuse remained true to a Marxism that
recognized the reality of a world outside the history of ideas. Jameson, however,
seems to see no problems in identifying himself as a straightforward Marxist. His
verbal gestures toward political militancy and modes of production, in fact, inti-
mate that he is a full-blooded Marxist of the old school, unlike the more cautious critical theorists of the Frankfurt School, to whom he owes much of his
orientation. But Jameson's style moves around problematic theoretical issues
much too easily. Any revival of Marxism that would aim at an impact beyond
the campus must begin, one would think, with a recognition of all the factors
that prevent Marxism from being more than an intellectual badge. If, however,
what attracts one to Marxism is not the opportunity to put theory into practice
but, rather, the chance to write books as a Marxist theorist who easily "subsumes other interpretive modes or systems" into the Marxist system (47), the
political difficulties facing revolutionaries need not occasion any rethinking.

The political importance of Jameson's Marxism is minimal, but such difficulties, though central to traditional, vulgar Marxism, require no acknowledgment in
a Jamesonian context; The Political Unconscious suffers from that belief in what
Freud called the "omnipotence of thought" (Totem and Taboo, 117) that seems
endemic to intellectuals and which no gestures of political militancy or obeisance
to Marxist fundamentalism can disguise.[6] On the other hand, the cultural impact
of Jameson's ideas is undoubtedly significant. Jameson remains a highly influential
theorist whose putative Marxism assures him a special niche on the cultural Left.
It is, therefore, worth considering with some care Jameson's proposal that all literary phenomena be interpreted in terms of ideology and utopia.

Although Jameson announces his conception with fanfare—"I would
argue that the problem of a functional or instrumental conception of culture is
basically transcended and annulled in the Utopian perspective which is ours
here" (293)—the idea that all cultural productions should be seen in the dual
light of utopia and ideology seems at first unoriginal and almost banal. (It is typical of Jameson's style that he dismisses the obvious parallel to Karl Mannheim's
Ideology and Utopia as mere "communicational noise and conceptual interfer-
ence" [296], not as a real problem that he needs to make an effort to clarify.) On

the one hand, on the other hand—every work contains something valuable today as well as something limited by the prejudices of time and place. Contrary to first impressions, however, Jameson's concepts of ideology and utopian desire are not merely empty, at least not by comparison to his concept of modes of production. They point to some definite views about history and culture and the relations between them.

For Jameson it is the "utopian" element of texts that is to be privileged, recuperated, valorized, to use the language of his school. The utopian elements of cultural works are valuable because they anticipate and thus make us aware of the need for a revolution that will go far beyond the political, which will be "the liberation of desire and of libidinal transfiguration" (67). Throughout *The Political Unconscious* Jameson speaks of utopian desire and utopian impulse. Always impulse, desire, and the utopian are connected and affirmed. Ideology, identified with consciousness and rationalization, receives far less attention.

It is true that Jameson "would seek to argue the proposition that the effectively ideological is also, at the same time, necessarily Utopian" (286). He declares that

> all class consciousness of whatever type is Utopian insofar as it expresses the unity of a collectivity. . . . The achieved collectivity or organic group of whatever kind—oppressors fully as much as oppressed—is Utopian not in itself but only insofar as all such collectivities are themselves figures for the ultimate concrete collective life of an achieved Utopia or classless society (291).

But Jameson's identification of ideology and utopia in this passage does nothing to ameliorate the insistent rhetorical identification of utopia with desire and impulse and of ideology with attempts at rationalization, with conscious ideals, thought—in short, with sublimation. Jameson tells us nothing about what form collective life might take in the utopia he envisions, but his emphasis on "libidinal revolution" (74), separated from any references to reason at all, suggests that Philip Rieff's comment is germane: "orgy is the one, only and original, totally democratic institution—the common utopia of all our gurus, 'fascist' and 'liberationist'" (162).

Jameson's ideas reveal their shallowness when compared with comparable theses of figures who are part of the tradition on which he draws: Lukàcs, Freud, and Marcuse. The bifurcation of culture into ideology and utopia recalls Lukàcs's thesis in *The Destruction of Reason* that modern culture could best be seen in terms of the conflict between reason and irrationalism. Despite the obvious limitations of Lukàcs's schematic study, his affirmation of reason and his fear of the irrationalist "liberation" of desire, which may lead to the unleashing of violence at least as easily as to the expression of universal love, seems to represent a much more accurate reading of the real dangers of the twentieth century, and not just of the era of Nazism, than does Jameson's "valorization" of desire—any kind of desire, apparently, as somehow valuable. Jameson's reading of Freud, despite its apparent sophistication, betrays an ignorance of what Freud was finally forced to acknowledge: that human nature is not simply innocent and pure, corrupted by social institutions alone; that desire can be destructive as well as loving; that the urge to aggression is as real as the urge to love. Although Lukàcs could never read Freud with understanding or sympathy, while Jameson continually uses Freudian terms and, the text suggests, has "sublated" Freud into his own larger system, it is Lukàcs's vision of history that seems closer to Freud's own.

Marcuse is the thinker whose use of Freud and whose affirmation of an erotic utopian vision seems closest to Jameson, and the differences between them are for that reason especially instructive. In *Eros and Civilization* Marcuse made a case for the critical value of a vision of erotic fulfillment, but he linked his argument to a consideration of the manifestations of the death instinct as well—acknowledging that desire can be destructive as well as creative. In *One-Dimensional Man* Marcuse analyzes the phenomenon of "institutionalized desublimation," which he says "appears to be a vital factor in the making of the authoritarian personality of our time" (74). As against the "liberation of desire" which allows "satisfaction in a way which generates submission and weakens the rationality of protest" (75), Marcuse affirms the critical function of sublimation:

> In contrast to the pleasures of adjusted desublimation, sublimation preserves the consciousness of the renunciations which the repressive society inflicts upon the individual, and thereby preserves the need for liberation. . . . In the light of the cognitive function of this mode of sublimation, the desublimation rampant in advanced industrial society reveals its truly conformist function (76).

Jameson fails to discuss the conception of desublimation, an understandable failure, since the very word sublimation, let along the concept or related ideas, fails, incredibly, to turn up anywhere in the text of *The Political Unconscious*. This omission, with Jameson's failure to mention aggressive impulses that are not utopian, vitiates his few words on "the ideological function of mass culture . . .

whereby dangerous and protopolitical impulses are 'managed' and defused, rechanneled and offered spurious objects" (287). Again, it is ideology—the element connected with deception and rationalization but also with reason and conscious thought—which is wholly the enemy, whereas "dangerous and protopolitical impulses" are assumed to be subversive and therefore good.

The influence of *The Political Unconscious* has been largely pernicious, both politically and culturally. The development of any movement for social change requires, at a minimum, that the people who make up such a movement are able to achieve a certain order in their private lives, are able to live with compromises and delayed gratifications. Only by doing so will they be able to achieve the sublimations necessary to envision ideals beyond the status quo. The distinction between personal life and social life, between culture and politics, must be recognized. Commercials and entertainment programs flood us with images of "libidinal gratification" and insist that life is not worth living if instantaneous gratification of every whim is not realized. The ability to envision possibilities for a better society and to act to bring them closer to reality depends on a willingness to find satisfactions in one's own life that are short of utopian. At a time when the satisfactions of ordinary life are extremely difficult to achieve, when the images of entertaining and advertising work to arouse utopian desires for immediate fulfillment, a thesis that suggests that only the utopian dimension of desire is worthwhile, that any use of reason is to be categorized as ideology, seems superfluous at best.

The failure to recognize difficulties, both conceptual and historical, is the common quality linking Jameson's style, in his Marxism and in his presentation of utopian desire. Together, these failures constitute a viewpoint whose self-proclaimed radicalism is weakened by its failure to recognize the very real problems most people face. For the vast majority of Americans economic problems remain pressing, while the satisfactions of ordinary human relationships are more and more difficult to achieve. It becomes more difficult to fulfill the everyday obligations, and thereby enjoy the rewards, of parenthood, of marriage, and of friendship. Jameson's call for a politics based on a commitment to utopian desire seems simplistic and arrogant. His Marxism invites the indignation of those confronted daily with the difficulties of both personal and collective life in the United States against an academic radicalism that claims to speak on their behalf but achieves easy rhetorical victories by ignoring their difficulties.

The decade after the 1981 publication of *The Political Unconscious* raised obstacles for any would-be Marxist, even those whose ambition did not go beyond a Marxism without difficulty, that is to say, a Marxism of the campus. It was during the 1980s, after all, that the actually existing socialism of the Soviet empire collapsed. In the United States, meanwhile, Ronald Reagan and George Bush won successive presidential elections. Jameson's *Postmodernism, or, The Cultural Logic of Late Capitalism* presents one means of coping with developments that would seem (1991) to present awesome difficulties for any Marxist who still believed in utopia as the goal and Communist revolution as the means. Jameson's key technique remains the simple refusal to acknowledge historical and political difficulties. Some of those who once hailed the Chinese "cultural revolution" have revised their judgments after memoirs and documents detailing the human cost of that era began to emerge. In 1991, however, Jameson found it possible to ignore the catastrophes of Chinese socialism. He remained buoyed by "the excitement of the immense, unfinished social experiment of the New China" (29). Ignoring the muffled groans of the victims and the eloquent narratives of refugees, what Jameson hears from China is music to his ears: "a collectivity which has become a new 'subject of history' and which, after the long subjection of feudalism and imperialism, again speaks in its own voice, for itself, as though for the first time"(29).

Just as Jameson finds no reason to rethink his enthusiasm for Mao, he likewise finds no difficulty in affirming traditional Marxism-Leninism. Sometimes Jameson affirms his loyalty by verbal signals, as in his use of "comrades" to refer, one supposes, to his colleagues in the revolutionary project. References to "comrades" may seem so campy that they disarm criticism, but Jameson's use of the term is worth considering. He feels a kinship with "the Russian comrades" (274), by whom he means not dissidents such as Sakharov but the pre-Gorbachev Politburo, while he rebukes the "more simple-hearted comrades" in academia who fear that his taste for postmodernist culture has blunted his revolutionary commitment (298). Jameson admits, that is, that both "the Russian comrades" and the "more simple-hearted comrades" have erred, but, since they are still comrades, at least their hearts, simple or otherwise, have been in the right place, that is, on the Left—in contrast, presumably, to all those standpatters who believe that Communist regimes have been a disaster and regard Marxism itself as an ideology that has served to justify the indefensible at least as much as any other contemporary philosophy or religion.

Although Jameson avoids making any full-scale political analyses in *Postmodernism*, he makes clear his continuing sympathy for the old regime in Russia and Cuba as well as China. He doesn't think it would be fair to make "the Russian comrades . . . bear all the responsibility for global history," but he cannot forebear suggesting that it was "the failure of the Khrushchev experiment" to "restore" the Soviet Revolution and "transform the party" that accounts for the diminishing appeal of socialism (274). Nothing, Jameson suggests, was wrong with Bolshevism itself. Some radicals have had qualms about their early support for Fidel Castro, but, for Jameson, Castro's "ultimate revolutionary victory" remains as unquestionably A Good Thing as ever (329). The apparent failure of socialism throughout the world might lead some to wonder if Marx really knew what he was talking about in predicting the inevitable triumph of socialism, but for Jameson it is simply a matter of revising the timetable. Turn from the unfortunately "foreshortened apocalyptic prophesies of *Capital* itself" to "the long temporal perspective of the *Grundrisse*" (206), and it is obvious that Marx has been right all along. If the book that Marx actually published during his lifetime is misleading, while the truth has to be dug out of an unpublished manuscript, that's the sort of difficulty that Jameson takes in stride.

Perhaps Jameson's failure to notice contemporary history can be explained as an effect of the disorienting power of the "cultural logic of late capitalism." The Bonaventure Hotel in Los Angeles, in particular seems to provide an overwhelming experience for Jameson.[7] The escalators of the Bonaventure offer an instance of the "dialectical intensification of the autoreferentiality of all modern culture" (42), while its "total space" doesn't simply become crowded, it induces "a new mode in which individuals move and congregate, something like the practice of a new and historically original kind of hypercrowd" (40). It's hard to find one's away around in the Bonaventure—at least this much of Jameson's description rings true. What rings false is Jameson's claim that the confusions of the lobby of the Bonaventure are in any way analogous to "the space of postmodern warfare" as exemplified in the war in Vietnam (44). Jameson uses Michael Herr's book on the Vietnam War, *Dispatches*, to argue that the "mystery of the new post-modernist space" is essentially the same in a Los Angeles hotel or a helicopter in Vietnam (45). Jameson's willingness to equate his thrilling bewilderment in a hotel lobby to the experience of soldiers in Vietnam offers a seemingly unsurpassable example of the way in which *Postmodernism* reduces all experience to interchangeable, equivalent texts. What Jameson says about postmodernism is surely true of his own prose: "it seems possible that in a situation of total flow . . . what used to be called 'critical distance' seems to have become obsolete" (70).

At least once Jameson suggests that the dominance of postmodernist culture is not absolute, but he suggests that alternatives are available only to "marginal groups" who inhabit a "Third World" within postmodern capitalism (159). The possibility that one might obtain a "critical distance" from contemporary society by referring to alternative perspectives from the past does not seem to occur to Jameson, perhaps because in his view postmodernist society marks a break with the past so absolute that the experience of earlier generations has nothing to teach us.

In *The Political Unconscious*, of course, it was Jameson's commitment to a libidinal utopia that defined him as a revolutionary. Jameson still feels that the "reinvention of the Utopian vision" remains central to "any contemporary politics"— that is a "part of the legacy of the sixties which must never be abandoned" (159). In *Postmodernism* that commitment may not be "abandoned," but it certainly gets short-changed in favor of the here-and-now delights of the US in the 1980s—MTV (theoretically significant as an instance of the "spatialization of music" [299]), hotel lobbies, videos, etc. Jameson is "a relatively enthusiastic consumer of postmodernism" for whom the Reagan years have had their upside: "Food and fashion have also greatly improved, as has the life world generally" (298–99). One would think that general improvement in the "life world" would constitute a significant development, one well worth examining in some detail, especially since it occurs under the aegis of what Jameson's subtitle calls "late capitalism," a term whose associations are with decline rather than improvement. For Jameson, however, the apparent contradiction between his official ideology, according to which Reagan's effect on U.S. society was disastrous, and his personal, intuitive sense that "the life world generally" has improved under Reagan presents no difficulty.

Jameson instead takes the opportunity to explain the virtues of his own kind of cultural studies by comparison to the cultural journalism associated with H. L. Mencken, Edmund Wilson, Dwight Macdonald, and other critics of an older tradition. Jameson describes his own kind of analysis as a "peculiar and rigorous conjuncture of formal and historical analysis," remarking with some satisfaction that his kind of "analysis" is unlikely to be confused with that "very different set of operations" that characterize "a cultural journalism oriented around taste and opinion" (298). Here he can rest easy. Jameson on architecture and postmodernism is not going to remind anybody of Ralph Ellison on *Tobacco Road* or Edmund Wilson on Grant's *Memoirs*.

Jameson's work involves, however, not only "analysis" but also "evaluation," and he does see the danger that his kind of evaluation might be confused with the straightforward evaluation of works that characterized the old cultural journalism. Although Jameson is generous enough to grant the "indispensable reviewing functions" of mere cultural journalism, his own sort of evaluation involves a different magnitude of significance altogether, one best evoked in Jameson's own prose:

> What I will call "evaluation" . . . no longer turns on whether a work is "good" [after the fashion of an older aesthetic judgment], but rather tries to keep alive [or to reinvent] assessments of a sociopolitical kind that inter-

rogate the quality of social life itself by way of the text or individual work of art, or hazard an assessment of the political effects of cultural currents or movements with less utilitarianism and a greater sympathy for the dynamics of everyday life than the imprimaturs and indexes of earlier traditions. (298)

In this passage Jameson offers three criteria that demonstrate the superiority of his version of cultural studies to the older "cultural journalism oriented around taste and opinion." First, his criticism doesn't examine the text in itself but, rather, attempts "assessments" of "social life itself" on the basis of the text. Second, his own work offers observations about the political impact of cultural developments "with less utilitarianism" than earlier practitioners. Finally, Jameson tells us, his work exhibits "a greater sympathy for the dynamics of everyday life" than that of earlier critics. At first the most surprising aspect of these assertions is their theoretical modesty. One might have expected Jameson to emphasize the superior insights possible for a critic who utilizes a "hermeneutic" that, he declared in *The Political Unconscious*, possesses an "ultimate philosophical and methodological priority" over all others (21). Without explicitly renouncing such grandiose claims, Jameson in *Postmodernism* claims merely personal virtues, virtues of style and outlook rather than theory. Perhaps he fears that claims of the superiority of Marxist theory that sounded most impressive in 1981 might ring hollow a decade later.

If one's first response is to note Jameson's unwillingness to make any theoretical claims in differentiating his work from earlier critics, on second thought one notices what an unfriendly terrain Jameson has chosen on which to assert the superiority of his version of cultural studies to that of the "earlier traditions" that he dismisses. Let us take Jameson's claims in turn. If one is to accept his claim that the use of a "text or individual work of art" to gain enlightenment on "the quality of social life" constitutes an advance over the old cultural journalism, one would have to ignore the vast array of instances in which Jameson is not only anticipated but surpassed. Jameson's thesis depends on the crude, tacit assumption that the old cultural journalists were all "new critics" concerned only about the text in itself. A random sampling of counterexamples might include Lionel Trilling considering the American sense of reality through looking at Dreiser and Parrington, Dwight Macdonald attacking middlebrow culture by way of his demolition of *Our Town*, or Ralph Ellison using Erskine Caldwell's *Tobacco Road* to illuminate the paradoxes of black-white relations in the United States.

Do Jameson's comments exhibit "less utilitarianism" than earlier cultural criticism? If utilitarianism is taken to mean a willingness to interpret art and literature solely in terms of their usefulness for scoring political points, then it is surely true that Jameson's *Postmodernism* and even his *Political Unconscious* are less utilitarian than much of the left-wing criticism of the 1930s. Jameson's *Postmodernism* is so little utilitarian that one can sympathize with the "simple-hearted comrades" who don't see what "hyperspace" has to do with social struggle. The despised new critics, however, were also notoriously free from blatant utilitarianism, while the *Partisan Review* critics broke with the Communist Party precisely because they refused to subordinate cultural criticism to political control. There is nothing exceptional about Jameson's relative lack of utilitarianism; what is unusual is Jameson's attempt to claim credit for both his detachment and his contribution to the cause of "permanent revolution in intellectual life and culture" and "a Utopian and revolutionary politics" (401).

Jameson's last claim to superiority rests on his self-professed "greater sympathy for the dynamics of everyday life." The validity of this claim depends on whose "everyday life" is under discussion. *Postmodernism* discusses a wide variety of phenomena, including hotels, an architect's private home, experimental videos, conceptual art, as well as the criticism of Derrida and Paul de Man, among others. Consideration of such topics may reveal a good deal about the everyday life of those who share Jameson's milieu, but it is doubtful that even the most strained extrapolation from such data would reveal much about the everyday life of most of us. In any case, Jameson's stress in both *Postmodernism* and in *The Political Unconscious* on utopian desire as the truly meaningful standard for political action— a standard for which total revolution constitutes the only adequate response—invalidates as hopelessly compromised the values and hopes of everyday life as lived by most people, in the United States and elsewhere.

No doubt few cultural critics would score very high if "sympathy for the dynamics of everyday life" were the criterion of judgment. Ralph Ellison is one of the few whose theory and practice are both straightforwardly democratic. Diana Trilling argued that members of the political and cultural avant garde should be judged by the same moral standards that apply to the rest of us. But H. L. Mencken, who would surely have classed Jameson with the prohibitionists and Woodrow Wilson as another proponent of the "messianic delusion," was as scornful as any Leninist could possibly be of the aspirations of the middle class—the "booboisie." Irving Babbitt saw the decline of Western civilization embodied in "an American of the present day reading his Sunday newspaper in a state of lazy collapse" ("Matthew Arnold," 112). Dwight Macdonald disparaged middlebrow culture, and Edmund Wilson in his latter years felt that the United States of the 1950s and 1960s had left him an alien.

Yet all these latter authors share with Ralph Ellison a willingness to criticize the particular vices of intellectuals themselves, to engage in cultural self-criticism. They all appealed from the follies of the intellectuals to standards that, at least in theory, were shared by the great majority of their compatriots. Against the "expansive desires" that Jameson champions, Irving Babbitt looks to virtues of more use in everyday life: "moderation, common sense, and common decency" ("What I Believe," 13). Mencken himself had "a sound respect for hard effort, for loyalty, for thrift, for honest achievement" ("Roosevelt: An Autopsy," 135), values that he could expect ordinary people to share when they were not bamboozled by a political or religious huckster. Lionel Trilling did not idealize "the people," but his critique of liberal intellectuals emphasized their failure to appreciate the weight of everyday contingencies. Trilling memorably articulated the sense of superiority that is one of the hidden attractions of the intellectual life:

> By intellectuality we are freed from the thralldom to the familial commonplace, from the materiality and concreteness by which it exists, the hardness of the cash and the hardness of getting it, the inelegance and intractability of family things. ("George Orwell," 144)

The absence of comparable passages from Jameson's voluminous oeuvre is significant enough. Beyond explicit statements, however, the quality of one's "sympathy for the dynamics of everyday life" may be gauged by one's prose. Those who avoid an esoteric vocabulary, who write in a public language that allows nonspecialists to understand and judge their arguments, implicitly declare their allegiance to a common culture and thus to what they have in common with other citizens. Even in his most radical phase during the 1930s and even in the bitterness of his last years, Edmund Wilson's prose demonstrated his commitment to standards that are common because they are widely shared if rarely attained. Jameson's prose everywhere conveys the message that its author is an adept who doesn't write old-fashioned cultural journalism but, instead, engages in "several new kinds of operations," including "transcoding" and "generating new codes," the latter of which Jameson calls "the production of theoretical discourse par excellence" (394).[8] It is possible to engage in imagined conversation with an essay of Trilling or Wilson, or even Mencken—though you both might be shouting—but it is hard to converse with somebody who is transcoding or producing theoretical discourse par excellence.

Chapter 11

The Critic as Exile:
On Edward Said

The great prestige of Edward Said derives in large part from his apparent success in making contemporary literary theory relevant to both the Third World and to revolution. When Fredric Jameson calls for a "cultural revolution" that "may be expected to project a whole new framework for the humanities, in which the study of culture in the widest sense could be placed on a materialist basis" (*Political Unconscious,* 96), he sounds more like an applicant for a grant than a Marxist revolutionary. When Terry Eagleton clinches a theoretical argument by asserting that his objections are shared by the "guerilla fighters of Guatemala" (*Literary Theory,* 143), the gap between academic and combatant is ignored but not bridged. Edward Said, however, is not only a University Professor at Columbia University, he also has been a voting member of the Palestinian National Council and an active participant in the struggles of "an anti-imperialist and anticolonialist Third World people" (*Question of Palestine,* 52). Said's books dealing directly with the relations between the so-called First and Third Worlds include *Orientalism, The Question of Palestine, Covering Islam,* and *Culture and Imperialism. Orientalism's* use of the theories of Michel Foucault provides a seemingly definitive refutation to those who argue that poststructuralist theory is incapable of generating politically significant cultural analysis.

Nevertheless, Said's work raises questions of its own. Although it is Said's use of Foucault that largely accounts for *Orientalism's* influence among literary theorists, it may be argued that the same theoretical framework vitiates any intended political implications. This thesis gains plausibility from a comparison between *Orientalism* and Said's less well-known but more directly political books, *The Question of Palestine* and *Covering Islam.* Although in the introduction to *The World, the Text, and the Critic* Said describes the three as a kind of trilogy dealing with "the history of relations between East and West" (27), there is a striking difference between *Orientalism* and the other two; when Said deals with immediate political questions in the latter two books, he drops Foucault and poststructuralist skepticism.

Said, of course, has always been more than a mere disciple of Foucault. In the essays collected in *The World, the Text, and the Critic* he has provided some of the most balanced and informed criticism available of Derrida, Foucault, and contemporary theory in general. Said, a figure whose left credentials are not in doubt, has demonstrated an ability to distinguish political substance from mere rhetoric. His shrewd criticisms spare neither his political allies nor the intellectual tendencies with which he is identified: "Right now in American cultural history, 'Marxism' is principally an academic, not a political, commitment" ("Introduction," 28). Said observes:

> Deconstruction, for example, is practiced as if Western culture were being dismantled; semiotic analysis argues that its work amounts to a scientific and hence social revolution in the sciences of man. . . . There is oppositional debate without real opposition. ("Reflections on American 'Left' Literary Criticism," 159–60)[1]

Such critiques heighten one's expectations about Said's own perspective, which he characterizes as "secular criticism." Said offers the stance of the "secular critic" not only as a description of his particular position but also as the proper stance for contemporary literary critics and theorists, and indeed for all intellectuals. The secular critic is suspended, in Said's formulations, between East and West, culture and system, First World theory and Third World revolution. Intellectuals must choose between acting as either "potentates" or "travellers"—who may be secular critics as well. The alternatives that Said offers to intellectuals provide a framework for considering his own career, from *Orientalism* to *The Question of Palestine* and *Covering Islam*, and from *Musical Elaborations* to *Culture and Imperialism*.[2]

The impact of Said's *Orientalism* surely derives from something more than the successful demonstration that most European scholarship dealing with the Islamic world has been ethnocentric, racist, and a servant of imperialism. Had it been a book that demonstrated so much by means of a careful comparison between the conclusions of influential "Orientalists" and the knowledge available to, but ignored or distorted by, those same Orientalists, it might have been an important work with significant political implications, but it would not have stirred the academic world. To accuse European and American Orientalists of a lack of fair-mindedness, disregard of pertinent facts, and a general failure of objectivity in regard to the Third World would be to identify oneself as a cultural conservative. For to make such accusations would be to admit that one still believed in the possibility of disinterested scholarship, in the cross-cultural validity of "fairness," and in the independent reality of facts. A book revealing an allegiance to such traditional norms would be unlikely to attract much notice, no matter how controversial its topic. Indeed, Said's *The Question of Palestine* and *Covering Islam*, which do affirm such norms, have not received nearly the attention expended on *Orientalism*, despite their polemical treatment of urgent, controversial political issues.

The most obvious difference between the critiques of *The Question of Palestine* and *Covering Islam* and the critique offered in *Orientalism* is that the latter employs Michel Foucault's ideas about the limitations of "representation" not simply to criticize one discipline but also to mount an attack on the very idea of a discipline and on scholarly knowledge itself. Even better, Said combines his advanced skepticism with undiminished political advocacy, creating a heady amalgam indeed. Said, however, nowhere reveals a capacity for actually integrating, rather than merely juxtaposing, the two positions. Instead, Said weaves back and forth, asserting an old-fashioned belief in moral truths and factual reality when he wants to criticize Orientalists for their distortions but emphasizing his rejection of the same concepts when he wants to affirm his membership in the theoretical avant-garde.[3]

Consider, for example, the question of the possibility of discovering and conveying truth about reality. Late in *Orientalism* Said affirms his official theoretical position; if "the real issue is whether indeed there can be a true representation of anything," then he must answer no, there cannot be, since "any and all representations, because they are representations, are embedded first in the language and then in the culture, institutions, and political ambience of the representer" (272). Given that general thesis, it follows that Said must dismiss the notion of "some Oriental essence" and the very idea that there "is such a thing as a real or true Orient" (322). Nevertheless, throughout *Orientalism* Said writes as though he does believe there is such a thing as reality, even an Oriental reality, and he blames the Orientalists for distorting or ignoring it. Said criticizes Orientalists for their distortion of what he identifies as "the East itself" (60), "Islam in itself" (60), "the Orient as it is" (104), and "the Orient as such" (127). He speaks of the "brute reality" (5) and "raw reality" (67) of the East, which he blames Orientalists for failing to convey, despite the difficulties of "representation" upon which he elsewhere insists so strongly. Richard Burton is attacked, for example, despite his "sympathetic self-association with the Arabs" (195), since "even in Burton's prose we are never directly *given* the Orient" (196). Said, however, offers no instances of prose by Arabs, Africans or anybody else, in which "the Orient"—or any other region—is "directly *given*."

Although Said does not achieve a theoretical integration of his two approaches, he integrates them rhetorically by describing the limitations of representation—in theory the limitations of any representation at any time—as though they are willful distortions that could have been avoided. In his discussion of Sylvestre de Sacy, Said seems to condemn procedures generic to any kind of scholarship, biased or objective: "In Sacy's pages on Orientalism . . . he speaks of his own work as having *uncovered, brought to light, rescued* a vast amount of obscure matter. Why? In order to *place it before* the student" (127). It seems that the italics are intended to insinuate that Sacy is doing something sinister. Said makes his point with a Foucauldian analogy:

> Knowledge was essentially the making visible of material, and the aim of a tableau was the construction of a sort of Benthamite Panopticon. Scholarly discipline was therefore a specific technology of power: it gained for its user (and his students) tools and knowledge which (if he was a historian) had hitherto been lost. (127)

The Panopticon analogy refers, of course, to a scanning tower in a prison. Said is implying that any gathering of texts into a volume to make them available for readers is the same kind of enterprise as the unseemly desire of a prison custodian to know all the details of the private lives of prisoners. Again, one would like to know what alternative Said would propose. If it is somehow wrong to "place before" the student original texts from another culture, what procedure would Said offer as an alternative? Or would he simply end scholarly inquiry? One wonders, given this clarification of Said's overall criticism of Orientalist scholarship:

> I mean to say that in discussions of the Orient, the Orient is all absence, whereas one feels the Orientalist and what he says as presence; yet we must not forget that the Orientalist's presence is enabled by the Orient's effective absence. (208)

This sounds like a serious criticism—presence and absence are certainly terms to conjure with in contemporary criticism—until one realizes that exactly the same point could be made about any writing on any subject, except perhaps diary notations.

If *Orientalism* is riven by opposing points of view, *The Question of Palestine* presents no such difficulties. Said's thesis here is that acceptance of the Israeli claim to the land of Palestine depends upon a preference for grandiose ideas and ideals over factual reality. In Said's presentation the priority of the Arab right to the land of Palestine is not based on any large idea, like the Jews' Zionism, but on the simple fact that the Arabs were physically present in Palestine before Israel became a state: "No matter how backward, uncivilized and silent they were, the Palestinian Arabs were on the land . . . these Arabs were usually described as uninteresting and undeveloped, but at least they were there" (9). In Said's formulation, the Arab Palestinians' existence is "an inconvenient fact" (13); their contemporary existence is a "present reality" that must be conjured away by "some argument about a 'higher' (or better, more worthy, more modern, more fitting; the comparatives are almost infinite) interest, cause, or mission" (15).

Said's argument stresses the extent to which intellectuals are peculiarly vulnerable to "self-serving idealism" that ignores the claims of factual reality (56). If only, Said seems to argue, intellectuals would attend to "the *specific*, detailed reality of the Palestinians" (118), they would not be seduced by the "large, global generalities" (143) by which the Zionist case is justified.

In *Covering Islam* Said does not stress so much the gap between grandiose ideas and ascertainable but unglamorous facts as he does the gap between easy generalizations and the complexity of reality. In his introduction Said refers to "the general problem of knowing and living in a world that has become far too complex and various for easy and instant generalization" (xii). He notes ruefully the appeal of "blanket solutions to messy detailed problems" (xiv) and pleads for "respect for the concrete detail of human experience" (xxxi).

It scarcely needs to be emphasized that Said's preference for complexity over simplicity, or for facts over ideas, cannot be justified on the basis of the advanced theory of *Orientalism*, in which the appeal to any reality, simple or complex, detailed or otherwise, is regarded as inherently inadmissible. Said seems to share some of the most radical of Foucault's assumptions, but, when he attempts to make a political case, he does not mention Foucault, and he writes as though poststructuralism and even structuralism had never arisen. Said's career, often pointed to as an example of the political relevance of poststructuralist theory, provides perhaps the most convincing example of the political nullity of that theory.

To draw this conclusion, however, is not to deny that Said's outlook possesses its own unity, one not defined by a commitment either to poststructuralist theory or even to the Palestinian cause. Said has characterized his own approach as that of secular criticism. At the end of *The World, the Text, and the Critic* he argues that this perspective should become that of intellectuals in general:

Once an intellectual, the modern critic has become a cleric in the worst sense of the word. How their discourse can once again collectively become a truly secular enterprise is, it seems to me, the most serious question critics can be asking one another. ("Conclusion," 292)

What is the meaning of this "most serious question"? What is secular criticism and how does it differ from other critical positions? Said's secular criticism seems attractive when he contrasts it to certain pseudoreligious tendencies in contemporary critical theory. He is suspicious of "grand ideas and their discourse" because such systems—like "religious discourse," according to Said— serve as agents "of closure, shutting off human investigation, criticism, and effort in deference to the authority of the more-than-human, the supernatural, the other-worldly" ("Conclusion," 290). Said finds in the contemporary critical scene "a dramatic increase in the number of appeals to the extrahuman, the vague abstraction, the divine, the esoteric and secret" (291).

What Said opposes to the temptations of such grandiose mystification is the independent critical consciousness of the resolutely secular critic, determined to remain "between culture and system." But what ground can the critic occupy? One might attempt to criticize a society by comparing its ideals to its practice, thus performing an immanent criticism—but Said is unwilling to adopt this strategy, which assumes that the ideals themselves may be legitimate. For Said any "culture" is merely "a massive body of self-congratulating ideas" ("Criticism between Culture and System," 202), which it is always the critic's task to deconstruct. The critic's tool, however—the "sovereign technique," or "system"—provides no surer access to truth than any culture, since "systems . . . perform essentially self-confirming tasks [which] allow for no counterfactual evidence" ("Traveling Theory," 230). There is, finally, no real difference between "cultures" and "systems" at all; Said insists that "cultures be understood as the systems they really are" ("Raymond Schwab," 267).

Given Said's impoverished conception of culture and his more persuasive skepticism about critical systems, the secular critic is left with no source of truth beyond the embattled individual self. In *Orientalism* Said argues that the ambiguities of representation mean that terms have significance only within some "common history, tradition, universe of discourse" (273), but he does not tell us what his own "history, tradition, universe of discourse" might be. Unwilling to place himself within the traditions of either Western humanism or those of Islam (or any alternative), Said allows himself a privileged freedom from contingency, the possibility of which it is the first business of Foucauldian theory to deny. But such an exemption from ordinary humanity is a dubious privilege.

Without the context that tradition provides, the secular critic's professed allegiance to the "norm" of "human freedom and knowledge" means little (*Orientalism* 327).

Said believes he is putting his cards on the table—"and here I shall be
explicit"—when he tells us that "criticism must think of itself as life-enhancing
and constitutively opposed to every form of tyranny, domination and abuse; its
social goals are noncoercive knowledge produced in the interests of human
freedom" ("Introduction," 29). But everybody, including bêtes noires of Said
such as Ronald Reagan, George Bush, and even Benjamin Netanyahu favor
"human freedom" and "noncoercive knowledge," and there is even a larger
majority, if that is possible, in favor of whatever is "life-enhancing." On the
other hand, nobody is on record as favoring "tyranny, domination and abuse."
The meaning of such abstract terms differs, however, depending on the context
in which they appear. When Said tells us that the critic must act "on behalf of
those alternative acts and alternative intentions whose advancement is a fundamental human and intellectual obligation" (30), he does not tell the reader anything about what those acts and intentions are beyond saying that they are
"alternative." Without situating secular criticism within a tradition that would
give a specific content to such terms, Said's "explicit" avowal amounts to little
more than assuring us that the secular critic will be one of the good guys.

The "worldliness" of the secular critic, nevertheless, does involve some
specific but sometimes incongruous associations for Said. On occasion the preferred connotations are unpretentious:

> "Worldliness" is a notion I have often found useful because of two mean-
> ings that inhere in it together, one, the idea of being in the secular world,
> as opposed to being "otherworldly," and two, because of the suggestion
> conveyed by the French word *mondanité*, worldliness as the quality of a
> practiced, slightly jaded savoir faire, worldly wise and street smart. ("Rep-
> resenting the Colonized," 212–13)

According to Said in this passage, the secular critic rejects the search for
absolute, spiritual truths but is compensated by a practical knowledge of actual
existence. Fair enough. Sometimes, however, Said makes larger claims, as when
he argues that the secular critic occupying "the Canaanite, that is, the exile position," is able

> perhaps more easily [to] feel compassion, more easily call injustice injus-
> tice, more easily speak directly and plainly of all oppression, and with less

difficulty try to understand (rather than mystify or occlude) history and equality. ("Michael Walzer's *Exodus and Revolution*," 178)

The secularist, or Canaanite, thus lays claim to a position of political misfortune whose compensations are moral superiority and intellectual insight. These are strong claims, urged with great intensity and skill. Although Said surely intends his descriptions to refer to himself in particular, he holds up the secular critic and even the Canaanite as valid models for intellectuals generally, modes of criticism available to those who summon up the necessary political will.

One difficulty with Said's presentation of the intellectual is that it seems internally contradictory. As an exile, or Canaanite, Said seems on familiar terms with truth and has little trouble in recognizing injustice as simply "injustice." The secular critic, one would have thought, would never simply call "injustice injustice" but would, instead, have to recognize, with the sophistication of "jaded" "*mondanité*," the complexity of earthly life when one is unaided by divine guidance and note that what one party calls injustice is usually seen by another as fair and equal dealing. Such apparent inconsistency suggests at least two limitations of the secular critic; the first is a matter of substance, the second a question of style.

As a secular critic, Said views both cultural and religious traditions as simply power formations to be resisted by the critical, oppositional intellectual. In analyzing the Israeli perspective as "An Ideology of Difference," Said begins by noting that in Israel "difference" takes various forms. Reasonably enough, Said mentioned the religious "form" first: "Theologically, of course, difference here means 'the Chosen People,' who have a different relationship to God than that enjoyed by any other group. But that sort of difference is, I confess, impossible for me to understand." Said then quickly moves to the "purely secular plane" (41). Unless, however, one is willing to attempt some sympathetic insight into Judaism as a religion and therefore into the concept of "the Chosen People," one can have no more than a shallow insight into the "ideology" of the Jewish state. Likewise, incidentally, one would be able to say little worth remembering about the culture and history of the Islamic world if one were to consider the concept of Mohammed as the specially chosen messenger of God a notion "impossible to understand."[4]

Not that the secular critic must undergo a religious conversion to achieve a sympathetic understanding of the cultural clash between Jew and Palestinian. Any cultural critic, however, should be able to employ historical analysis to carry out a study of religious and cultural traditions not merely as screens for domination but also as possible sources of real insight. Herbert Marcuse once differentiated critical theory from the sociology of knowledge on the grounds that sociology was interested only in reducing past philosophies into their social relations, whereas "when critical theory comes to terms with philosophy, it is interested in the truth content of philosophical concepts and problems. It presupposes that they really contain truth" ("Philosophy and Critical Theory," 147–48). Said, on the other hand, seems more interested in the sociology of knowledge, arguing that the fundamental task of "critical consciousness or criticism" is "to occupy itself with the intrinsic conditions on which knowledge is made possible" ("Criticism between Culture and System," 182). Said's unwillingness to accept any cultural or religious tradition as a source of insight as well as an agent of domination severely limits his capacity for sympathetic understanding of not only Israel but also the Third World and, indeed, any society. He is left with a self unchecked by allegiance to any traditions, a self subject to sudden, inexplicable lapses.

The characteristic activity of intellectuals, and surely of secular intellectuals, is debate. Intellectuals should not settle arguments by appeals to force, fraud, or the assertion of divine knowledge—only by an appeal to ideas and argumentation. Thus, one's conduct in debate offers a demonstration of one's notions about the intellectual life itself. Said's stance in polemics frequently bears little resemblance to worldliness, or *mondanite*. His characteristic tone is one of righteous indignation, the voice of one confronted by opponents who are either knaves or fools, probably both. Name-calling, for this voice, is a respectable alternative to discussion, since one's opponents do not deserve the minimal respect required for intellectual debate to take place. Thus, in "The Essential Terrorist" Said refers to "the utterly ninth-rate P. J. Vatikiotis," while characterizing Bernard Lewis, Elie Kedourie and Vatikiotis as "guns-for-hire." After all, they have each contributed an essay—"a slice of mendacity" (156), in Said's phrasing—to an anthology on terrorism with whose premises and political slant Said disagrees. Said, however, does not merely criticize such authors for differing with him politically. He also asserts that they have failed as intellectuals and humanists: "What happened to the precision, discrimination and critical humanism that we celebrate as the hallmarks of liberal education and the Western heritage?" (158). The reader may judge whether Said's own polemics further a discourse of "precision, discrimination and critical humanism." But perhaps the most striking example of Said's style in debate occurs in his "Response" to criticism of his essay arguing that Zionism is "An Ideology of Difference."

Robert Griffin, whose critique Said attacks most vehemently, makes several attempts in his own piece to meet Said halfway, even while challenging

Said's view of the relations between Israel and the Palestinians. Griffin suggests that, "as one reads through the various documents, the various histories, one discovers that there is more than enough blame and shame to go around" (622). He notes: "From my perspective, no resolution is possible without recognizing the principle of Palestinian self-determination. This means that Israel should negotiate a withdrawal from the occupied territories as soon as possible." In closing, Griffin emphasizes, "I do not want to close off the possibility of dialogue from my side" and realistically notes that "the Arab-Israeli conflict dwarfs any dispute between Said and myself in an academic journal" (625). His strongest personal comment on Said is offered in the context of a concession to Said's political views:

> We might consider why it is that Mr. Said feels the need to resort to half-truths, misrepresentation, and open falsehood in order to build a convincing case. There is absolutely no need to put in doubt so carelessly one's credibility and intellectual integrity. One need only draw on Meron Benevenisti's detailed research to demonstrate that the continued military occupation of the West Bank is repressive, unjust, untenable. (622)

Said begins his reply to the essay by referring to "Robert J. Griffin, whose lies, calumnies, and solemn idiocies inhabit a semideranged world entirely his own" ("Response," 638). Griffin's differences cannot result from conflicting perceptions; instead, Griffin's views about the relations between Israelis and Palestinians are different from Said's "obviously because he has neither the wit nor the moral courage" to agree. Said speaks of Griffin's "shamelessness . . . snideness and outright prevarication" (639) and asserts his pity for "poor Griffin"'s "incompetence and ignorance as a scholar (if that is what it he is)" (640).

From his eminence as University Professor at Columbia University, Said mocks the academic status of his opponent: "So we must finally ask, who is this Robert J. Griffin who has never in his life written a published word on Palestine, and is only, to the best of my knowledge, the author of two (or is it three?) below-average articles on Dr. Johnson?" (645). In concluding his response, Said explicitly refuses to accept Griffin as "a partner in dialogue and community" and refers to him as something less than human, a "creature," an "Israeli-worshipping paragon" (645) who is not a person but instead "an ideological simulacrum" (646).

One may agree with all the political and historical points that Said makes and yet feel that such writing narrows the possibility for intellectual interchange, not just between proponents of Israel and adherents of the Palestinian cause but also between partisans of divergent views on any controversial issue. If Said's discourse is accepted as a legitimate means of debate against an adversary, provided only that one believes intensely enough in the rightness of one's cause, then polemical exchange will degenerate into mere culture war. Intellectual life depends on a willingness to recognize a distinction between debate and actual warfare; it depends on upholding norms appropriate to debate that are unheeded in combat. Griffin explicitly calls attention to the difference between the two—"the Arab-Israeli conflict dwarfs any dispute between Said and myself in an academic journal" (625)—while Said attempts to argue for the moral equivalence of the two dimensions: "His response to me is therefore the verbal equivalent of the Israeli occupation, an equivalent whose specious arguments and time-wasting verbosity cover up the shameless killing and oppressing of Palestinians" (646).

It is fair enough for Said to refer to the "intellectual warfare" that is "a central aspect of the world of interpretations" (639), but such phrases make sense only if it is recognized that intellectual warfare has its own rules. When Said violates the rules of intellectual warfare, he lays himself open to the objections that Cardinal Newman made to Charles Kingsley more than a century ago.

Kingsley, in Newman's view, assumes that everyone who is a Catholic must be "either a knave or a fool" (99); Said seems to make a similar assumption about anyone who speaks on behalf of Israel, whatever concessions he or she might make to the rights of the Palestinians. Newman objects not merely to Kingsley's arguments but also to his "method of disputation," using an analogy to war:

> I am at war with him; but there is such a thing as legitimate warfare: war has its laws; there are things which may fairly be done, and things which may not be done . . . he has attempted a great transgression; he has attempted (as I may call it) to *poison the wells.* (108)

That is, by impugning his opponent as either a knave or a fool, or both, Kingsley hopes

> to poison by anticipation the public mind against me, John Henry Newman, and to infuse into the imaginations of my readers, suspicion and mistrust of everything that I may say in reply to him. This I call *poisoning the wells.* (109)

One "poisons the wells" of public debate when one writes in such a way as to suggest that all those who do not share a view that one believes to be politically correct must be either knaves or fools, or both. The effect of doing so is not merely to discourage debate on the topic in question but also to undermine intellectual life in general. If what Said seems to believe about the Palestinian-Israeli controversy—that proponents of one side hold the moral high ground while the other side is composed of fools and knaves—comes to be regarded as the usual situation on controversial issues, public debate and intellectual discussion would lose their reason for being, to be replaced by the alternatives: force and fraud.

The theoretical divergence between Said's poststructuralist critique of representation in general and his belief that, in the case of the Palestinians, the facts speak for themselves to all people of goodwill parallels the divergence in attitude between the secular critic with his or her "*mondanité*, worldliness as the quality of a practiced, slightly jaded savoir faire" and the Canaanite whose "exile position" provides both moral and intellectual superiority to other people. In practice Said's secular criticism has the effect, if his own polemics are to be taken as examples, of diminishing the life of the mind by rejecting the notion that intellectual debate should be carried on by reasoning rather than by name-calling. It may be argued that the seriousness of Said's cause justifies his language and even that his vehemence testifies to the authenticity of his emotions. One might reply that the "precision, discrimination and critical humanism" that Said considers "the hallmarks of liberal education and the Western heritage" cannot be fostered when proponents of views with which one disagrees are considered beyond the pale of civilized discourse. Ideas may be weapons, but the very existence of the republic of letters depends on honoring the distinction between armed combat and the intellectual warfare that, as Said notes, "is a central aspect of the world of interpretations."

Despite occasional polemical overkill, Said is often better than his theory. The poststructuralist stance of *Orientalism* provides no principled means of differentiating between the attempt to understand and the drive to control, both because there is no reality to understand and because knowledge itself is identified, after Foucault, with power. As a partisan for the Palestinian cause, however, Said has no qualms about references to facts, to fairness, or to justice. It would be easy to discount such appeals as merely expedient, but to do so would be to ignore Said's real, if troubled, commitment to the possibility of an intellectual life beyond politics. A reader of his 1991 Academic Freedom Lecture at the University of Cape Town in South Africa, entitled "Identity, Authority and Freedom: The Potentate and the Traveller," must recognize in

Said a powerful champion of academic and intellectual freedom against the claims of both the Left and Right.

It is not surprising that in that address Said informs his audience that the dangers to academic freedom in the United States have come mostly from conservatives nor that he caricatures *The Closing of the American Mind*, telling his South African listeners that Allan Bloom wants universities to educate only "a small, carefully prepared and instructed elite" in the works of "only a small handful of works by the Greeks and some French Enlightenment philosophers" (5). What might surprise Said's critics, or those who know him only from brief television interviews, is his willingness to criticize as well the politicization of universities throughout the Arab world after independence. Whatever the historical explanations, Said regards it as an unmitigated disaster that "political conformity rather than intellectual excellence" has come to dominate many Arab universities (7).

Said is willing, furthermore, to bring forth as an ally the same Cardinal Newman whose reflections on polemical morality have been adduced against Said. Admirably, if inconsistently with his official theory, Said quotes Newman to suggest the possibility of a search for truths that are more than contingent on behalf of something beyond power. Said emphasizes that Newman's conception of the intellectual life transcends the goals of "coercion, or direct utility, or immediate advantage or dominance" (15). Said cautions his audience that Newman, of course, placed "the highest premium on English, European or Christian values" (16). Nevertheless, suggests Said, Newman's statement of his ideal transcends the limitations of the cardinal's place and time. Perhaps Newman's ideal is only the result of a "slip," but it is a slip that should be cherished.

Said's conception of the possibility of transcendence-by-slip is worth quoting, if only because its eloquence gains when one remembers how often its author has dismissed the possibility of transcendence on any terms:

> Sometimes, even though we may mean to say something, another thought at odds with what we say insinuates itself into our rhetoric, and in effect criticizes it, delivers a different and less assertive idea than on the surface we might have intended. This happens when we read Newman. Suddenly we realize that although he is obviously extolling what is an overridingly Western conception of the world, with little allowance made for what was African or Latin American or Indian, his words let slip the notion that even an English or Western identity wasn't enough, wasn't at bottom or at best what education and freedom were all about. (16)

As against the "hermeneutics of suspicion" exemplified in *Orientalism*, Said in "The Potentate and the Traveller" generously gives Newman the benefit of the doubt and is rewarded with a conception of intellectual possibility beyond the Foucauldian boundaries. Academics, says Said, should see themselves as migrants, or travellers, journeying beyond their own "ethnic identity, culture, and traditions" (17) "to enter a ceaseless quest for knowledge and freedom" (19). The notion that "women should read mainly women's literature, that Blacks should study and perfect only Black techniques of understanding and interpretation, that Arabs and Muslims should return to the Holy Book for all knowledge and wisdom" (17), seems to Said only an inverse racism.

Perhaps a critic can offer to Said the generosity he extends to Newman. Throughout Said's oeuvre resounds an attack on Western culture as the handmaid of Western imperialism. Over and over again Said suggests that academic values such as disinterestedness and universality have not only failed in practice but are also impossible in theory. Said's writings sometimes offer, however, a counterpoint to these themes, of which the lecture at Cape Town is a distinguished example. If Said often criticizes Western values, he also appeals to them. If in theory he disclaims the possibility of transcending one's contingent status, in practice he has often honorably overcome his own partisanship and articulated universal principles.

Perhaps some of Said's ambivalence can be traced to his conception of the intellectual life, a conception that, as he formulates it in "The Potentate and the Traveller," seems both noble and limiting:

> In its essence the intellectual life—and I speak here mainly about the social sciences and the humanities—is about the freedom to be critical: criticism *is* intellectual life and while the academic precinct contains a great deal in it, its spirit is intellectual and critical, and neither reverential nor patriotic. For one of the great lessons of the critical spirit is that human life and history are secular, that is, actually constructed and reproduced by men and women.

Said's conception has the nobility that derives from a pride that refuses the prop of any particular "cultural, national or ethnic identity" (11). On the other hand, a one-sided emphasis on criticism alone as the essence of the intellectual life leaves that life vulnerable to the destructive momentum inherent in any one-sidedness. For, if criticism alone is to be prized, then it is easy enough to criticize and dismiss the ideals of the intellectual life itself; mere skepticism is more likely to lead to the arbitrary worship of strange gods than to an examined life.

Perhaps attitudes such as wonder, reverence, and respect for tradition are not as alien to the intellectual life as Said implies. If they do not constitute its essence, perhaps the critical spirit does not either. The critical spirit is an indispensable constituent in the life of the mind, but it is not the only one. Perhaps the intellectual life has no essence; in regard to other matters Said himself typically regards an "essentialist" outlook as inherently flawed.

In his Cape Town lecture Said presents the "potentate and the traveller" as "images" that offer contrasting models for academics and intellectuals. In the first, "the academic professional is king and potentate," a ruler who insists on the "*authority*" you exercise in "your domain." The potentate seems to achieve a certain "detachment," but it is the distance of a monarch who exercises "mastery" over a kingdom. Under the guise of discussing his or her subject, the potentate engages in little more than "self-adulation and uncritical self-appreciation" (18). This image sums up the picture of the European scholars of the Middle East presented in Said's *Orientalism*. Whatever "detachment" their writings might appear to have exhibited from the prejudices fanned by imperialism, for Said their goal was never simply understanding but always mastery, instead. Said's traveller, on the other hand, is not a ruler nor even a tourist; he or she is a "migrant," (17), one who "crosses over, traverses territory, abandons fixed positions." For the former the "search for knowledge" is finally a "search for coercion and control over others," while the latter regards "knowledge as something for which to risk identity." While the potentate views his subject with "detachment and mastery," the traveller acts "with dedication and love" (18). Said's picture of the traveller is an appealing one, just as his portrait of the potentate is forbidding; the reader has no difficulty in deciding which image Said favors. The very persuasive power of the two images, however, raises its own difficulties.

Does a division of intellectual life into two images, one good and one evil, foster the attitudes celebrated by the image of the traveller? A contemporary of Newman's, John Stuart Mill, thought that a true "philosophical tolerance" required a recognition of the fundamental legitimacy of "antagonist modes of thought" ("Coleridge," 295). On behalf of this thesis Mill argued that English culture could only gain from a willingness to listen to both Jeremy Bentham, "the great questioner of things established" ("Bentham," 242), and to Samuel Taylor Coleridge, who "considered the long or extensive prevalence of any opinion as a presumption that it was not altogether a fallacy . . . at least proof of an adaptation in it to some portion or other of the human mind" ("Coleridge," 291–92). The ability to appreciate the power of the alternative approaches summed up in the portraits of Bentham and Coleridge provides the only way, argues Mill, in which "liberality in matters of opinion" becomes something other than "a polite synonym for indifference between one opinion and another" (295).

Said's invitation to divide the world of letters into potentates (bad) and travellers (good) seems unlikely to foster the "liberality" that Mill commends. Another difference must be noted as well. Whereas Mill looks for the divergent truths to which Bentham and Coleridge draw attention, truth seems the last thing that Said's traveller will discover. Instead, he or she encounters "a variety of disguises, masks, rhetorics" (18), to all of which one must be sensitive but to none of which is accorded the respect that ensues from a willingness to consider the possibility that their claims might actually be true. Despite such qualifications, however, Said's image of the ideal academic traveller still remains worth celebrating as an instance of honorable inconsistency; the contemporary radical "lets slip" an old-fashioned liberality, ignoring for the moment the objections of Foucauldian theory and the constraints of politics.

Writing about music provides Said another occasion for moving beyond the radical skepticism of *Orientalism*. In *Musical Elaborations* Said adopts the stance of neither a traveller nor a potentate; he writes, instead, as a lover of music, "a fully committed *amateur*" (xxi), a word, Said advises, "to be taken first in its literal sense" (7). As a true "amateur," a lover of music, Said cannot accept the Foucauldian reduction of things to power alone. He knows beyond any doubt that at the very least "*not all* music can be experienced as working toward domination and sovereignty" (xxi). Any "theoretical totalization" that reduces life and art to a simple, overriding pattern (55), Michel Foucault's ambitious attempt included (50), must be rejected. Even the works of a composer such as Richard Wagner, whose doctrines are both obtrusive and repellent, cannot be reduced to its politics. Great art, even art that includes nasty or dangerous affirmations, is simply too complex and too rich to be judged by politics alone. Such, at least, is Said's verdict on Wagner's *Die Meistersinger.*

> Read and heard for the bristling, tremendously energetic power of the *alternatives* to its own affirmative proclamations about the greatness of German art and culture, *Die Meistersinger* cannot really be reduced to the nationalist ideology its final strophes stress. It has set forth too much in the way of contrapuntal action, character, invention. (61)

In the introduction to *Musical Elaborations* Said declares that he brings to musical criticism the standpoint of the new "cultural studies," the new insights made available by "deconstruction, cultural history, narratology, and feminist theory" (xvi). Fortunately, perhaps, what his little book offers, instead, are the reflections of "a fully committed *amateur*."

Said seems much more willing to allow personal experience to overrule doctrine when discussing music than when confronting literature or literary criticism. In *Culture and Imperialism*, nevertheless, he comes much closer to embodying his own ideal of the intellectual traveller than the theoretical constraints of *Orientalism* allowed. In *Culture and Imperialism* Said quietly drops the major thesis of his earlier book, the notion that members of one culture cannot achieve any real knowledge about another culture. In *Orientalism* Said could find no European scholar, not one, who had overcome the insurmountable obstacles that confronted the Western student of "the Orient." In the later work Said takes it for granted that an Englishman such as Basil Davidson has the ability to offer valuable insights about African culture (see, e. g., 196, 209–10).

Indeed, Said now explicitly denounces the notion that cultures can only be understood by insiders. The recognition of "all culture as hybrid" seems to him "*the* essential idea for the revolutionary realities today" (317). Warning against the temptation to revel in "the emotional self-indulgence of celebrating one's own identity" (229), he warns against the cult of "identity, always identity, over and above knowing about others" (299). The institutionalization of "paranoid nationalism" throughout the world, so that students everywhere are taught only to "celebrate the uniqueness of *their* tradition (usually and invidiously at the expense of others)," appears to Said the most dangerous contemporary cultural tendency, and it is against this impulse that his own book is written (xxvi). Said thus refuses the easy task of merely attacking imperialism itself, which few now defend, and takes up the much more contentious task of criticizing "identity politics" wherever he finds it (219). In doing so, Said lives up to the idea of the independent intellectual traveller sketched out in his Cape Town lecture.

Throughout *Culture and Imperialism* the presentation of imperialism in imaginative works ranging from *Mansfield Park* to *The Stranger* is counterposed to the picture of imperialism derived from works of history and politics, and particularly from the writings of anti-imperialist activists such as C. L. R. James and Frantz Fanon. In an honorable desire to keep the book from becoming merely another contribution to "the rhetoric of blame" (18), Said repeatedly emphasizes his own conviction that the books he is considering remain masterpieces, whatever their relation to imperialism. At a time when influential academics consider any "privileging" of one text above another an infallible indication of right-wing tendencies, Said's straightforward judgments reveal an impressive independence of spirit. Said confesses that he is one of those who "believe that some literature is actually good, and that some is bad," and even admits that he believes that "reading a classic" is probably a better way of spending one's time than "staring at a television screen" (319). Noting that *Great Expectations* and *Nostromo* are "very great" novels (xiv), Said announces his intention to first appreciate the works to be criticized as "great products of the creative or interpretative imagination" (xxii). He carries out this project most successfully and surprisingly in his analysis of Rudyard Kipling's *Kim*, a novel that, despite its embrace of British rule over India, Said considers a "great work of art" (67), a novel that "belongs to the world's greatest literature" (145).

Just as Said emphasizes his own refusal to accept any one culture as the source of all authenticity, or truth, so he refuses to accept being pigeonholed as an advocate of either "radical skepticism" or "deferential reverence of the status quo" (318–19). He concedes that his views about the relative value of television and the classics classify him "as conservative as anyone" on such matters (319). It is not only in aesthetics, however, that Said reveals an affinity for conservative views. In the concluding pages he offers a political program that seems deeply conservative, and none the worse for that: "The two general areas of agreement nearly everywhere are that personal freedoms should be safeguarded, and that the earth's environment should be defended against further decline" (330).

Ralph Waldo Emerson believed that the civil war between "Conservatism" and "Innovation" rages in "every man's bosom . . . every hour" ("The Conservative," 173). In *Orientalism* Said's sympathies lie almost entirely with Innovation, and the rhetorical energy of the book derives from that straightforward indignation, although the radical skepticism of its theoretical formulations undermines the logic of its criticisms. In the sweep of the book's rhetoric, however, the dismissal of truth claims simply provided more ammunition for attacking the West rather than raising a question about the status of the attack itself. In *Culture and Imperialism* things are more complex. The Conservatism of important aspects of Said's program has been ignored by most critics, whether hostile or friendly, but the importance of cultural conservation remains a persistent motif throughout the book. Said, of course, is best known as a partisan of Innovation, and throughout *Culture and Imperialism* his "innovations" make up his central arguments, while his conservative inclinations appear mainly as qualifications. The larger importance of *Culture and Imperialism* depends on Said's success in integrating these two opposing impulses.

Often Said presents himself as a proponent of Innovation alone. His courageous and thoughtful critique of nationalism is undermined when he offers as an alternative "the decentering doctrines of Freud, Marx, and Nietzsche" (266). This trio of innovators has certainly given the twentieth century a lot to think about, but it is not clear that their "doctrines," either separately or together, provide a basis for a country's culture. We have already seen two societies based on versions of the doctrines of two of the thinkers cited by Said, but Stalin's Russia and Hitler's Germany are surely not models of true liberation. The virtues of "decentering" as a basis for nation-building are not obvious, to say the least. Said, however, seems to think that it is good, even liberating, when "the crisis of the Third World" induces throughout society the kind of skepticism that otherwise would have to be learned in graduate seminars:

> In having to give up traditional beliefs, the newly independent states rec-
> ognize the relativism of, and possibilities inherent in, all societies, systems
> of belief, cultural practices. (325)

Frantz Fanon is the prophet of liberation whom Said cites most often and most favorably, but here Said's optimism seems greater than Fanon's, without Fanon's historical justification. The unashamed brutality of arbitrary power seems a much more likely result of the "relativism" that Said celebrates than anything that could be described as liberation. Saddam Hussein of Iraq, for example, seems unencumbered by any "traditional beliefs" that might restrain his power, and he is only one of many tyrants of the present or recent past who might be cited.

In *The Wretched of the Earth* Fanon himself did not detail the steps by which a just society would be created, offering only the pious hope that after national independence is achieved "a new history of Man" will begin (255), in which presumably all the old errors will be left behind. Fanon does specify that the new society will be socialist, since

> the choice of a socialist regime, a regime which is completely orientated
> towards the people as a whole and based on the principle that man is the
> most precious of all possessions will allow us to go forward more quickly
> and more harmoniously. (78)

Said, unfortunately, does not attempt to update or correct Fanon's ideas about the ideal society. Fanon was writing *The Wretched of the Earth* at a time when the struggle to achieve national independence was still being fought, and the intensity of those battles resonates through his book. Today, however, there should be no need for additional proof that the "violence committed by the people" on which Fanon relied to make "it possible for the masses to understand social truths" is not a sovereign remedy for all difficulties (117). If it is acknowledged that the attempt "to set afoot a new man" (255) in the Third World since Fanon wrote has only demonstrated the persistence of a human nature not noticeably transformed by political events, then it follows that Fanon's vision of liberation requires a good deal of supplementation. Said fails, nevertheless, to offer any amendment or criticism of Fanon's work, despite the benefit of thirty years' hindsight.

The mention of Saddam Hussein brings up a motif that recurs throughout *Culture and Imperialism*, Said's polemic against U.S. involvement in the Gulf War. His treatment of this theme provides an example of both the strength and the limitation of Said's approach. "The United States' clash with Iraq and Iraq's aggression against Kuwait concerning oil" are offered as two "obvious examples" of irresponsible power (20). Said characterizes Desert Storm as "ultimately an imperial war against the Iraqi people" (301), while nevertheless condemning "Saddam Hussein's brutal occupation of Kuwait" (131). Surely, such evenhandedness does not come easily for one who sees himself as a defender of the Arab world against a misinformed, prejudiced West. In criticizing both the United States and Iraq, Said lives up to his own ideal of the traveller, the migrant, the exile who is unwilling to accept the certainties of any culture as absolutely sacred.

Said's evenhandedness, however, has its own price. In condemning both Iraq and the United States, Said refrains from suggesting what actions he himself would advocate. Clearly, he believes Saddam Hussein was wrong to take over Kuwait. What response, then, should the United States have made? None, since any action would be a manifestation of imperialism? Sanctions alone? *Culture and Imperialism* risks no such specifics. Any choice, even if only on paper, would involve getting one's hands dirty, since any choice would require something beyond the purity of simple opposition to "coercive domination." As long as Said himself refuses to make such choices, at least in words, it is easy enough to dismiss his criticism of those who do choose, in actions as well as words.

If Said retains a disabling purity by refusing to sketch his own political choices, he holds onto an ideological purity that is much more disabling. Until Said is ready to move beyond the "relativism" of "all systems of belief" (325) and straightforwardly declare the source of his moral judgments, it is difficult to take him seriously as a cultural and political critic. Said notes with sorrow the wide support for Saddam Hussein in the Arab world, a support that seems to endorse a philosophy of "exterminism, the notion that if you do not get your way or something displeases you it is possible simply to blot it out" (299). The impulse to destroy what displeases is a constant temptation for human beings—

checked most effectively, if still only partially and intermittently, by prohibitions deriving their authority ultimately from religious traditions. Said's own
allegiance, however, is to a secular world in which the authority of religions and
even of cultures gives way to a recognition of the arbitrary, contingent nature
of all traditions. On the basis of such skepticism, even when enriched with "the
decentering doctrines of Freud, Marx, and Nietzsche" (266), there does not
seem to be any principled means of opposing any point of view, even exterminism. Perhaps the widespread support for the exterminism that Said deplores
derives at least partially from the relativism that he finds so liberating.

Said repeatedly pays tribute to the aesthetic greatness of the European novels that he criticizes for their complicity with imperialism. In doing so, he is
attempting a praiseworthy balancing act, a political criticism that does not deny
the artistic integrity of the works. Said's "perfect example" of the hidden connections between literature and imperialism is Jane Austen's *Mansfield Park*.
Uninterested in simply proving that Jane Austen did not write novels of social
protest, Said wants not merely to debunk but to read the novel "with a newly
engaged interest" (68), to open up "a fascinatingly expanded dimension to
Mansfield Park" (84).

Said, however, fails to live up to this admirable goal. His discussion of
Mansfield Park centers around a key passage in the novel's conclusion, when Sir
Thomas Bertram, the owner of a plantation in Antigua as well the proprietor of
Mansfield Park, comes to realize where he has gone wrong. Said quotes the pas-
sage at some length:

> Here [in his deficiency of training, of allowing Mrs. Norris too great a role,
> of letting his children dissemble and repress feeling] had been grievous
> mismanagement; but, bad as it was, he gradually grew to feel that it had
> not been the most direful mistake in his plan of education. Some thing
> must have been wanting *within*, or time would have worn away much of
> its ill effect. He feared that principle, active principle, had been wanting,
> that they [his children] had never been properly taught to govern their
> inclinations and tempers, by that sense of duty which can alone suffice.
> They had been instructed theoretically in their religion, but never required
> to bring it into daily practice. To be distinguished for elegance and accom-
> plishments—the authorized object of their youth—could have had no
> useful influence that way, no moral effect on the mind. He had meant
> them to be good, but his care had been directed to the understanding and
> manners, not the disposition; and of the necessity of self-denial and humil-
> ity, he feared they had never heard from any lips that could profit them.

(*Mansfield Park*, 448, qtd. in *Culture and Imperialism*, 91–92 [the passage in brackets within the quotation is Said's own explication.]

Sir Thomas, in other words, has been a success as a proprietor and has managed to see that his children received a conventional education; nevertheless "some thing must have been wanting *within*"—the successful man of affairs, perhaps because of his very strengths as a businessman and administrator, has ignored what the author calls "the necessity of self-denial and humility." These are qualities that a man of affairs might well deem appropriate for women, children, and slaves but not for himself. It is central to the moral impact of the novel that Sir Thomas Bertram learns finally that "self-denial and humility" are necessities not only for others but also for himself. Only if he forgoes his pride enough to admit his own errors and his own responsibility for his children's errors will he be able to pass on to his own children the "sense of duty" and the commitment to "principle, active principle" that have been lacking.

Said interprets the passage quite differently:

> What was wanting *within* was in fact supplied by the wealth derived from a West Indian plantation and a poor provincial relative, both brought in to Mansfield Park and set to work. . . . A principle "wanting *within*" is, I believe, intended to evoke for us memories of Sir Thomas's absences in Antigua. (92)

Determined to demonstrate "that the morality in fact is not separable from its social basis" (92), Said suggests that the moral insight of the passage is rendered nugatory by Austen's implicit endorsement of slavery. His interpretation, however, is not supported by the quotation he himself offers for analysis. It could not be "the wealth derived from a West Indian plantation" that can supply "what was wanting *within*," because *within,* in context, refers to moral qualities inside Sir Thomas's own self, not the "grievous mismanagement" of others. Mere wealth, the novel suggests, can by itself provide no guarantee of right conduct. The obvious contrast to "wanting *within*" is not, as Said suggests, Sir Thomas's "absences in Antigua" but, rather, his "mismanagement" of others. This mismanagement has resulted in errors that are "grievous" but, nevertheless, comparatively unimportant next to Sir Thomas's own failure *within.*

If Said's goal were simply to bring out hidden connections between the personal morality on which Jane Austen focuses and questions of political morality, he could have found what he was looking for in the passage he quoted. The passage endorses not slavery but "self-denial and humility"—not for slaves and not even for women or children only but also for Sir Thomas Bertram himself. It is not too great a stretch to suggest that a morality that emphasizes the virtues of "self-denial and humility" does not provide a firm basis for either imperialism or for the ownership of slaves. A true sense of "humility" might well lead to the conviction that one has no right to own other human beings or to run the affairs of another country, while recognition of the virtue of self-denial might reconcile one to the loss of whatever wealth the forgoing of slave ownership or slavery might entail. Said himself notes that "everything we know about Austen and her values is at odds with the cruelty of slavery" (96), but he makes no attempt to connect that knowledge with his interpretation of *Mansfield Park*. He reiterates what is obvious— that *Mansfield Park* makes no overt protest against imperialism or slavery—while missing the opposition that lies just below the surface. Said, that is, will not grant Jane Austen's *Mansfield Park* the same capacity for "contrapuntal" movements that he claims for Richard Wagner's *Die Meistersinger.*[5]

Why would a reader of Said's intelligence and integrity miss the implicit contrast between a morality stressing self-denial and humility and the belligerent self-assertion encouraged by imperialism and slavery? One can only guess that Said is determined to convict Jane Austen and *Mansfield Park* of complicity with evil not only in the obvious sense that her novel fails to condemn slavery but on the basis of a far more ambitious argument, according to which the novel's deepest moral intuitions amount to implicit endorsements of slavery. Said praises *Mansfield Park* for its elucidation of "the fine points of moral evaluation" (95), but he seems unready to learn anything about morality from Jane Austen. And, indeed, the notion that Edward Said, defender of the Palestinian cause, advocate for Arabs, Muslims, and the entire Third World—a figure who speaks in *Culture and Imperialism* on behalf of "an emergent non-coercive culture" (334), against "the untrammelled rapacity, greed and immorality of the North" (283), could learn anything about morality from Jane Austen, whose novels betray no desire to change either England or the world, must seem incredible to a reader who accepts the self-portrait provided by *Culture and Imperialism.*

The issue here is not so much the tendency of Said's moral earnestness to slide into self-righteousness as it is his continuing unwillingness to ground his insistent moral-political assertions on anything beyond vague aspirations toward "liberation" and a "non-coercive culture." Refusing to connect his own views to any traditions in literature, philosophy, or religion, Said identifies himself only as a "secular intellectual," not as a liberal, a Marxist, or a Christian, and not even as a proponent of Arab traditions. Said's problem is not that his background spans two cultures—that is, indeed, an advantage—but that his intellectual stance is based on a determination to avoid entangling alliances with any traditions at all. This refusal encourages Said to present himself as entirely high-minded, seeking only truth and justice, untouched and unimplicated in the guilt that all traditions must bear by virtue of their histories. At his best Said grapples with the dilemmas of multiple allegiances. All too often, however, he eludes such difficulties by moving to a moral high ground far beyond ordinary mortals, anomalous territory for a proponent of worldly, secular criticism.

Chapter 12

The Two Branches of the Law and Literature Movement: A Critique of Stanley Fish

The "law and literature" movement has at least two branches. The division is not along political lines, since political radicals and conservatives are to be found in both camps. One branch, however, might be described as culturally conservative, while the other argues for a cultural radicalism that is usually but not always tied to a left political program. The conservatism of the former resides in its belief that the cultural inheritance of human beings, including works of literature, does provide insights of permanent value that might enrich and humanize the study of the law. The second branch, basing itself on contemporary literary theory rather than on literary works, has attempted to apply the theorist's claim that all literature is rhetorical rather than referential to the law. The traditional assumption that great works of the past provide access to truths about human beings and their world is rejected, along with "truth" itself as a meaningful category of discourse. Taking literature as a paradigm of a discourse that, properly understood, makes no truth claims at all and has no reference outside itself, this branch proposes to study legal writings on the basis of the literary paradigm.

Stanley Fish's *Doing What Comes Naturally: Change, Rhetoric, and the Practice of Theory in Literary and Legal Studies* has a special interest because Fish, Chair of the Department of Literature as well as Professor of Law at Duke University, shares the presuppositions of the latter camp but nevertheless rejects the political radicalism which, for many (especially adherents of Critical Legal Studies), is the raison d'être behind their work of cultural deconstruction. A short outline of the conflicting positions of the two branches will serve to bring out the unusual role that Stanley Fish is playing as one of the most prominent critics of the cultural assumptions of the first branch and of the political conclusions of the second.

J. Allen Smith's essay on "*Job* and the Legal Profession: An Example of the Relationship of Literature, Law and Justice" offers an example of the cultural conservatism of one wing of the law and literature movement. Here, as elsewhere, it is misleading to equate cultural conservatism with an unthinking acceptance of conventions; in arguing for the relevance of the Book of Job to legal studies, Smith is battling the conventional "unwillingness of lawyers to use truths when they appear in the form of myth and poetry" (665). Nevertheless, the very assertion that myth and poetry can provide truths would be taken by cultural radicals as an assertion of belief in a "ground" that must be rejected, or "deconstructed." The belief that literature refers obliquely to actual existence and is thus capable of presenting truths about human life, is one of the fundamental assumptions of the first camp, while its rejection is one of the starting points of the second.

Thus, even Robin West's use of the work of Franz Kafka to critique the assumptions of Richard Posner's "law and economics" approach would have to be rejected by the second group, though Posner himself is one of their favorite targets. West's argument depends upon the thesis that the work of Kafka can actually tell us something about real human life. "Kafka's characters," she argues, "are strikingly recognizable . . . we have no trouble seeing ourselves and our neighbors in the inner worlds" of Kafka's figures (387). In contrast, Richard Posner's view of human beings is vitiated by its failure to make contact with actual human life as we know it: "The inner lives and motivations of Posner's characters . . . are strikingly unrecognizable. They are not we, and their stark inner lives are not ours" (388). West ends her critique with an assertion that "moral theory . . . must be about truth." The truth about "the essence of the experience of being human" (428), she argues, cannot be found in the "inadequate picture of human nature" on which Posner's work depends (424), but it can be illuminated by a study of the works of Franz Kafka. West's belief that great works of literature, such as Franz Kafka's *Trial*, can tell us something about human life, as well as her belief in truth itself, stamps her project as culturally conservative in the larger sense of the term.

The cultural radicals not only disallow attempts to move from literature to life; they argue that the literary work itself has no stable, independent existence and thus cannot be used as a basis for any judgments at all. One cannot settle arguments about life or law by reference to a literary text, since there is no boundary between the text itself and competing interpretations. In Stanley Fish's words, "There is no distinction between what the text gives and what the reader supplies; he supplies *everything*" ("Why No One's Afraid of Wolfgang Iser," 77). In Fish's view any attempt to settle disputes by reference to a text, whether the text is the Book of Job or Kafka's *Trial*, inevitably begs the question. Any reference to any text by any participant in a debate is determined by the particular theoretical perspective of that participant; no use of the text can count as independent evidence, since any use is informed by one of the approaches under dispute. The same is true for the Constitution of the United States; Fish argues that it is impermissible to object that a judge's bias leads him or her to decisions based on personal preferences rather than the Constitution, both because "the agent is always and already situated" and because the Constitution is "always an already-interpreted object," without any independent existence of its own ("Fish v. Fiss," 128, 130).

From such a perspective James Boyd White's project in *When Words Lose Their Meaning* seems empty, since its thesis depends on a belief in the existence of texts as independent entities. In his preface White asserts that each of the works he will study—*The Iliad*, Jane Austen's *Emma*, Burke's *Reflections on the Revolution in France*, among others—

> teaches us how it should be "read" in the large sense in which I will use
> that term: it teaches us how it should be understood and lived with, and
> this in turn teaches us much about what kind of life we can and ought to
> have, who we can and ought to be. (ix–x)

In contrast to Smith, West and White, Stanley Fish is "a card-carrying anti-foundationalist." Fish's "anti-foundationalism" requires that human discourse be considered as rhetorical rather than referential. For Fish, "another word for anti-foundationalism *is* rhetoric," and the debate in which he is engaged against the proponents of transcendence or an independent reality "marks one more chapter in the long history of the quarrel between philosophy and rhetoric, between the external and the temporal, between God's view and point of view" ("Anti-Foundationalism," 347).

Not that Fish denies the existence of something beyond language; he merely argues that human beings possess no independent criterion of truth, no unmediated access to a standard by which assertions in law, literary studies, or anything else can be judged. The essays in *Doing What Comes Naturally* are devoted to the working out of the implications of that thesis, so much so that every essay, declares the author, is "the same" (pref., ix). Taking Fish at his word, the following exposition considers *Doing What Comes Naturally* as a single argument, not as a collection of separate essays.

By his own definition Fish is part of the "intellectual left," which he characterizes as "all those who have contributed to the assault on foundationalism" ("Anti-Professionalism," 225). Nevertheless, Fish is more than ready to criticize other leftists when their pursuit of revolutionary ideals leads them to forget that those ideals have no more "foundation" than any right-wing ideology. Fish is convincing when he notes that acceptance of the "anti-foundational thesis" does not have the revolutionary political implications that both proponents of Critical Legal Studies and some deconstructionist literary theorists would like to find there. After all, if antifoundationalists reject the possibility of transcendental grounding as such, the rejection surely applies to revolutionary versions of Truth, Beauty, and Justice as well as to those sanctioned by tradition. The antifoundationalist critique cuts both ways—as Fish, to his credit, acknowledges and emphasizes.

Fish goes on to make a more general point. Not only does the theory of antifoundationalism lack the radical political implications with which many of its practitioners seek to endow it, but "theory" in general, in both law and literature, "has no consequences" ("Consequences," 325). In saying this, Fish is not denying that "theory talk" has consequences; what he is denying is the possibility of the existence of a realm of theory independent enough to serve as a judge of practice, a set of criteria by which arguments may be settled. Just as there is no unmediated, uninterpreted reality by which arguments may be settled, likewise there is no realm of theory that provides "external and independent guides" to practice (323). Any use one makes of theoretical guidelines itself requires an interpretive choice that cannot itself be justified by theory without begging the question under consideration. Theory, argues Fish, in itself is incapable of settling questions. Questions are only settled by rhetorical struggle.

There is still another sense in which Fish argues that his views are without consequences. Affirming their lack of political implications and their inability to solve interpretive disputes, he argues that they have no consequences for individuals:

> The foundationalist right worries that if people hearken to me and my kind they will be moved to divest themselves of all standards and restraints; the anti-foundationalist left worries that if people are persuaded by the "no consequences argument" they will leave off trying to divest themselves of standards and constraints. I reply that constraints are not something one can either embrace or throw off because they are constitutive of the self and of its possible actions. ("Introduction," 27)

Even if Fish succeeded in convincing law schools and English departments that their beliefs about law and literature were "groundless," without foundation, nothing would really change, since "one's beliefs do not relax their hold because one 'knows' that they are local and not universal" ("Critical Self-Consciousness," 467).

The modesty of Fish's claims is disarming. Yet one wonders if Fish protests too much. At first glance his comment on, for example, Franklin Roosevelt's attempt to expand the membership of the Supreme Court, appears innocuous, a mere truism:

> The fact that Roosevelt was in fact blocked is not to be explained by saying that a "lesser" strategy was foiled by a legitimate one, but by saying that the political forces always at work in the system exist in ever-changing relationships of strength and influence. ("Fish v. Fiss," 132)

This is not particularly illuminating, and it certainly does leave plenty of room for continued debate. Yet, if Fish's formulation resolves nothing, it does propose a particular vision of the world within which the debate will continue. For Fish, Roosevelt's scheme was simply politics as usual in a world in which "political justifications are the only kind there are" ("Consequences," 340). Fish does make the admission that, if one accepts his thesis, "certain kinds of objections would no longer have very much force and certain kinds of appeals would no longer seem tainted" ("Still Wrong After All These Years," 350).[1]

Based on his analysis of Roosevelt's "court-packing" scheme, one might suppose that objections based on moral considerations "would no longer have very much force" and appeals to "political justifications," on the other hand, "would no longer seem tainted," though presumably political appeals that included references to moral principles would indeed be "tainted."

Should such a change be welcomed? While Fish devotes a great deal of energy to minimizing the negative consequences of a general acceptance of his views, he does not tell his readers what the positive results might be. One result that seems to emerge from the acceptance of Fish's perspective is the collapsing of distinctions that many take to be important. According to Fish, there is no real difference between making a decision based on reflection and acting on gut instinct, between acting by one's own choice (whether reflectively or impulsively) and acting under the threat of a gunman, or between rhetoric and force as agents of change.

There is no real difference between acting on the basis of self-critical reflection and acting impulsively, since Fish defines reflective self-consciousness out of existence. For Fish self-reflection is not real unless "it exists in a realm wholly independent of the realms that are the objects of its severe and searching action" ("Critical Self-Consciousness," 448). Since antifoundationalism refuses to recognize any "realm" exempt from the situatedness of all human life, "critical self-consciousness is at once impossible." (464).

What is gained if Fish's rejection of the possibility of self-reflection is generally accepted? One positive result would be that those who claim to speak on the basis of "critical self-consciousness" would not be able to make ex cathedra assertions but, instead, would have to see their proposals considered on the same plane as those of less-exalted beings. Fish's pointed question to those who claim to speak on behalf of a critical—and therefore superior—consciousness is surely always relevant: "How do the proponents of critique know that what they urge is in the service of all mankind and not merely a function that they themselves happen, at the moment, to desire?" ("Critical Self-Consciousness," 448–9).

If Fish appeals to common experience when he warns against the presumption of those who arrogate to themselves a wisdom superior to that of others, his rationale for doing so violates the common perception that sometimes some people are able to achieve some distance from even their most cherished beliefs. The belief that this is possible is based not on a theory of a realm outside human history but, rather, on experience both personal and historical.

A famous example of the kind of self-criticism that Fish defines out of existence is celebrated by Matthew Arnold in his 1864 essay on "The Function of Criticism at the Present Time." Arnold's example is taken from the last paragraph of Edmund Burke's "Thoughts on French Affairs," a work written after the more famous *Reflections on the Revolution in France*, "at the very end," as Arnold puts it, "of his [Burke's] fierce struggle with the French Revolution, after all his invectives against its false pretensions, hollowness, and madness, with his sincere conviction of its mischievousness" (267). In a passage that Arnold calls the "return of Burke upon himself," Burke envisions the possibility that, after all, the French Revolution may not only succeed but may, for some reason unknown to him, be favored by divine will, so that

> they who persist in opposing this mighty current in human affairs, will appear rather to resist the decrees of Providence itself, than the mere designs of men. They will not be resolute and firm, but perverse and obstinate. ("Function of Criticism," 267; *Thoughts*, 386)[2]

Arnold praises the passage from which this quotation is excerpted as a signal example of "living by ideas." Arnold celebrates Burke's ability to raise doubts

about his own beliefs at a time when it is most difficult and most necessary—
"when one side of a question has long had your earnest support, when all your
feelings are engaged, when you hear all round you no language but one, when
your party talks this language like a steam-engine and can imagine no other"
(267).

Fish cannot legislate such passages as Burke's "return upon himself" out of
existence, but he does contend that they must be characterized not as the result
of critical reflection on one's beliefs but only as evidence of a change in those
beliefs. Readers will, of course, judge for themselves. If one is willing to deny
that Burke has achieved a critical distance in regard to his own ideas, in recognizing the possibility that the French Revolution was the work of Providence
and that his own opposition to it might possibly be better described as "perverse
and obstinate" rather than "resolute and firm," then one is likely to agree with
Fish about "the thesis that being situated . . . means that one cannot achieve a
distance on one's own beliefs" ("Critical Self-Consciousness," 467). On the
other hand, if the "return of Burke upon himself" seems an example of the kind
of critical distance toward their own beliefs that human beings can occasionally
achieve, then the reader would have to note that Fish's "thesis" seems at odds
with experience.

Running even more strongly counter to experience is Fish's contention
that, finally, there is nothing "to distinguish the rule-centered legal system from
the actions of the gunman" ("Force," 504), since, if one feels "constrained" by
a legal system or by the threats of a gunman pointing his revolver at one's head,
the feeling of constraint is, in both cases, "finally" an illusion. After all, argues
Fish, "*there is always a gun at your head.*" Those who might feel unusually
"coerced" or "compelled" by the threats of a gunman can take comfort in the
reflection that "in the end we are always self-compelled, coerced by forces—
beliefs, convictions, reasons, desires—from which we cannot move one inch
away" (520). Since we have no ability to think for ourselves, to reflect freely and
change our minds based on that reflection, we have no freedom to lose. We are
always "coerced by forces," and whether those forces are manifested by a .45
revolver or a given "community of interpretation" makes no difference—no
difference, that is, from the viewpoint of Fish's philosophy.

Waiving the obvious objections that common sense might raise to a philosophy that prevents one from making distinctions in theory that even its
author might recognize in practice, it is worth noting the impoverished view of
history on which the blurring of such distinctions depends. Throughout the
essays of *Doing What Comes Naturally* Fish appeals to history, arguing that his
opponents cannot help "devaluing history and historical process" ("Anti-Professionalism," 222), whereas "anti-foundationalism teaches . . . that human his-

tory is the context within which we know" ("Consequences," 324). The trouble is that Fish seems satisfied with repeating this assertion, rather than making use of history to analyze or clarify any actual difficulties in law or literature. When he does make an effort at historical interpretation, he does so in a remarkably crude way. For example, one would expect a complex historical analysis would provide the only way of answering the question of what social relations have led to the current legal systems of England and the United States. One would have to consider several revolutions and wars, the impact of technology, and many other questions. But Fish answers the questions "Who gets to make the rules? . . . who gets to say who gets to make the rules?" without the bother of any long historical discussion. He assumes that, whatever the particulars of the historical experience of any specific society, the answer to the question of who it is who makes the rules and who gets to say who gets to make the rules is going to be the same: "something like 'whoever seizes the opportunity and makes it stick'" ("Force," 504). If the world can be usefully explained according to such formulas, then, of course, there is very little to differentiate one legal system from another, or even any legal system from any individual with a gun. A judgment about whether the refusal to make such distinctions is an intellectual gain or loss will probably influence one's readiness to accept Fish's outlook.

One might argue that it is inappropriate to consider what the consequences of Fish's philosophy might be, since arguments should be judged on their merits, not on our preference for one result rather than another. It is not open for Fish himself to urge such restraint, however, since he rejects altogether the belief in such a thing as "the authority exerted by arguments that make their way simply by virtue of a superior rationality" ("Fish v. Fiss," 135). For Fish all arguments are rhetorical arguments, and "rhetoric is another word for force" ("Force," 517). Thus, there is no real distinction between an argument that makes its way on its merits and one that derives its "authority" from the prestige of its source:

> To put the matter starkly, interpretation is a form of authority, since it is
> an extension of the prestige and power of an institution; and authority is a
> form of interpretation . . . it is not possible to distinguish between them as
> activities essentially different in kind. ("Fish v. Fiss" 135)

If one accepts the view of the world that emerges from Fish's essays, this conclusion is not surprising. Since throughout *Doing What Comes Naturally* Fish rejects the notion of any independent reality that might provide a "transcendent" basis for judgment, he attempts to avoid any explicit characterization of his own worldview. Nevertheless, at least once Fish does offer a straightforward description of how he himself views the world. Arguing that, once one renounces the possibility of critical reflection, nothing really is lost, he asserts that "one is in the position one was always in, the position of seeing the world as a field of possibilities to be seized by whatever means your situation recommends" ("Critical Self-Consciousness," 465). This is, apparently, the outlook that remains once the illusions of transcendence have been debunked. Presumably, it was the view of those unnamed historical agents who make legal systems because they are able to "seize an opportunity and make it stick" ("Force," 504). It is surely one possible way of viewing life, but it is by no means the only plausible perspective on existence. At least in Fish's hands, what one might call the "seize the world" view of life seems to lead to an impoverished view of human beings, society, and history.

The polemical essays that make up *There's No Such Thing as Free Speech* demonstrate again that Stanley Fish is a dangerous opponent in debate. Fish asserts that it is because "our neoconservative Jeremiahs" are "so self-righteous" that they cannot be swayed by "something so paltry as *evidence*" ("Speaking in Code," 97). In criticizing adherents of free speech, Fish argues that free speech idealists ignore "the real world of consequences" ("Jerry Falwell's Mother," 125). Perhaps they do, and maybe neoconservatives are self-righteous, but it ill befits a renowned antifoundationalist skeptic like Stanley Fish to clinch his arguments by appealing to such archetypal foundations as the "real world" and "*evidence.*" Fish's characterization of Dinesh D'Souza seems a revealing self-portrait: "In a sense, then, he doesn't mean anything by his words—he doesn't stand by them—for he regards them as merely instrumental" ("Speaking in Code," 97).

If Stanley Fish is a dangerous opponent, he is perhaps even more worrisome as an ally. Defending affirmative action in "You Can Only Fight Discrimination with Discrimination," he begins by rejecting the appeal to overriding moral principles on which the conventional defense relies. Reminding us that "fairness is itself a contestable concept" (73), he argues that the effect of civil rights progress "has not been to eliminate partiality but to alter its shape" (75). The followers of Martin Luther King Jr. might have thought that they were struggling to eliminate prejudice and discrimination, but Fish insists that they were deluding themselves, since "You Can Only Fight Discrimination with Discrimination."

The success of Fish's attempt to defend civil rights while robbing the movement of its moral content may be judged by his attempt to defend Martin

Luther King's "I Have a Dream" speech from misinterpretation by "conservative ideologues" ("Speaking in Code," 95). King's moving hope that "one day
my four little children will . . . not be judged by the color of their skin, but by
the content of their character" is misused, argues Fish, by those who assert that
King was affirming color blindness as a universal ideal. According to Fish, the
"power" of the famous passage derives mainly from its rhetorical devices, not
from any declaration of binding moral principles:

> he [King] crafted an utterance whose power derived largely from its
> rhetorical and stylistic features, the balance of parallel phrases counter-
> pointed by a heavy use of alliteration and assonance, "not the color of their
> skin, but the content of their character" (the extra syllable of "character"
> bringing the whole to a nicely cadenced close). (99)

Fish concludes his analysis of the speech by arguing that in the "I Have a
Dream" speech King intimated virtually the opposite of what he seemed to say;
Martin Luther King, in Fish's interpretation, declared, or at least insinuated to
his followers that *"the color of their skin has in some measure been the content of their
character"* ("Speaking in Code," 100). If someone objects that Fish's attempted
defense of King seems to drain the famous speech of all meaning, Fish can reply
that he is treating the speech in the same spirit that he elsewhere has advocated
for the interpretation of the Constitution; he asserts in *Doing What Comes Naturally* that "the Constitution cannot be drained of meaning because it is not a
repository of meaning" ("Fish v. Fiss," 139). And it is evident that Fish does not
regard the "I Have a Dream" speech as a "repository of meaning."

What makes this putative defense of Martin Luther King especially perverse is that elsewhere in *There's No Such Thing as Free Speech* Fish offered quite
a different analysis about a case that raises the same interpretive issues. Asserting
that the ideal of color-blindness has now become a shibboleth of opponents of
civil rights, Fish argues that the ideal itself should be discarded in favor of his
own thesis that the choice is only between "alternative forms of discrimination"
("You Can Only Fight Discrimination with Discrimination," 77). In "The Law
Wishes to Have a Formal Existence" Fish makes a different point about the
same issue of interpretation. He points out that the parol evidence rule has been
circumvented in a number of ways by clever attorneys. Does this historical pattern suggest that the parol evidence rule has had no effect and should be discarded? Examining cases such as *Masterson v. Sine*, Fish says no:

> The important fact about Masterson is not that in it the court succeeds in
> getting around the parol evidence rule, but that it is the parol evidence

rule—and not the first chapter of Genesis or the first law of thermody-
namics—that it feels obliged to get around. (151)

The parol evidence rule is therefore "constraining even if it is not, in the strict
sense, a constraint" (152).

It was open to Fish to make the same point about Martin Luther King's
great speech. If even those whom Fish believes to be "bigots" can only make
their point by appealing to King's speech, if they must argue on behalf of
"color-blindness" rather than straightforward white supremacy, then surely the
principles of Martin Luther King remain a force in the land. Interpreting King's
speech as a rhetorical exercise and undercutting all appeals to moral principle,
Fish seems a dangerous ally for the cause of civil rights and, one might add, for
any other cause or principle. Perhaps we can do without principles—in an
appendix Fish claims he himself manages without them (298). On the basis of
the essays in *There's No Such Thing as Free Speech,* however, there is little reason
to find his example particularly compelling.

Doing What Comes Naturally is a more substantial work that *There's No Such
Thing as Free Speech,* but its essays offer no persuasive rationale for Fish's perspective. Though his antifoundationalism is premised on a rejection of the possibility of transcendence, he offers no arguments about why transcendence is
impossible or unthinkable. Fish's assertion of the impossibility of self-critical
reflection depends upon a definition of terms that need not be accepted by
those who have been fortunate enough to encounter at least a few examples of
such reflection, whether in literature or life. What Fish does succeed in doing is
demonstrating that those who share the antifoundationalist outlook cannot use
its critique only against views they dislike. They must apply their critique to
their own ideals as well. In making this case repeatedly and emphatically, Fish
has performed an important intellectual service, engaging in the sort of cultural
self-criticism that his own theorizing virtually defines out of existence. His success should alert those who hope that the growing academic and intellectual
influence of law and literature will contribute to the creation of a more humane
society to the possibility that it is the culturally conservative branch of the
movement that offers the best chance for the realization of their hopes.

Part 5

Cultural Conservatism, Political Liberalism

Chapter 13

Best-sellers of Cultural Conservatism: E. D. Hirsch and Allan Bloom

The popular success of both *Cultural Literacy* by E. D. Hirsch and *The Closing of the American Mind* by Allan Bloom requires an explanation beyond a renewed public interest in educational policy. The reviewers' comments on both books and, especially, the linking of the two in the public mind—despite obvious differences in style, conception of culture and political implication—suggest that the two works were taken as interventions in the cultural civil war that, since the 1960s, has pitted conservatives against radicals. All the differences between Hirsch and Bloom were largely overlooked in light of the one important perceived similarity: both were taken to speak for the conservative, traditionalist side of the cultural civil war.[1]

Although the immediate relevance of *Cultural Literacy* and *The Closing of the American Mind* stemmed from the willingness to view them as affirmations of one side of an ongoing debate, the significance of both books today derives from their attempts not simply to carry on the debate but also to redefine its terms. Even though both Hirsch and Bloom stressed their commitment to democracy, their best-sellers were mainly praised by the political Right and, more often than not, denounced by political leftists.[2] Were they misunderstood, or do their explicitly democratic sentiments merely conceal the inherent authoritarianism of their versions—of any version—of cultural conservatism? Does the furthering of democracy require an assault on traditional values and high culture or a rethought commitment to those values and that culture? At least raising such issues prevents one from assessing *Cultural Literacy* and *Closing* simply on the basis of the catchwords with which they have been attacked and defended. An examination of each book in light of its style, its particular version

of cultural conservatism, and its political implications may not only illuminate
the works themselves but also offer some clues to the larger questions.

The style of *Cultural Literacy* comes as a surprise to one who assumes that
no book on educational policy gets to be a best-seller without conjuring up an
apocalyptic vision of present disasters alleviated only by the certainty of overwhelming success if the book's revolutionary changes are implemented. Either
Hirsch had not read such books, or he was not trying to write a best-seller. At
any rate, he ignores the rules of the genre. He tells us immediately that his goal
is not revolutionary. In the first sentence of the book Hirsch states that the
reforms he urges are needed "in order to achieve a higher level of national literacy" (1). He calls for improvement, not transformation. Hirsch's goal is not to
use the schools to create a new kind of human being or even to bring back
old-fashioned values but, rather, simply to increase the percentage of adults who
are culturally literate.

Even more surprising, Hirsch refuses to present himself as a lonely voice of
wisdom surrounded by professional fools and knaves. Hirsch's politeness to all
those whom he cites, even those with whom he disagrees, is so unusual that one
critic was moved to look for a nefarious political motive behind such mild language: he argues that Hirsch is cleverly assuring a favorable reception for the
book among academics.[3] In any case, Hirsch surely gives up a lot of easy rhetorical effects when he fails to damn the "educational establishment" or even "progressive education." With his rejection of "skills" teaching, even skills such as
"critical thinking," in favor of the educational virtue of sheer information,
Hirsch is clearly at odds with the Deweyan progressives. Yet Hirsch goes out of
his way to indicate the goals he shares with John Dewey and his followers:

> The reorientation of the schools to practical social goals was intended as a
> generous and humane goal in the writings of John Dewey, Clarence D.
> Kingsley, William H. Kilpatrick, and other leaders of the progressive
> movement. . . . Dewey was in some respects on the side of the tradition-
> alists, many of whom, for their part, continue to honor his aims of plural-
> ism and social utility. (122)

If Hirsch is respectful to those with whom he disagrees, he also makes clear
how much his argument owes to the specialized studies of others. Hirsch does
not present himself as a researcher on the cutting edge of knowledge. The studies he cites emphasizing the active quality of reading and the concomitant need
of the reader to make use of information outside of the text itself during successful reading seem to correlate with the latest developments in "reader-

response theory," but Hirsch does not mention this connection. He would rather stress the affinities with common sense he finds in the research. Far from being a lonely prophet in the wilderness, Hirsch appears as a synthesizer, even a popularizer.

The unpretentiousness that marks Hirsch's style likewise informs his version of cultural conservatism. Hirsch's call for "cultural literacy" does not depend on a belief in the exclusive wisdom of the Western tradition. He argues that cultural literacy is especially important for the disadvantaged, because it increases the opportunity to "break the cycle" of poverty (xiii). Hirsch wants individuals to be able to "participate in the literate national culture" because to do so allows one to be effective, "in whatever direction one wishes to be effective" (23). John Dewey himself could not have affirmed a more pragmatic goal. *Cultural Literacy* is not a get-rich-quick primer, but Hirsch does assume that the primary difference that the achievement of cultural literacy would make for most people would be an economic difference. He is not so dissatisfied with human beings that he would judge education by its ability to induce a spiritual transformation. Furthermore, Hirsch is unwilling to argue that the cultural tradition whose assimilation he is urging offers a single or unambiguous model of spiritual achievement.

Only once does Hirsch suggest that the educational reforms he urges will help bring about better human beings—and then he assumes that moral growth will come about not by absorbing the teaching he prescribes but, rather, by reacting against it:

Children can express individuality only in relation to the traditions of their society, which they have to learn. The greatest human individuality is developed in response to a tradition, not in response to disorderly, uncertain, and fragmented education. (126)

Hirsch has already pointed out that "conservatives who wish to preserve traditional values will find that these are not necessarily inculcated by a traditional education, which can in fact be subversive of the status quo" (24). But this point itself is made only in passing. Hirsch's goal is not to create superior human beings but simply to allow more people to have the advantages now possessed by those who are already culturally literate. Nor does Hirsch present the culturally literate as a spiritual elite; they are simply people who are better able to cope with the modern world than those who are not so equipped.

The strongest claim that Hirsch is ready to make is on behalf of the American "civil religion," whose documents he urges should be learned in school.

Again, however, he bases his affirmation on pragmatic grounds rather than the validity of its ideals; the "civil religion" is valuable because it promotes "coherence":

> The American civil religion, as expressed in our national rites and symbols, is in fact a central source of coherence in American public culture, holding together various and even contradictory elements of its tradition. (99)

As for the morality of our particular national tradition, Hirsch feels no need to offer any brief: "There is no point in arguing about either our civil religion or our vocabulary. They are our national givens, our starting points" (103). It is important to note that Hirsch is not arguing that either the coherence or the "given" quality of the civil religion makes debate unnecessary or impossible. On the contrary, Hirsch cites the pages of the *Black Panther*, "a radical and revolutionary paper if ever this country had one" (22), to illustrate how awareness of the documents of the civil religion may serve revolutionary rhetoric.

Hirsch's entire project may be summed up, in his own words, as "the demystification of literate culture." High culture may be plausibly seen as dependent on breeding, on family tradition, on a certain way of life, as long as the elements of that culture are thought to be intrinsically mysterious and ineffable, spiritual qualities that the mob can only profane. Once cultural literacy is defined in terms of "a few hundred pages of information" (143), few will be willing to argue that it must remain inaccessible to those from other lands, to the poor, to those from deprived or unstable homes. Hirsch's notorious list of "What Literate Americans Know," so easy to ridicule, has the goal of reducing the requirements of cultural literacy to the printed page, open to any reader.

Although Hirsch is unwilling to use the authority of cultural tradition to erect a uniform spiritual standard for individuals, he does affirm his own commitment to a democratic society. If cultural literacy does nothing more than promote wider economic opportunity, that in itself will be a democratic gain— "the achievement of greater social and economic equity" (143). But Hirsch goes further. He argues in his conclusion that enactment of the reforms he favors will not only make possible greater personal and national prosperity, it will also, by "enabling all citizens to participate in the political process," bring "us closer to the Ciceronian ideal of universal public discourse—in short, achieving fundamental goals of the founders at the birth of the republic" (145). Those goals once assumed an aristocratic culture in which gentlemen farmers would debate with one another. Hirsch's call for cultural literacy attempts to reconstitute that ideal in a society without an aristocracy and without the shared way of life that agriculture once made inevitable. Against those who argue that true culture requires leisure and breeding, Hirsch argues for a cultural literacy accessible to all. Against those who argue that the "Ciceronian ideal" is impossible in a technologically complex society, Hirsch argues that "the more computers we have, the more we need shared fairy tales, Greek myths, historical images, and so on" (31). At least we need them if, like Hirsch, we wish to "reinvigorate the unspecialized domain of literate discourse" (31) without also reinvigorating a leisure class free to specialize in such conversation while the rest of us tend to the machines.

If the style of *Cultural Literacy* departs from the mode typical of best-selling cultural diagnoses, Allan Bloom's *Closing of the American Mind* energetically fulfills genre expectations. Bloom speaks in apocalyptic tones with the authority of a prophet, strongly suggesting that most of his professional colleagues are fools, knaves, or cowards. No doubt just these characteristics go far to explain both the book's popular success and its dismissal by many academics. But it is a mistake to consider Bloom's work simply as an example of the cultural bestseller. It is worth taking the book seriously—which does not mean taking it at face value—in order to sort out what is valuable and what is meretricious in Bloom's analysis of the social consequences of relativism, in the version of cultural conservatism that he offers as an alternative to contemporary relativism, and in the implications of his point of view for democracy.

Bloom opens his introduction by asserting, "There is one thing a professor can be absolutely certain of: almost every student entering the university believes, or says he believes, that truth is relative" (25). This relativism inculcates an openness that for Bloom is merely an "openness to closedness" (39), since it denies beforehand any attempt to use reason to arrive at a judgment that is something other than a mere statement of individual preference. The "openness" promoted both in the classroom and in popular culture encourages not independent judgment but, instead, "accepting everything and denying reason's power" (38). Bloom argues that the current relativism leaves individuals defenseless against the sheer presentness of the status quo. For Bloom, "Openness, as currently conceived, is a way of making surrender to whatever is most powerful, or worship of vulgar success, look principled" (41).

Bloom's objection to relativism is not so much that it allows the individual to choose as that its American version tends to render all choices equally principled, equally meaningless. Decisions about the most important personal issues thus take on the moral dignity of the choice of brandnames at a supermarket: "America has no-fault automobile accidents, no-fault divorces, and it is moving with the aid of modern philosophy toward no-fault choices" (228).

Although the premature ecstasy induced by rock music or drugs seems to stand for values utterly opposed to a putative civility based on indifference, Bloom notes that a taste for the "orgiastic state of feeling" likewise induces passivity in everyday life and makes passion similarly irrelevant (74). Nor is the culture of rock less hypocritical than that of the adults: the same popular music that emphasizes universal love also includes "nasty little appeals to the suppressed inclinations toward sexism, racism and violence" (78), so that songs like "We Are the World" present only a "smarmy, hypocritical version of brotherly love" (74). But Bloom's major objection to the culture of rock is the same objection he makes to the culture of relativism: both create a climate in which it is virtually impossible to "have a passionate relationship to the art and thought that are the substance of liberal education" (79).

In contrast to a culture that legitimizes but also trivializes all decisions as merely aspects of one's "lifestyle," Bloom opposes the tragic vision that provided the context for Nietzsche's promulgation that "God is Dead" and for Max Weber's sober recognition that Westerners were henceforth condemned to make fateful decisions without guidance from any external authority, whether divine or scientific. Against an easygoing America that wants to believe in the universal efficacy of "conflict-resolution," Bloom asserts the dignity of "the harsh conflicts for which men were willing to die" (228). He admires nineteenth-century atheists more than modern-day secularists because atheists once "took religion seriously and recognized that it is a real force, costs something and requires difficult choices" (216). For Bloom the essence of the serious life is the making of difficult choices:

> A serious life means being fully aware of the alternatives, thinking about them with all the intensity one brings to bear on life-and-death questions, in full recognition that every choice is a great risk with necessary consequences that are hard to bear. (227)

There is much about Bloom's criticism of contemporary society that rings true. It is hard to disagree with Bloom's dictum that "In philosophy and morals the hardest and most essential rule is 'You can't have your cake and have it too'"(229), and he is surely right to note that the appeal of many contemporary attitudes derives from their apparent ability to have it both ways. On the other hand, if Bloom's position itself is examined from the point of view of this "hardest and most essential rule," problems emerge. Bloom's critique has many points in common with the leftists he criticizes. A comparison of Bloom's ideas with those of Herbert Marcuse, denounced by Bloom for writing "trashy culture criticism with a heavy sex interest" (226), is instructive.

Bloom's attempts to distance his position from "the old alliance of Right and Left against liberal democracy" (32), "the fatal old alliance between traditional conservatives and radicals" (104), by various rhetorical means—including contemptuous dismissals of Marcuse and the entire Frankfurt School—seem questionable when the obvious parallels between some of his most striking ideas and those of Marcuse are noted.[4] Bloom's thesis that the "openness" of American culture makes real debate almost impossible was anticipated more than twenty-five years ago in Marcuse's controversial essay on "Repressive Tolerance." Likewise, Bloom's argument that the sexual titillation of contemporary movies, television, and music cripples rather than promotes true liberation was preceded by Marcuse's concept of "repressive desublimation," developed in *Eros and Civilization*, first published in 1955. The title of Marcuse's best-known book, *One-Dimensional Man* (1964), refers to the same absence Bloom finds in modern society, the loss of the "second dimension" of art and thought.

But Bloom's critique suffers from more serious flaws than a resemblance to the ideas of his adversaries. In opposition to the openness of "do your own thing," Bloom opposes the dignity of hard choices made in tragic awareness. Why are "hard" choices better than ones made lightly? From what Bloom tells us, the ones made with tragic awareness are no more likely to be right than those made with casual irresponsibility. The sense of tragedy that moves Bloom so deeply arises precisely because, according to the school whose views he seems to share, once "God is Dead" there is no objective basis to make one choice rather than another. Thus, the only reason for preferring that people experience decisions as difficult and tragic rather than as "options" to a lifestyle is simply that one has an aesthetic preference for one "style" of decision making over the other.

On the other hand, if there is really an objective reason that one can come to know through knowing nature, as Bloom sometimes seems to suggest there is, following his master Leo Strauss, decisions lose their existential anguish, their quality of being tragic and fateful. They become, in a word, easy. For Plato everybody desires the good; the only problem is finding out what the good is. Once you know it, though, choosing it really requires no choice at all. Bloom seems to want to follow the ancient Greeks but also the modern Germans. He wants to have it both ways, to have his cake and eat it too. We are supposed to be moved by the existential pathos of those who make difficult choices, but we are also supposed to follow the dictates of an objective reason to be found in nature.

Marcuse, and the Marxian tradition in general, have difficulty in avoiding inconsistency here as well. The harmony of the Communist utopia would seem to render individual character ultimately obsolete, yet social critics such as

Adorno and Marcuse deplore the blunting of strong character in mass society. In *Sincerity and Authenticity* Lionel Trilling commented that Marcuse's clear preference for strong though flawed personalities revealed a theoretical inconsistency deriving from what Trilling called "an aesthetic of personality. He likes people to have 'character,' cost what it may in frustration" (166). Since Bloom cannot easily renounce a Nature that is the only source for his concept of reason, his own preference for strong personalities seems likewise at odds with his (Straussian) theory.

This conflict is worth noting, since Bloom's account of the importance of philosophy does not stress its intellectual significance but, rather, its effect on one's "sensibility," its spiritual impact. Throughout "the philosopher" is differentiated from others not on the basis of theoretical achievement but on the acquisition of a superior spirituality. When Bloom speaks of "the philosophic conversion" (71), he refers not to the achievement of new insights or even to the learning of a critical detachment but, instead, to a particular emotional experience, something akin to a religious conversion. For Bloom philosophy is not so much an intellectual perspective as an "experience, one of liberation." Philosophers recognize other philosophers because "they share the experience and are able to recognize it in others" (271).

Bloom is less than forthcoming about exactly what the qualities of the experience shared by philosophers involve, beyond saying that the feeling "is one of liberation." Since this is the same response that any pothead could make to a question about how it feels to smoke a joint, one would think he would wish to tell us more. All that Bloom can tell his audience, the nonphilosophers, is that it's a feeling they will never have. Bloom adds that even modern philosophers, the genuine ones, "were perfectly conscious of what separates them from all other men, and they knew that the gulf is unbridgeable" (290). Bloom himself insists that "the philosophers in their closets or their academies have entirely different ends than the rest of mankind" (291). Although Bloom comments on the way Louis Armstrong's "smiling face" singing Kurt Weill's "Mack the Knife" symbolizes the ignorant, "astonishing Americanization" of German culture (151), his own answer to the question of the essence of philosophy resembles the answer Armstrong is said to have made to an onlooker who wanted to know the essence of jazz: "If you have to ask, you'll never know."

Presenting philosophy as an experience rather than a continuing investigation, Bloom offers his own personality as a basis for authority rather than the cogency of his arguments. We know he is one of the "knowers," since he tells us so: "The substance of my being has been informed by the books I learned to care for. They accompany me every minute of my life" (245). Bloom's sweeping assertions about contemporary life, such as "The dreariness of the family's spiritual landscape passes belief" (57) or "The eroticism of our students is lame" (132), seem rhetorically justified by the contrast that Bloom presents between the passive shallowness of contemporary culture and his own caring, expressed in an indignation sustained over the entire book. Such passion is effective as rhetoric, but Bloom himself explains why it is less than effective as scholarly and especially philosophic discourse. Commenting on the radicals of the 1960s he writes

> Indignation may be a noble passion and necessary for fighting wars and righting wrongs. But of all the experiences of the soul it is the most inimical to reason and hence to the university. Anger, to sustain itself, requires an unshakable conviction that one is right. (327)

Yet indignation is not what most obscures Bloom's reason. Although Bloom asserts that "indignation is the experience of the soul "most inimical to reason," it could be argued that contempt is even more destructive, since contempt assumes that the object of one's scorn is not worth understanding. Yet for Bloom contempt is thought of only as a source of insight: "An experience of profound contempt is necessary in order to grasp our situation, and our capacity for contempt is vanishing" (195). Bloom's own contempt is displayed not only in his dismissals of ideas and people but, arguably, in his attitude toward his readers, whom he seems to assume are either not interested or not able to understand the reasoning that might support his assertions.

Despite Bloom's boasted contempt for the whole modern scene, it seems clear that his best-seller is often in tune with contemporary trends, including those Bloom disparages most strongly. Anyone willing to locate the essence of philosophy not in reflection but in experience, and an experience of liberation at that, is not entirely out of touch. When one adds that this experience is essentially incommunicable to those who have not had it, and that insight for Bloom is characterized not by articulate discourse but by "the primary natural experience" (238), then it seems clear that Bloom is inventing a typically contemporary form of philosophy, one that pays tribute both to the modern cult of experience over reason and to the current distrust in the ability of discourse to formulate truths common to all.

The weakness of Bloom's book once it is considered on the level of philosophical thought instead of seen as a collection of sometimes brilliant *aperçus* unified by indignation rather than argument may be seen by a comparison with another book covering much the same philosophical ground, Jürgen Habermas's *Philosophical Discourse of Modernity*. Both books emphasize the significance of the Enlightenment, and both deal with modern culture's attempt to cope with a reason that seems cut off from personal emotion and from tradition and religion as well. For both Habermas and Bloom, Nietzsche and Heidegger are pivotal, ambiguous figures.

The differences between the two books are even more striking, however, than the similarities. Most obviously, Habermas considers seriously and in detail the writings and arguments of those with whom he disagrees. Bloom dismisses Jacques Derrida, for example, in a few phrases. His deconstruction is "the last, predictable stage in the suppression of reason and the denial of the possibility of truth in the name of philosophy." It proceeds from "a cheapened interpretation of Nietzsche" and is merely "a fad," one that "appeals to our worst instincts" (379). And that is all that Bloom says about Derrida. Habermas himself is very critical of Derrida and on much the same grounds as Bloom. Habermas, like Bloom, believes that deconstruction effects a "denial of the possibility of truth in the name of philosophy." But Habermas is not satisfied simply to attack Derrida. Instead, he makes a careful immanent critique, arguing that Derrida, despite his attacks on "logocentrism," fails to "extricate himself from the paradigm of the philosophy of the subject" (166)—that is, of the logocentric, subject-centered reason that Derrida wishes to attack. Further, although Derrida attacks a philosophy of origins, Habermas notes that "Derrida by no means breaks with the foundationalist tenacity of the philosophy of the subject" (178), since he retains as his foundation the notion "of an originative power," even though this power is thought of as "temporally aflow" (179). Most important, Habermas points out that Derrida's critique of logocentrism is inherently self-contradictory, "since subject-centered reason can be convicted of being authoritarian in nature only by having recourse to its own tools" (185). Thus, Derrida's attempt to privilege rhetoric over logic would require him "to relativize the status of his own project" (187,) if Derrida were to be consistent to his own truth.

The contrast in style between Bloom and Habermas can be stated simply: Habermas offers reasons for his views, while Bloom simply asserts his theses, offering only the implicit authority of his own spiritual depth. To the shallowness of contemporary relativism Bloom opposes the authority of the "substance of my being . . . informed by the books I learned to care for" (245). Yet Bloom's authority is not derived from his erudition but, rather, from undergoing the conversion that separates the "knowers" from the rest of us. Hirsch argues that "literate culture is the most democratic culture . . . it excludes nobody; it cuts across generations and social groups and classes" (21). But even assiduous study of the great books would not give one the authority that Bloom locates in the knowers alone, since that derives from a spiritual experience.

Bloom's refusal to offer explanations for his views seems to imply his own acceptance of what he reports as Nietzsche's thesis: since human beings are essentially unequal, disagreements do not depend for their resolution on questions of logical validity but, instead, on the force of distinctions such as "authentic-inauthentic, profound-superficial, creator-created." Bloom's style suggests that he believes his book will become an example of the process by which "the individual value of one man becomes the polestar for many others whose own experience provides them with no guidance" (201).

On the other hand, Habermas's style reflects his willingness to offer reasons and thereby allow the reader to participate in the ongoing debate, while his own theoretical solution to the contradictions of a subject-centered reason derives from his analysis of "everyday life." As Habermas shrewdly notes, in a comment that applies to Bloom as well as to Derrida, everyday life is an arena that those under the influence of Nietzsche "contemptuously slide over . . . as something derivative or inauthentic" (339). Habermas argues that the means for offering an alternative to the subject-centered reason of the Enlightenment is to be found in an analysis of "intersubjective understanding as the telos inscribed into communication in ordinary language" (311). In everyday life Habermas finds evidence that decisions can be reached—as they should be in philosophy—on the basis of "the unforced force of a better insight" (305), on "the unforced force of reason" (341). Habermas achieves one of his most important insights when he refers to the dangers of an "elitist contempt for discursive thought" (186). The idea that contempt for discursive reason is elitism, perhaps the most seductive and dangerous version of elitism, seems especially important today. Habermas is thinking especially of the continuing appeal of the later Heidegger, who "with the gestures of the seer and an abundance of words" (184) avoided internal contradiction by fleeing "to the luminous heights of an esoteric, special discourse, which absolves itself of the restrictions of discursive speech generally" (185).

The invocation of Heidegger by both Bloom and Derrida betrays their susceptibility to this version of elitism. Both adopt rhetorical strategies that recall Heidegger's implicit "claim to the authority of the initiate" (*Philosophical Discourse of Modernity*, 185). Beyond the force of the reasons offered for his arguments, Bloom asserts an authority that seems to derive from a supposed closeness to an essential Being found either in Nature or in the Great Books. And one wonders how much of Derrida's present mystique derives from the force of that discursive reasoning whose authority he disparages as logocentrism and

how much from the belief, inculcated by various rhetorical devices, that he possesses the initiate's special ability to scent the aroma of the spoor of the absent
present of that same Being.[5]

Both *Cultural Literacy* and *The Closing of the American Mind* endorse versions
of cultural conservatism. Hirsch and Bloom seem, however, to have virtually
opposing views of the culture they wish to conserve. Hirsch wishes to demys-
tify the elements of "literate culture" (143). His list of dates, names, phrases, and
topics can be attacked as a trivialization of the living reality of culture. On the
other hand, Bloom finds the essence of true culture in ineffable experiences
impossible to communicate to the nonknowers. Yet, despite their differences
and apparently against the intentions of their authors, both books have been
enlisted in the continuing civil war in American life between cultural conservatives and radicals. Both Hirsch and Bloom have added something new to the
battle. Hirsch has demonstrated that at least some versions of cultural conservatism are compatible with a commitment to democracy and even with political radicalism. Bloom has revealed how both ideas and rhetoric once associated
with leftist criticism can be appropriated by conservatives. The success of *The
Closing of the American Mind* has demonstrated that Marcuse-like cultural criticism can hit a new audience with the force of revelation when its insights are
separated from their old quasi-Marxist theoretical framework. Bloom has also
demonstrated that the "authenticity" once manifested in works such as *Soul on
Ice* may become a rhetorical weapon for conservatism as well as for cultural radicalism. He has also confirmed, however, the limitations of authenticity as a
basis for a repossession of the cultural past.

Neither Hirsch nor Bloom has articulated a cultural conservatism that both
responds to the experience of the present and remains in touch with the greatness of the past. Hirsch's conservatism is a cautious pragmatism, commonsensi-
cal but without any larger meaning. Hirsch cannot really make use of his conception of past culture as "humankind's accumulated wisdom about human
nature" (125–26) without engaging in a much more serious critique of his own
time and society than he is ready to do in *Cultural Literacy*. Bloom, on the other
hand, is serious enough, but he too is unable to treat past high culture as accumulated wisdom, since he is so eccentrically narrow about what constitutes the
genuine tradition. Yet these criticisms should not have the last word. There are
ways in which both *Cultural Literacy* and *The Closing of the American Mind* point
beyond themselves, once they are considered in contexts beyond their immediate arguments.

Hirsch's fleeting references to the American civil religion, for example,
may provide a pointer for moving the discussion beyond Hirsch's own argu-

ments. Hirsch asserts that the civil religion should be utilized simply because it is there, because it is what we are stuck with. It is true that, if Hirsch's advocacy of cultural literacy is attacked as an attempt to suppress diversity, a defense of civil religion risks being dismissed out of hand. Hirsch himself emphasizes the minimal nature of his call for cultural literacy by contrasting the stronger claims of the civil religion. American public culture, he argues, may be thought of as a spectrum, on which

> at one end is our civil religion, which is laden with definitive value tradi-
> tions. Here we have absolute commitments to freedom, patriotism, equal-
> ity, self-government, and so on. At the other end of the spectrum is the
> *vocabulary* of our national discourse, by no means empty of content but
> nonetheless value-neutral in the sense that it is used to support all the
> conflicting values that arise in public discourse. (102)

Hirsch emphasizes that this "vocabulary," acquaintance with which defines his notion of cultural literacy, is not a tool of domination but, rather, "an instrument of communication among diverse cultures" (104). Considering the degree of suspicion the call for cultural literacy has aroused, it is understandable that Hirsch has been unwilling to go further and argue for the continuing importance of the civil religion, despite his evident sympathy with its commitments. Hirsch's caution, however, has done little to challenge those who regard the framework of a common, public culture or shared heritage as a technique of domination. Better, it would seem, to articulate openly and forcefully the reasons why our heritage is not simply "an instrument of communication" but also an inheritance worth salvaging and reviving in its own right.

Robert Bellah, the originator of the notion of civil religion as a factor in American culture, and a proponent of "some sort of decentralized democratic socialism" (*Covenant,* 136), argues in "Civil Religion in America" for the continuing importance of the civil religion on the basis of its affirmation that "the rights of man are more basic than any political structure" (4), its "awareness that our nation stands under higher judgment" (17), and its prophetic tradition extending from Thoreau through the civil rights movement and beyond.[6] Acknowledging that the "civil religion has not always been evoked in favor of worthy causes" (14), Bellah declares that it is all the more important that "critical Americans . . . not leave the tradition of American idealism entirely to the chauvinists" (*Covenant,* 162).

The "American bible," as Hirsch approvingly notes, "is constantly being brought up to date through new additions" (101), and he specifies Martin

Luther King's "I Have a Dream" speech as the most recent addition. If in rejecting the civil religion we also end the possibility of such "additions," then we
should, at the least, consider all the possibilities before cutting ourselves off from
such a tradition. Perhaps, like Lincoln in the Second Inaugural, we can still
entertain the hypothesis of a God who judges nations, if not to guide our metaphysical speculations at least to judge ourselves by standards beyond those of
realpolitik. We might, that is, adopt the civil religion as a working hypothesis—
at least until we find a substitute for what still provides the broadest bridge linking, in Robert Bellah's words, "the profoundest commitments of the Western
religious and philosophical tradition and the common beliefs of ordinary Americans" ("Civil Religion," 15–16). If neither the "commitments" nor the "common beliefs" have any particular significance, cultural literacy wouldn't seem to
matter much either, since it is hard to see what we would have to talk about
anyway.

   If E. D. Hirsch's call for cultural literacy can be underwritten by a commitment to the civil religion stronger than one Hirsch himself seems willing to
make, it is also true that an appreciation of the virtues as well as the flaws in
Bloom's *Closing of the American Mind* may depend on placing Bloom's book in
a context different than the philosophical tradition that he proposes as
definitive. It may be worth considering *Closing* as a work of literature—not as a
means of discounting its explicit arguments, but as a way of getting at its fundamental strengths as well as its flaws.

   In the foreword to *The Closing of the American Mind* Saul Bellow found that
Bloom was "willing to take the risks more frequently taken by writers," daring
to discuss the "truest truths" in a "profoundly personal" way (12). The "republic of letters" was once capacious enough to include history, biography, and
philosophy, not to mention sermons and political oratory, as well as poetry, literature, and drama. *The Closing of the American Mind* can be read as an intellectual autobiography, a "confession" in the tradition of *The Education of Henry
Adams,* Thomas Mann's *Reflections of a Nonpolitical Man,* or the *Confessions* of
Rousseau and Saint Augustine.

   Yet perhaps the drama of Bloom's work can best be captured by a comparison to an American novel, *The Great Gatsby* by F. Scott Fitzgerald. Like
Bloom, the protagonist is a midwesterner who finds on the shores of the Great
Lakes a world utterly unlike the rest of the Midwest. Like Bloom, James Gatz is
more than willing to undertake the personal transformation that entrance to that
world requires. James Gatz becomes Jay Gatsby as soon as he meets the mil-
lionaire Dan Cody at Little Girl Bay, off Lake Superior. Cody's yacht "represented all the beauty and glamour in the world" to the young midwesterner

(100–101). Gatsby's enchantment with the possibilities represented by that yacht leads him to "the service of a vast, vulgar, and meretricious beauty" (99). This "service" ends, of course, in Gatsby's own disillusion and death. Nor has Gatsby harmed only himself: his association with Meyer Wolfsheim of the "Swastika Holding Company" (171) suggests that Gatsby was complicit in a variety of crimes, including murder, bootlegging, and perhaps fixing the World Series. Nevertheless, knowing all this, Nick Carraway cries out to Gatsby: "They're a rotten crowd. . . . You're worth the whole damn bunch put together" (154). This is said in the heat of the moment, yet it is Nick's collected reflection that Gatsby possessed "some heightened sensitivity to the promises of life . . . an extraordinary gift for hope, a romantic readiness," which allows him to assert, thinking over the whole story, that "Gatsby turned out all right at the end" (2).

Of course, *The Closing of the American Mind* does not suggest that Allan Bloom is intoxicated with wealth, but his first sight of the University of Chicago seems as determinative an event as Gatsby's sighting of Dan Cody's yacht: "When I was fifteen years old I saw the University of Chicago for the first time and somehow sensed that I had discovered my life." Just as the yacht stands for a world beyond North Dakota, a world beautiful and complete in itself, so the "fake Gothic buildings" of the University of Chicago are different from anything Bloom has seen before in a "Middle West . . . not known for the splendor of its houses of worship or its monuments of political glory." For the first time the fifteen-year-old Allan Bloom saw structures "evidently dedicated to a higher purpose, not to necessity or utility, not merely to shelter or manu-facture or trade, but to something that might be an end in itself" (243).

Unlike Gatsby, however, Allan Bloom was not so transfixed by his first vision of possibility that he became incapable of further discrimination. Gatsby remains "faithful to the end" to his first vision—the sort, says Fitzgerald, "that a seventeen-year-old boy would be likely to invent" (99). Bloom, on the other hand, comes to learn that the buildings "were fake, and that Gothic is not really my taste" (243). He tells himself that the university is "after all only a vehicle for contents in principle separable from it" (245). Still, he does not renounce his original discovery that possibilities unknown or obscure in the outside world reside in the university: "For me the promise of these buildings was fully kept" (244). Bloom retains, that is, despite his anger—which is all most of his critics have noticed—"an extraordinary gift for hope, a romantic readiness" to dis-cover spiritual greatness, true philosophy, true friendship at the university, the same institution denominated already in the 1960s as the "multiversity" by a pragmatic Clark Kerr.

Undoubtedly, Bloom's exhilaration blinds him to much that others see. He refers quite straightforwardly to "the philosophers" who, ancient and modern, "were perfectly conscious of what separates them from all other men, and they knew that the gulf is unbridgeable" (290). Fitzgerald's famous comment about the rich in the opening of "The Rich Boy" is equally Bloom's thesis about "the philosophers": "They are different from you and me. . . . They are different" (177). Jay Gatsby never wavered in his acceptance of that faith. F. Scott Fitzgerald, however, was quite capable of seeing through the aura of the very rich, as "The Rich Boy" itself demonstrates. There is nothing in *The Closing of the American Mind* that suggests that Bloom was capable of any comparable skepticism about the philosophers.

And yet Bloom's wholehearted commitment to his vision of the philosophical life as the life most worth living, narrow and flawed though that vision may be, allows him to articulate insights that any less grandiose vision would not have allowed. It may not be true that "men may live more truly and fully in reading Plato and Shakespeare than at any other time, because then they are participating in essential being and forgetting their accidental lives" (380). "Essential being" may not be what one "participates" in when reading Shakespeare or even Plato. Bloom's use of the inclusive masculine is open to objection. After all the criticisms are made, however, it still seems likely that one who accepts some version of this assertion is more likely to attain generosity of mind than those whose beliefs are bounded by the orthodoxies of the present, "politically correct" or not. And generosity of mind will be a key intellectual virtue in working out a cultural conservatism that will uphold the moral standards declared in American civil religion. Whatever Bloom's flaws, he retained in *The Closing of the American Mind* a sense of wonder, and of possibility, that goes far to redeem the limitations of his best-seller.

Chapter 14

On Cultural Self-Criticism

The academic respectability of contemporary "cultural studies" depends on the assumption that there is a master key that turns the lock to all cultures and all history, though practitioners disagree among themselves about its specific nature. Only those who believe in the reality of such a master key are likely to share the faith that a Ph.D. degree in cultural studies entitles one to pronounce on cultural phenomena in general, despite the variety and complexity of human affairs and history. The authority of academic credentials is not the greatest difficulty, however, with the master key syndrome. More important, a critic who employs a theory that explains everything forfeits the possibility of considering independent evidence and thus loses the opportunity to correct or qualify one truth with another. This forfeiture occurs whether the theory is Marxist, feminist, poststructuralist, some combination of these, or another, perhaps one less favored in academic circles—for example, the notion that knowledge of a particular sacred text absolves one from the need to learn anything else. Discussion rather than a mere war of words occurs when we can appeal from one tradition to another, from one discipline to another, from theories to common sense, from personal experience to accumulations of historical experience. The current popularity of cultural studies therefore has a significance beyond the university, since the campus affirmation of totalizing approaches strengthens those off-campus, on both Right and Left, who have already rejected discussion in favor of political and cultural warfare.

If a recovery of the older criticism can contribute to an amelioration of the culture wars, it will not be through the discovery of a neglected master key but, rather, through a revival of the capacity for "cultural self-criticism," a phrase that Leszek Kolakowski coins in the introduction to his *Main Currents of Marxism* in an attempt to explain the approach he pursued through the three volumes of the study. Kolakowski points out that, even if it is possible to carry on the history of ideas "outside ideology," it is not possible to place "ourselves outside the culture within which we live" (4). Recognizing this, however, does not lead Kolakowski to abjure the possibility of reasoned judgment altogether. Instead, he invokes the concept of cultural self-criticism, offering as an example not a work of analysis but, instead, a novel, Thomas Mann's *Doctor Faustus*. The passage is worth quoting at some length:

> Thomas Mann was entitled to say that Nazism had nothing to do with German culture or was a gross denial and travesty of it. In fact, however, he did not say this: instead, he inquired how such phenomena as the Hitler movement and Nazi ideology could have come about in Germany, and what were the elements in German culture that made this possible. Every German, he maintained, would recognize with horror, in the bestialities of Nazism, the distortion of features which could be discerned even in the noblest representatives (this is the important point) of the national culture. Mann was not content to pass over the question of the birth of Nazism in the usual manner, or to contend that it had no legitimate claim to any part of the German inheritance. Instead, he frankly criticized that culture of which he was himself a part and a creative element. (4)

As a former Marxist and Communist, Kolakowski is not interested in denouncing Marxism or Communism but, rather, in understanding the intellectual sources of twentieth-century Marxist regimes. Similarly, a Christian who rejected the notion that Saint Paul was "personally responsible for the Inquisition" and did not believe that the Inquisition was the inevitable result of Christian doctrines, nevertheless might "seek to discover what it was in the Pauline epistles that gave rise, in the fullness of time, to unworthy and criminal actions" (4–5). The careful analyses that make up the three volumes of *Main Currents of Marxism* bear out Kolakowski's claim that the work is indeed an attempt to understand Marxism from within, an exercise in cultural self-criticism rather than in sermonizing and denunciation. This chapter highlights the ways in which critics from Mencken to Ellison have carried out American versions of cultural self-criticism after considering some ways in which the contemporary intellectual climate discourages the practice.

First, however, some possible misconceptions should be noted. Just because the criticism of American culture has a special saliency when carried out by Americans, it does not follow that critiques or even denunciations by others have no cogency or moral standing. Likewise, there seems to be no valid reason why Americans should be precluded from offering criticism as well as praise about other countries or about cultures originating elsewhere. General acceptance of the notion that only Arabs are qualified to criticize Arab culture, that only Africans can make judgments about Africa, and that only citizens of the United States have the right to raise questions about U.S. policy would render intellectual discourse impossible. Arguments should be rebutted on their merits, not by attacking the origins of their author. It is also true, however, that discussion of cultural, moral, and religious matters becomes more serious when those who have most at stake take part. We attach greater moral weight and grant greater credence, other things being equal, to those who criticize "from within." Michael Walzer, in *The Company of Critics,* rightly prefers the "specificity and force of an older social criticism" to the "palaver of the critic-at-large," who gains the moral high ground by refusing to acknowledge any allegiances to actual societies and human beings (228).

To repeat, the point is not that criticism "from without" should be proscribed. It is that criticism by a critic sociologically or culturally outside the phenomena criticized usually gains in depth and persuasive power if analysis is preceded by an attempt at understanding and imaginative identification—an attempt, in other words, to "get inside." Although it may be impossible for one person to experience entirely the feelings of another, imaginative identification equal to the purposes of acute criticism and high art is possible: we have the essays and the art to prove it. (A willingness to carry out such a preliminary mental experiment does not necessarily imply final acceptance—Thomas Mann's essay on Adolf Hitler, "A Brother," illustrates how identification can lead to understanding but not necessarily to sympathy.)

If, then, the value of cultural self-criticism is appreciated, another misunderstanding looms. Since self-criticism is a good thing, must it follow that those who criticize their own society most vociferously are the most profound critics? Surely not, if only because the more sweeping the denunciations of one's own culture, the more self-righteous the critic. No outright assertions of purity need be made, since the inverse rhetorical logic of denunciation implicitly correlates the height of the denouncer's moral perch with the depths of iniquity he or she discovers. It is no small part of the literary achievement of the critics in the humanist tradition that none, even implicitly, presents him- or herself as a candidate for sainthood or even for President. Each manages to offer a persona that claims intelligence and cultural acumen while avoiding the pose of lonely goodness in a world of sinners.

Critics in the humanist tradition are more likely than others to sustain their moral balance in print, because they draw authority from the cultural heritage rather than from the self alone. In contrast, when Leslie Fiedler and Susan Sontag turned against traditional humanism, both found it necessary to claim a unique personal purity as the basis for cultural authority. Susan Sontag was ready to welcome the destruction of the United States, worrying only that "the rest of the planet" ("What's Happening in America," 204) might be dragged down as well. As she herself honorably noted in *Illness as Metaphor*, her assertion that the white race "*is* the cancer of human history" amounted to a call for genocide (203). This verbal gesture had no significant practical effect; it did, however have the rhetorical effect of claiming a unique moral superiority above other citizens of the United States, and especially above other white people, for their author, Susan Sontag. In *Illness as Metaphor* and *AIDS and Its Metaphors*, on the other hand, Sontag claims no unique moral status. Her goal in writing is now "to alleviate unnecessary suffering" (*AIDS*, 101), a purpose that is certainly moral enough but which arouses no controversy, fails to shock, and can be approved by the most uptight, middle-class philistine. In these books Susan Sontag's writing is as brilliant as ever, but now she writes to deflate the avant-garde mythology that she once affirmed so eloquently.

Paradoxically, the writings in which Susan Sontag and Leslie Fiedler move to the front of the avant-garde now seem dated; those that make no attempt to be contemporary retain their interest. Fiedler's early essays hold up in part because he then identified himself with the targets of his criticism. He concluded his critique of "the liberal-intellectual" with a parenthetical but important affirmation: "It is perhaps unnecessary to say that I consider myself one of this group" ("McCarthy and the Intellectuals," 68n). Later, however, Fiedler claimed a unique innocence for himself, asserting that the events of his life should be viewed as episodes in an "endless war . . . between the dissenter and his imperfect society" (*Being Busted,* 7). In *What Was Literature?* Fiedler appears as an innocent entertainer, a jester "paid to allay boredom" (34).

The essays in Fiedler's latest collection, *Fiedler on the Roof: Essays on Literature and Jewish Identity* (happily, the subtitle reflects the essays within more accurately than the title) make up some lost ground, reaffirming his earlier self-definition "as a liberal, intellectual, writer, American and Jew" (pref., *An End to Innocence*, xiii). Moving from James Joyce's *Ulysses* to the Book of Job, Fiedler takes up again the humanist task of passing on the cultural heritage to another generation. One of the best reasons for doing so appears at the end of the book, in the quotation Fiedler offers from his grandfather explaining why he took the young Fiedler to a synagogue on High Holy days: "Not because I believe, but so you should remember" ("In Every Generation," 181). For the self aiming at autonomous innocence, memories are only an encumbrance. The memories to which literature and the historic religions provide access are troubling as well as inspiring, but it is the possession of such memories that distinguishes human beings from (innocent) beasts.

Many on the cultural Left believe that jettisoning the past is a means of liberation. Cultural conservatives such E. D. Hirsch and Allan Bloom agree that the cultural heritage—the great religions and the masterpieces of literature, art, and philosophy—should be preserved, but they have difficulty in envisioning how the past can be brought to bear on the present. In *Cultural Literacy* Hirsch scarcely aims at cultural criticism, since his goal is to propose certain educational reforms adapted to U.S. society as it is. This goal does not preclude Hirsch from making value judgments, as in his affirmation of "the Ciceronian ideal of universal public discourse" (145), but the book as a whole is governed by a simple acceptance of the national mores, based not upon principle but on a tactical refusal to raise fundamental questions. If Hirsch argues that Americans should become aware of their own history, it is not because he is ready to make a case for the virtues of our traditions. He even seems to consider the mere willingness to debate about one's culture to be evidence of either immorality ("chauvinism") or ignorance ("provincialism"): "It is cultural chauvinism and provincialism to believe that the content of our [national] vocabulary is something either to recommend or deplore by virtue of its inherent merit" (107).

Bloom was more than ready to consider the "inherent merit" of many aspects of the national vocabulary. *The Closing of the American Mind* is a powerful (though flawed) exercise in cultural criticism because it is also a spiritual autobiography. Bloom's dramatic portrayal of his midwestern, American identity as a kind of Jay Gatsby of the intellect makes his indictment of the national culture an exercise in cultural self-criticism, not a mere sermon. The wholesale dismissal of *The Closing of the American Mind* by those who think of themselves as leftist intellectuals reveals more about the intensity of the culture wars than it does about the book itself. The book, nevertheless, cannot serve as a model for other works, since its source of authority is so personal, while its explicit cultural standard—"the philosophers"—is beyond scrutiny or comparison. Between Bloom's philosophers and the rest of humanity "the gulf is unbridgeable," since "the philosophers . . . have entirely different ends than the rest of mankind" (290–91). The revival of cultural self-criticism, then, cannot depend on the examples of Hirsch and Bloom.

Among the practitioners of the new cultural studies Edward Said stands out for his willingness to criticize what he holds dearest and what he most wishes to defend. Said's forthright and courageous critiques of anti-intellectualism and authoritarianism in the Muslim world demonstrate his personal integrity. On the other hand, Said's theoretical perspective prevents him from using his personal insights to develop his cultural self-criticism into more than scattered comments. Even in "Orientalism Reconsidered," an essay specifically designed as a reflection on the responses to his book *Orientalism*, Said refused to discuss the possibility that there might be a discrepancy between his doubt that "there can be a true representation of anything" (272) and his vehement indictments of Western scholars because they did not tell the truth about the Orient. Said's indictments of Western culture in *Orientalism* are sweeping, but they are blunted, because he never identifies an alternative tradition from which his own insights are derived. Throughout his writings Said presents himself as an "oppositional" intellectual, an eternal "exile." The effect of such a stance is to suggest that his criticism derives only from his isolated moral purity, not from any set of standards or traditions that could be shared. On those occasions when Said forgets about postmodernist theory and drops his pose as the last honest man, however, he can be a thoughtful and insightful critic.

Like Said, Richard Rorty and Stanley Fish are hampered from reaching the insights of the older cultural criticism by their common commitment to dogmatic skepticism. Their shared "antifoundationalism" asserts emphatically that the literature, philosophy, and religion of the past have nothing to teach, since all discourse is merely a manifestation of the struggle for power. This view is presented most baldly by Fish, but it enfeebles the work of Said and Rorty as well. One is forewarned against looking for instances of self-criticism in Fish, since he defines the phenomenon out of existence.

In the Preface to *There's No Such Thing as Free Speech* Fish declares his opposition to "the game I call 'moral algebra,' a game that is played by fixing on an abstract quality and declaring all practices that display or fail to display that quality equivalent" (ix). On the basis of Fish's description of the game of "moral algebra," it is hard to imagine anybody wanting to play. The folly of affirming that any one attribute, especially an "abstract" one, is of such overwhelming importance that it renders "equivalent" activities that otherwise might be very different seems obvious. Fish, however, seems to be intimating not just that some comparisons about the moral status of differing activities are unwarranted but also that no comparisons at all are possible. Every question is a particular one, and the solution in every case must be equally particular. No appeal to general moral principles is allowed.

Consider an instance of the kind of moral algebra that Fish rejects. Suppose one opposes a particular government, perhaps because it is politically reactionary or because it discriminates against coreligionists. Suppose further that the regime, which one opposes on other grounds, begins to torture political prisoners. Fish would certainly agree that opponents would be smart to oppose the regime on the basis of its use of torture. Opposition to torture is a rhetorical strategy that often gains a broader support than merely political arguments. Suppose now that a regime that one supports, perhaps because it is "progressive" or perhaps because it establishes one's favored religion, begins to torture its prisoners. No moral problem would occur for Fish, although rhetorical difficulties might ensue. Only those who engage in moral algebra would find themselves forced to confront their opposition to one regime that uses torture with their support of another regime that also uses torture. We practice moral algebra when we measure ourselves and our allies against the same moral yardstick that we apply to our opponents. The game of moral algebra, it appears, is Fish's name for the practice of "self-criticism," a mental activity that he believes to be impossible and which he certainly does his best to discourage.

It is fair to note that Fish, in practice, has served as an acute critic of the pretensions of other antifoundationalists. He has pointed out that those who reject the authority of established values have no reason to expect others to accept the authority of their own revolutionary set of preferences. Fish has even taken note of some of the difficulties that ensue when literary critics, inspired by "some grandiose new name like Cultural Studies," become "claimants to universal competence" ("Why Literary Criticism Is like Virtue," 12). In doing so, Fish honorably contradicts his assertion, in the same article, that "there is no such thing as critical self-consciousness" (14). Indeed, Fish often engages in cultural self-criticism, since he is more than willing to question trends within the antifoundationalist cultural Left, of which he himself is a leading member.

Richard Rorty, like Fish, has warned other cultural leftists against their theoretical and political pretensions; he was not afraid in 1991 to affirm that John Dewey and Sidney Hook were right to believe that "the Cold War was a good war" ("Just one more species," 6), and he even had the temerity to say some good words about E. D. Hirsch, while offering only "Two Cheers for the Cultural Left" at a 1988 conference at Duke University that was, in effect, "a rally of this cultural left" (227). Most important, he has insisted on the virtues of liberal societies in comparison to the alternatives. Unfortunately, the antifoundationalism that Rorty shares with Fish has led the former to propose a version of liberalism in which principles are replaced by preferences, or tastes. And, since Rorty accepts the proverbial notion that "there is no arguing about taste," it is difficult to subject his version of liberalism to any extensive self-criticism.

Fredric Jameson's *Postmodernism, or, The Cultural Logic of Late Capitalism*, published in 1991, may be compared to Kolakowski's *Main Currents of Marxism*, published a decade earlier, in at least one respect: both respond to the decline of

Marxism and Communism, the worldwide collapse of which was well on its way when Jameson wrote his April 1990 introduction to *Postmodernism*.[1] It is as alternative approaches, however, that the two works may be most usefully compared. In assessing Jameson's response in *Postmodernism* to the fall of Communism, it is worth remembering that Jameson's status is based on his reputation not as a mere literary critic but also as a Marxist. On the back cover of *The Political Unconscious* Hayden White hailed Jameson as "the best Marxist critic writing today," and on the back of *Postmodernism* Terry Eagleton calls him "America's leading Marxist critic." As a Marxist and revolutionary, Jameson is presumably concerned about those societies whose recent history has been shaped by revolutions undertaken in the name of Marxism. A few dates, therefore, are relevant. Gorbachev came to power in 1985 and was displaced in 1991, while Communism collapsed throughout Eastern Europe during the fall of 1989. In early 1990 there were clear signs that Soviet Communism was coming to an end. According to Charles Fairbanks,

> The most decisive step of all was taken in February 1990, when the CC [Central Committee of the Communist Party] voted for Gorbachev's proposal to end its monopoly of power, agreeing in principle to a multi-party system, and to end its opposition to private property, thus abolishing the core of Leninism and the core of Marxism in one three-day meeting. (54)

Jameson's retention of the term late capitalism in the book's subtitle—at a time when common sense would have suggested that "late" should be applied to "Communism" or "Marxism-Leninism" rather than to "capitalism"—provides a representative instance of his reluctance to reconsider his premises in the light of events. Jameson might have responded to the breakdown of Soviet Communism by emphasizing that his revolutionary Marxism has nothing to do with Leninism. That response would have involved difficulties, since Leninism seems to be the only version of twentieth-century Marxism that can actually produce revolutions, but at least it would have indicated Jameson's awareness of the obligations of his stance. Instead of rethinking, however, Jameson decided instead to merely redefine, offering an explanation of his retention of late capitalism that defies the straightforward Marxist sense of the term. Jameson's introduction of April 1990 warns that the appearance of late capitalism in his subtitle should not be taken to mean "anything so silly as the ultimate senescence, breakdown, and death of the system as such." Instead, late capitalism just means, uncontroversially, "the sense that something has changed, that things are different" (xxi). It is, in fact, "something like a literal translation of the other expression, *postmodernism*" (xxi). Blandly equating late capitalism with postmodernism, the use of which requires no investment in Marxist thought at all, Jameson is apparently determined to have his cake and eat it too. He presents himself as both "a relatively enthusiastic consumer of postmodernism" (298), enjoying the improvement of "the life world generally" during the Reagan decade (299), and as the kind of revolutionary Marxist who still looks forward to the rising of the "international proletariat" (417). *Main Currents* and *Postmodernism* may indeed have something in common, but they are also opposites. One is an exemplary work of cultural self-criticism, another a manual in how to avoid it.

It is always difficult to raise questions about one's own ideas and one's own side; Jameson is not the only theoretician unwilling to question his own theories. Stanley Fish's message provides a rationalization attractive to many who are not antifoundationalists. Unappealing to the individual, unwelcome for the group, cultural self-criticism cannot exist, let alone flourish, without the encouragement that examples can provide. Critics such as Lionel Trilling, H. L. Mencken, Irving Babbitt, Dwight Macdonald, Diana Trilling, Edmund Wilson, and Ralph Ellison have many claims on our attention, but in an era of cultural civil war the examples of cultural self-criticism that they offer are particularly valuable for critics and academics unwilling to be recruited into the culture wars. Avoiding the self-righteousness so common among both Left and Right today, these critics share a suspicion of grandiose moral rhetoric; they recognize and counter the special appeal such rhetoric possesses for literary intellectuals such as themselves. All make sharp criticisms of American culture, but they do so from within, as participants in the culture that they are criticizing.

Lionel Trilling's book *The Liberal Imagination* attempts to correct the rigidities of liberal doctrine by reference to the complexity and variety available through literature. In his later career Trilling became less and less sure that modern literature, at least as taught and presented through criticism, did indeed provide the necessary correctives to the general culture. *The Liberal Imagination* suggested that literature should witness against a doctrinaire rationality, but in *Beyond Culture* Trilling proposed that the values implicit in modern literature and art required balancing from the "rational intellect":

> In our adversary culture such experience as is represented in and proposed by art moves toward becoming an idea, even an ideology, as witness the present ideational and ideological status of sex, violence, madness, and art itself. If in this situation the rational intellect comes into play, it may be found that it works in the interests of experience. (Preface, n.p.)

"On the Teaching of Modern Literature" is explicitly autobiographical. As a professor "committed to an admiration of modern literature" (27), rejecting neither modernism nor the academy, Trilling questions his own continuing attempt to carry out "the socialization of the anti-social, or the acculturation of the anti-cultural, or the legitimization of the subversive" (23). He notes his own "queer respect" for those students who remain untouched by the "adversary culture," who write papers full of "bad grammar" and "general incoherence" but whose repulsion from modernism he recognizes as "authentic" (23–24). Trilling's ironic readiness to confer the honorific term on an unreflective acceptance of middle-class pieties illustrates his own growing suspicions about the slogans of the adversary culture. In the closing pages of *Sincerity and Authenticity* (1972) Trilling notes how the then new influence of Foucault works in accord with the zeitgeist to insure "a happy welcome from a consequential part of the educated public" for "the doctrine that madness is health, that madness is liberation and authenticity" (171). Trilling engaged in cultural self-criticism throughout his career; in the 1940s he called upon literature to reply to the "easy rationalistic optimism" of liberal psychology ("The Function of the Little Magazine," 94), while later he attempted to correct the ideologies deriving their authority from literature by an appeal to mind.

The writer whose criticism seems to be least useful in learning how to consider that one might be wrong is H. L. Mencken. Mencken's literary pose was always one of supreme confidence in his own intelligence and a comparable certainty of the stupidity of almost everybody else. What saves Mencken's criticism from an insufferable elitism is his refusal to present himself as morally superior to others. He does not demonize his opponents; he simply ridicules them. His criticism, therefore, does not lend itself to hate campaigns or even to bigotry. Mencken, indeed, was one of the most effective opponents of the Ku Klux Klan at a time when it was a national power. Mencken's humor arises from the disproportion between the vehemence of his criticism and the nonchalance of his stance. One might expect the sweeping criticisms he offers to be followed by urgent proposals for reform, by a calling of the troops to battle before universal disaster strikes. Instead, Mencken follows his descriptions of a cultural wasteland with a horselaugh. The obvious implication is that he himself is no better than he should be and that, just maybe, his descriptions can be taken with a grain of salt rather than accepted as literal fact.

Mencken's criticisms of American culture remain powerful in large part because they are written in an American idiom, by a writer whose persona is entirely American. Mencken's style dramatizes his unwillingness to stand apart

from American life, neither escaping from the country like the "exiles" of the
1920s nor retreating into the vestiges of the genteel tradition, as he unfairly
assumed Irving Babbitt was doing. In *The American Language* Mencken offers a
counterpoint to his wholesale condemnations of American culture. Mencken is
describing his own style as he captures what he sees as the essence of the American language:

> The American, from the beginning, has been the most ardent of recorded
> rhetoricians. His politics bristles with pungent epithets; his whole history
> has been bedizened with tall talk; his fundamental institutions rest far more
> upon brilliant phrases than upon logical ideas. And in small things as in
> large he exercises continually an incomparable capacity for projecting hid-
> den and often fantastic relationships into arresting parts of speech. (92)

Although Mencken sadly concludes that "profanity is not an American art,"
noting that son-of-a-bitch, for example, has "no lift in it, no shock, no sis-
boom-ah" (317), in general he praises the American language as a supreme
example of creativity, imagination, and intelligence. Phrases such as "to fill the
bill," "to fizzle out, and "to make tracks" demonstrate to Mencken "the
national talent for condensing a complex thought, and often a whole series of
thoughts, into a vivid and arresting image" (142). The contrast between the
English *cinema* and the American *movie* offers a proof of the "superior imagina-
tiveness and resourcefulness" of American, according to Mencken: "*Movie* is
better than *cinema*; and the English begin to admit the fact by adopting the
word; it is not only better American, it is better English" (95).

In the essay "On Being an American" Mencken asserted that his own criticisms of American culture were more sweeping than those of any of the "fugi-
tive Young Intellectuals" (90) who were escaping to Europe because they
avowedly found "life intolerable for them at home" (89). Summing up his own
criticisms in language indeed difficult to surpass, he castigated the American
people as "the most timorous, sniveling, poltroonish, ignominious mob of serfs
and goose-steppers ever gathered under one flag in Christendom since the end
of the Middle Ages." Nevertheless Mencken was not about to join the Young
Intellectuals in exile, nor was he about to see himself as victim of American life.
Instead in Whitmanian language he pronounced himself "a loyal and devoted
Americano . . . contentedly and even smugly basking beneath the Stars and
Stripes" (90). For Mencken the United States "is incomparably the greatest
show on earth" (121). Here, says Mencken, "is the land of mirth, as Germany

is the land of metaphysics and France is the land of fornication" (124). And, as these quotations suggest, Mencken himself is one of the foremost contributors to that mirth.

His own hyperbolic language, with its Whitmanesque piling-up of phrases, is part of the circus that he both cherishes and despises. The following description of American life is written with love as well as contempt, its style partaking of the same extravagance that it describes:

> And here, more than anywhere else that I know of or have heard of, the daily panorama of human existence, of private and communal folly—the unending procession of governmental extortions and chicaneries, of commercial brigandages and throat-slittings, of theological buffooneries, or aesthetic ribaldries, of legal swindles and harlotries, of miscellaneous rogueries, villainies, imbecilities, grotesqueries, and extravagances—is so inordinately gross and preposterous, so perfectly brought up to the highest conceivable amperage, so steadily enriched with an almost fabulous daring and originality, that only the man who was born with a petrified diaphragm can fail to laugh himself to sleep every night, and to awake every morning with all the eager, unflagging expectation of a Sunday-school superintendent touring the Paris peep-shows. ("On Being an American," 92)

Mencken himself suspects that in passages such as this one he has something in common with his targets. Perhaps, he suggests, "I yield to words as a chautauqua lecturer yields to them, belaboring and fermenting the hinds with his Message from the New Jerusalem" (92). Throughout Mencken's writings he does indeed "yield to words," participating in the national circus, putting on a show, enjoying himself thoroughly. Mencken is criticizing a culture that he himself shares and expresses, a culture of which his own style is one of the most striking manifestations. Where his imaginative afflatus fails, when he does not "yield to words," as in his diaries or the posthumous *Minority Report*, Mencken's mere opinions have little to recommend them. The criticism that made him famous, however, stands up today, unpoisoned with the bitterness and self-righteousness that so often emanates from partisans on both sides of the culture wars.

Irving Babbitt's "new humanism" emphasized the unavoidable necessity of recurrent self-examination, since even the best of us is a divided self, caught between our aspirations and our appetites. More profoundly, Babbitt pointed out how often our noblest aspirations, for example the humanitarian impulse to serve all humanity, can become an excuse for the acquisition of power. Babbitt noted how the notion of the "white man's burden" was used as an excuse for conquest and how Woodrow Wilson's desire to "make the world safe for democracy" justified entry into World War I. Babbitt argued that democracy in the United States needed criticism more than celebration, pointing out how a great celebrator of democracy like Walt Whitman moved easily to an endorsement of imperialism.

Aware that the most grandiose ideals are most easily converted into justifications of great evils, Babbitt urged that humanists aim at the more attainable virtues of "moderation, common sense, and common decency" ("What I Believe," 13). To achieve such qualities is a considerable accomplishment, though not so exceptional as to qualify one as either a hero or a saint— but then Babbitt's humanist does not aim at setting himself above the rest of humanity. For Babbitt the necessity of the "inner check" is ongoing; he recognizes no spiritual elite whose superiority allows them to ignore the moral sanctions that the masses must obey. Though Babbitt is often thought of as a cultural dogmatist who urged the uncritical acceptance of past authority, those who read his actual writings know that he was more than willing to adopt a critical perspective toward the Western tradition itself—without, however, simply rejecting the tradition altogether. He hoped to contribute to the recovery "in a positive and critical form" of "the soul of truth in the two great traditions, classical and Christian, that are crumbling as mere dogma" ("English and the Discipline of Ideas," 69). For Babbitt the task of preservation and that of critical analysis are one and the same.

In the essays that make up "The Responsibilities of Peoples" Dwight Macdonald insisted that the only meaningful moral criticism of whole peoples begins at home—must be, on some level, self-criticism. Macdonald's arguments are aimed at the policies of the conquering Allies, but in other essays in *Memoirs of a Revolutionist* he points out that it is not only conquerors who avoid self-criticism. A former Trotskyite himself, Macdonald quotes the leader of the American Trotskyist party, James Cannon, assuring his followers in 1944 that "when the history of his epoch is written . . . they'll discover that the only really moral people were the Trotskyists" ("Trotskyism I," 274). Some Trotskyists, however, turn out to be immoral—those, like James Farrell, who dare to raise questions about the tactics or strategy of the party's leaders. According to Cannon, criticism of the party from within "is at bottom an expression of the capitulatory skepticism of the petty bourgeois" ("Trotskyism II," 276). Not even Macdonald's own political agreements and personal sympathy with the Trotskyists, not even his belief that they are "victims of a monstrous frameup by the Roosevelt administration" (274) prevents him from pointing out how easy it is for victims to share the arrogance of the powerful.

In Macdonald's later writings his notion of self-criticism loses some of its point, since he seemed to distinguish himself and his audience from the masses who consume popular culture. In a number of respects, however, even in *Against the American Grain*, Macdonald remains faithful to the spirit of his original perspective. Like Mencken, Macdonald occasionally insinuates that his taste or his intelligence is better than the next person's, but he makes no attempt to assert or even insinuate moral superiority to others. Those who know *Against the American Grain* only by its title might suppose that the book is one of those indictments against a whole people that Macdonald opposed during World War II—only this time on cultural rather than moral grounds. That would be a mistake. Macdonald's target is not folk culture and not even mass culture; instead he zeroes in on "midcult" because "it pretends to respect the standards of High Culture while in fact it waters them down and vulgarizes them" (37). When, for example, James Gould Cozzens's *By Love Possessed* inspires a reviewer to demand, "Hemingway and Faulkner, move over!" (191), Macdonald moves in. Macdonald's special targets are "the products of lapsed avant-gardists who know how to use the modern idiom in the service of the banal" (51). The modernist masterpieces were produced by an avant-garde whose claims to cultural superiority were backed up by their work. The appeal of Midcult stems from its ability to confer the same sense of cultural superiority without going through the puzzlement and difficulty that inevitably attends working through the masterpieces whose techniques are appropriated. Macdonald's criticism is a criticism from within, in the sense that his standards are the pretensions of the midcult writers themselves, the standards set by the works of the great modernists.

In the 1940s Diana Trilling's ability to make "double judgments" allowed her to oppose Nazism and still judge anti-Nazi novels on their literary merits. In the 1950s she could question the mystique of Allen Ginsberg while pointing to the Beats' similarites to "the intellectuals who most overtly scorn them " ("The Other Night at Columbia: A Report" 163), pausing even to wonder about "the troubling contrast" between the emotions of pity and terror aroused by the Beats' poetry reading and the "orderly scene" of her own "comfortable living room," with its atmosphere of "disciplined achievement and well-earned reward" (172–73). In the 1960s her study of the Columbia student rebellion raised questions not only about the motivations of the students but also about those, like herself, who are moved by the "revolutionary content" of modernist literature but shocked when "the moral substance of contemporary art" is "translated into actuality" ("On the Steps of Low Library," 93–94). Diana

Trilling does not deprive either Beats or protestors of their common humanity; the criticisms she offers are indeed penetrating, and one can understand why those who identify with Beats and protestors might be outraged by her essays. Yet a careful reading reveals how closely she links her critiques of her ostensible subjects with a criticism of her own milieu and its political and cultural assumptions.

In the introduction and throughout its first half, *Patriotic Gore* is a debunking indictment of the notion, so flattering to the national pride, that the Civil War through blood sacrifice proved America's commitment to freedom for all. Wilson goes so far as to suggest that "the cause of the South is the cause of us all." In the second half, however, the myth of the Confederacy is subjected to a debunking of its own. The hero of the conclusion, Oliver Wendell Holmes Jr., appears as a champion of republican virtue. The reductive Darwinism of the introduction is undercut by the work's tracing of the complexity and diversity of individual motives and actions, but the national political traditions are never rehabilitated in any very significant way. Thus, Wilson discusses the Gettysburg Address merely as an example of "lucidity, precision, terseness" (649) while ignoring its ideas altogether. The closing portrait of Oliver Wendell Holmes Jr. is weighted by the implicit parallels to the life of Wilson's own father, who, like Holmes, had somehow "got through with honor that period from 1880 to 1920!" ("The Author at Sixty," 235), and to Wilson himself, who recognizes in Holmes a fellow citizen of "the great world of thought and art" (781) who was able to believe what Wilson has come to doubt but cannot entirely reject: "that the United States had a special meaning and mission to devote one's whole life to which was a sufficient dedication for the highest gifts" (796). There is much to question about *Patriotic Gore*, much in American history that Wilson either leaves out or ignores, but such valid criticisms should also take into account the extent to which the work constitutes a self-criticism of Wilson's earlier dream of a world ruled by intellectuals. As one reads and rereads *Patriotic Gore*, one's sense of American culture and American identity is not diminished but enriched—chastened, indeed, like the prose style of the postwar North—but enriched and deepened by Wilson's portrayal of the vicissitudes induced by the Civil War and its aftermath.

Ralph Ellison's literary and cultural criticism proceeds from the insight formulated by the protagonist of *Invisible Man* in the epilogue as he confronts the mysterious deathbed advice of his grandfather:

Could he have meant—hell, he *must* have meant the principle, that we were to affirm the principle on which the country was built and not the men, or at least not the men who did the violence. Did he mean say "yes" because he knew that the principle was greater than the men, greater than the numbers and the vicious power and all the methods used to corrupt its name? Did he mean to affirm the principle, which they themselves had dreamed into being out of the chaos and darkness of the feudal past, and which they had violated and compromised to the point of absurdity even in their own corrupt minds? Or did he mean that we had to take the responsibility for all of it, for the men as well as the principle, because we were the heirs who must sue the principle because no other fitted our needs? Not for the power or for vindication, but because we, with the given circumstance of our origin, could only thus find transcendence? (561)

Throughout his two collections of essays, *Shadow and Act* and *Going to the Territory*, Ellison takes "the sacred democratic belief that all men are created equal" ("Twentieth-Century Fiction," 28) as his starting point. He is ready to recognize, with the antifoundationalists, that these transcendent principles "are really man-made, legal fictions," but he immediately adds, "That doesn't stop them from being precious; that doesn't stop them from being sacred" ("Perspective of Literature," 328). Ellison's criticism of American society is thus an immanent criticism; he notes the variety of ways in which Americans have failed to live up to ideals that almost all are willing to recognize as sacred. In this Ellison is one with Frederick Douglass, Martin Luther King Jr. and the James Baldwin of *Notes of a Native Son* and *Nobody Knows My Name* and in opposition to those who would condemn not only violations of the principles but also the principles themselves.

Self-criticism, even cultural self-criticism, is not easy. To criticize or correct oneself, to recognize the possibility that one might be wrong, are not procedures that seem to flow naturally from simple impulse. To raise questions about the views of those around us—for an academic, say, to consider the illusions particularly tempting to academics—is an activity more likely to lose friends than win them. If this study emphasizes the flaws of contemporary cultural studies and the virtues of an older tradition, that is because the academic reputation of the contemporary work seems inflated, while critics in the latter group are unjustly neglected. These distortions result in large part from the intensity of the campus culture wars. In academic cultural studies, to be "Left" affords one the presumption of innocence, while to admit that as a tenured professor one is a middle-class American is to make a startling confession of complicity with evil. It seems doubtful that the cultural self-criticism of which academics are most in need is to be found in the new programs in cultural studies, which tend to systematize and confirm the practitioners' sense of themselves as a beleaguered moral elite surrounded by masses of sexists, racists, and logocentrists.

The larger society, however, might benefit from the new cultural studies, whether its practitioners retained their politics or not, if they would forgo their characteristic wholesale denunciations of entire epochs and traditions, the corresponding affirmations of innocence for a few, and the jargon intelligible only to an in-group. If such renunciations were joined to a willingness to learn from history, the new cultural studies would begin to look a lot like the old—which would be an advantage for both academia and the country. This book praises the older tradition not only because it deserves praise, though that is true enough, but in the hope that a renewed awareness of the possibilities of cultural self-criticism might encourage partisans of both the Left and Right to raise questions about their own "side" without necessarily changing sides. There will always be sides in culture as well as politics, but we would all benefit from an attempt to replace cultural warfare with debate, including debate with ourselves.

Chapter 15

Conclusion:
Cultural Conservatism,
Political Liberalism,
and the Ideal of Diversity

The notion that the individual has rights simply because he or she is a human being is the core notion of political liberalism. The principle of "human rights" has spread across the world, and the ideal of democracy is, if anything, accepted even more widely. The political ideas associated with liberal democracy have no contemporary rivals. Monarchy, fascism, Communism, and theocracy (the strongest competitor) have, at most, only limited appeal in local situations. Francis Fukuyama may be wrong that we have reached "the end of history," but the more mundane point that at present the ideal of liberal democracy, the notion of human rights, provides the basis for worldwide political legitimacy seems undeniable. The Charter of the United Nations may be honored more in the breach than the observance, but the consensus on behalf of human rights that it symbolizes is not matched by any comparable agreement on any other set of principles.

One reason that we have not arrived at the end of history is that the triumph of political liberalism has not been matched by any similar consensus about morality, culture, or religion. Catholic and Protestant, Jew and Muslim, secularist and fundamentalist, argue and sometimes fight. Nationalisms and tribalisms dispute and often war with one another in Europe, Africa, Asia, and South America. In North America, Canada is riven by language-driven conflict, while in the United States the era of "culture wars" has been under way for some time.

Academic "cultural studies" responds to contemporary ideological divisions in two ways. On the one hand, cultural studies presents itself as an advance on the traditional humanities because it knows the values the older tradition

231

accepted as authoritative are based finally on nothing more than brute power. Since cultural studies recognizes the "contingency" of all points of view, traditional attempts to "privilege" some literary works as "masterpieces" are rejected, as are attempts to enshrine the validity of some particular set of moral or political values. On the other hand, cultural studies is also driven by a commitment to radical cultural and political change. These two stances would seem to contradict each other, but many proponents of cultural studies embrace both.

Douglas Kellner's essay "Toward a Multiperspectival Cultural Studies" provides a representative example of this contradictory stance. Kellner argues that cultural studies preserves a severe neutrality that "allows us to examine and critically scrutinize the whole range of culture without a priori prejudices toward one or another sort of cultural text" (7). No taboos are to be allowed, no dogmas unquestioned, and no theory or approach is to be ruled out in advance. Cultural studies, he asserts, differs from traditional disciplines because it refuses to "privilege certain cultural forms and approaches to culture while excluding others" (10). Kellner favors an openness to diverse approaches, a combining of "Marxist, feminist, structuralist, post-structuralist, postmodernist, reception theory, psychoanalytic" (13) approaches, among others. He points out that the "polysemic" nature of "cultural texts" is now "generally accepted" (12). Such texts require "multivalent 'readings" as well as readers with a "multiplicity of subject positions" (12). Only cultural studies, with its "superdisciplinary approach" (5), is equal to the challenge of today's postmodern, multicultural world. Traditional humanist approaches that privilege some values and exclude others reveal their limitations when compared to "multiperspectival" cultural studies.

If Kellner is sure that cultural studies represents intellectual progress because it avoids the certainties of older views, he is equally convinced that its virtue resides in its radical political agenda. For Kellner the most important thing to know about anything is whether it is "progressive" or "reactionary." But is it progressive? The willingness to place this question at the center of one's scholarly agenda is for Kellner the essence of cultural studies:

> The key criterion for distinguishing the difference between the cultural studies approach and other approaches to culture lies in the political commitments of cultural studies and the integration of study of culture with progressive politics. (22)

In examining a popular film such as Bruce Willis's *Die Hard*, the key issue for Kellner is whether the audience's pleasure was "progressive or reactionary, emancipatory or destructive" (18). He worries about the "ways that pleasure can bind individuals to conservative, sexist, or racist positions" (19). Because audiences insist on enjoying the wrong things, or perhaps enjoying the right things for the wrong reasons, cultural studies scholars have to work hard "to distinguish critical and oppositional from conformist and conservative moments in a cultural text" (7). In dealing with such complexity, Kellner at least has the security of knowing that to be conservative is always to be conformist, sexist and racist, while to be progressive is always to be "critical and oppositional."

Cultural studies is not alone in attempting to embrace both skepticism and certainty. One way to avoid the necessity of choosing between these alternatives is to find an umbrella that seems to cover both. But what concept could signal both an awareness of postmodernist skepticism and a commitment to social betterment? Throughout cultural studies and in the official rhetoric of many universities the one idea that alone seems invulnerable to criticism is the notion of diversity as an ultimate value. Certainly, much of the popularity of diversity as a "god-word" derives from its rhetorical usefulness. The term is ideal for administrators, because it seems to offer something for everybody and take away nothing. The essence of the seductive appeal of diversity as an ideal in itself is the implicit suggestion that choices do not have to be made. It is possible, after all, to have one's cake and eat it too.

Richard Rorty, here as elsewhere in close touch with the zeitgeist, celebrates contemporary society because it is "more sensitive to the desirability of diversity, than any other of which we have record" ("Heidegger, Kundera, and Dickens," 81). The opposition to diversity, in Rorty's representative account, derives ultimately from religious sources. Religion encourages believers to think that they themselves have discovered absolute truth while those outside the communion live in error. Rorty believes so strongly in diversity that, as noted in chapter 1, he is eager to see religion "eradicated" so thoroughly that religious intuitions would simply disappear (intro., *Consequences of Pragmatism*, xxxvii); then religion would no longer have to be debated, since people would simply "*stop having* such intuitions" (xxx). Rorty thus contemplates, without apparent qualms, a cultural "cleansing" more absolute than anything yet attempted, even in totalitarian states, in order to make the world safe for diversity.

It is far from clear that such a cleansing would result in more diversity. Indeed, in the interests of the very goals of social justice on behalf of which the notion of diversity has been called to perform its powerful rhetorical service, it might be well not to allow religious thought to be eradicated from cultural memory. The implications of the notion of diversity as an ideal may be better understood through a consideration of the philosophical and theological assumptions associated with the conception of diversity as an end in itself. For it is not only in the late twentieth century that diversity has been affirmed as an ultimate ideal. Arthur O. Lovejoy, in his great classic of intellectual history, *The Great Chain of Being*, demonstrates that the history of diversity as an ideal—or, as he calls it, the "principle of plenitude,"—has been intertwined from the beginning with the history of what others have since called Western "logocentrism."

Today diversity is usually employed as a device for combating racism. The notion of diversity is indeed a powerful rhetorical tool, but it is also a treacherous one for those seeking justice and racial equality.[1] Racism is an evil, and the ability to recognize the equal dignity of individuals of diverse races and colors is a gain not only for justice but also for culture. A study of the history of diversity suggests, however, that it is a dangerous mistake to frame the discussion so that the affirmation of racial equality is made to depend on the acceptance of diversity as a controlling value. Far better to defend justice and equality on the liberal principle of equal rights, a notion whose legitimacy is accepted throughout the world. Lovejoy's narrative reveals that the logical consequences of accepting diversity as a supreme ideal include the acceptance and even the glorification of suffering, injustice, and hierarchy as necessary means to the "maximization of diversity" (182).

Lovejoy traces the history of diversity as an ideal as far back as the *Timaeus*, a dialogue in which Plato envisions a "Demiurge" who creates the visible universe. In Lovejoy's words, "Plato's Demiurge acted literally upon the principle in which common speech is wont to express the temper not only of universal tolerance but of comprehensive approbation of diversity—that it takes all kinds to make a world" (51). Plato's notion of the Idea of the Good turns out to contain within itself what Lovejoy calls the principle of plenitude, which he defines as

> the assumption that no genuine potentiality of being can remain unfulfilled, that the extent and abundance of the creation must be as great as the possibility of existence and commensurate with the productive capacity of a "perfect" and inexhaustible source, and that the world is the better, the more things it contains. (52)

The Great Chain of Being traces the fateful linking of two seemingly opposed conceptions—the ideal of pure goodness and the ideal of infinite diversity—through Western philosophy and religion. A justification of God based on diversity as an ideal in itself does not need to attempt to minimize suffering and injustice but can actually affirm their necessity for the sake of a higher good. Lovejoy notes that the indiscreet Peter Abelard only articulated more explicitly what was already hinted in conventional theology when he wrote,

> For as a picture is often more beautiful and worthy of commendation if some colors in themselves ugly are included in it, than it would be if it were uniform and of a single color, so from an admixture of evils the universe is rendered more beautiful and worthy of commendation. (72)

As Lovejoy puts it, "The goodness of this best of possible worlds consists, not in the absence of evils, but rather in their presence—consists, that is, in the actualization of what Abelard calls the *rationabilis varietas* which requires them" (72). The Leibnizian notion that ours is "the best of all possible worlds," ridiculed so devastatingly in Voltaire's *Candide*, depends on the premise that the greatest good is not to be found in human happiness or even in holiness but, instead, in "the maximization of diversity."

Although the Great Chain of Being may seem an antiquated notion, its consequences, including the notion of diversity as an ideal in itself, are still with us. Lovejoy argues that the novel conception that distinguishes the nineteenth and twentieth centuries from their predecessors is "the substitution of what may be called diversitarianism for uniformitarianism as the ruling preconception in most of the normative provinces of thought" (294). Those who regard the celebration of diversity as the most up-to-date affirmation of enlightened multiculturalism would do well to study Lovejoy's history. The conception of diversity, Lovejoy demonstrates, has been used repeatedly as an explanation and justification for suffering, injustice, and even war. Often, as in the earlier passage from Abelard, the notion of diversity allows one to transmute moral difficulties into aesthetic advantages. Many adherents of "the God of Things as They Are" (222) have found it convenient to imagine

> the Cosmic Artist as cramming his canvas with diversified detail to the last infinitesimal fraction of an inch; as caring far more for fullness and variety of content than for simplicity and perfection of form; and as seeking this richness of coloring and abundance of contrast even at the cost of disharmony, irregularity, and what to us appears confusion. (296–97)

Thomas Mann's articulate conman, Felix Krull, delighted the king of Portugal when he explained the social implications that result when one considers diversity from an aesthetic point of view:

By his very existence the beggar, huddled in rags, makes as great a contribution to the colourful picture of the world as the proud gentleman who
drops alms in his humbly outstretched hand, carefully avoiding, of course,
any contact with it. And, Your Majesty, the beggar knows it . . . It takes
the instigation to rebellion by men of ill will to make him discontented
with his picturesque role and to put in his head the contumacious notion
that men must be equal. (*Confessions of Felix Krull* 329)

The Great Chain of Being, despite its exploration of the ways in which
diversity, or the principle of plenitude, has been used as a justification of the
world as it is, does not leave one with the impression that the conception should
simply be "eradicated." Instead, Lovejoy concludes,

The discovery of the intrinsic worth of diversity was, in both of its aspects,
and with all of the perils latent in it, one of the great discoveries of the
human mind; and the fact that it, like so many other of his discoveries, has
been turned by man to ruinous uses, is no evidence that it is in itself without value. (313)

At the same time, Lovejoy makes clear that the attempt to use diversity as a governing principle in politics, culture, or education is finally impossible, since "to
say 'Yes' to everything and everybody is manifestly to have no character at all"
(312). Lovejoy's own characterization of the dilemmas facing us between the
absolutes of diversity and uniformity is eloquent:

The delicate and difficult art of life is to find, in each new turn of experience, the *via media* between two extremes: to be catholic *without* being
characterless; to have and apply standards, and yet to be on guard against
their desensitizing and stupefying influence, their tendency to blind us to
the diversities of concrete situations and to previously unrecognized values; to know when to tolerate, when to embrace, and when to fight. And
in that art, since no fixed and comprehensive rule can be laid down for it,
we shall doubtless never attain perfection. (312)

The ideal of diversity, like the opposing ideal of utopian equality, will
always retain its appeal, because it seems to relieve us of the necessity of making
consequential choices. So far, however, no formula or methodology has been
found that can liberate human beings from the obligations of their humanity.
Even if, for example, one takes the Ten Commandments to be binding, one

must still decide every day what "Honor thy father and thy mother . . . " (Exod. 20:12, KJV) means in practice. (Prohibitions are clearer but still require decisions. There is comparatively little dispute, if not unanimity, about what "Thou shalt not commit adultery" means [20:14]; on the other hand, exactly what is excluded by the command "Thou shalt not kill" continues to be widely debated [20:13].) Secular formulas, such as the Kantian "treat every individual as an end rather than a means," likewise provide no direct answers for the dilemmas of everyday life.

The importance of cultural criticism becomes clear when one recognizes that no absolutes, whether religious or secular, can absolve individuals or societies from the responsibility of making choices. Literary critics cannot provide specifics where religion and philosophy offer only monumental generalities, but they can make available the insights literature provides about the moral and political dilemmas individuals and societies inevitably must confront. The political opinions of the cultural critics in the older tradition differ widely. H. L. Mencken was contemptuous of democracy but adamant about personal freedom, especially freedom of speech. Irving Babbitt affirmed a "unionist tradition" of "constitutional democracy" in opposition to Jeffersonian liberalism. Dwight Macdonald moved from Trotskyism to radical pacifism to support for the cold war to an affirmation of student radicalism in the 1960s. Lionel Trilling criticized "the liberal imagination" but did not question the validity of political liberalism. Ralph Ellison called for the realization in practice of American ideals of democracy and equality. Edmund Wilson's 1930s enthusiasm for Communism gave way to a bitter distrust of all centralized authority. Diana Trilling continues to affirm a liberalism without qualifiers.

Despite the variety of their political opinions, these critics share a common opposition to the contemporary notion, so popular in cultural studies, of the supremacy of politics over culture. Instead, their critical works demonstrate the ways in which political categories can be leavened and qualified by literature. Despite their differences in political opinions, then, the cultural criticism of all shares a common affinity for a liberal polity. Culture has been subordinated to politics not only in the academic enterprise of cultural studies but also in ideal societies such as Plato's Republic and in the totalitarian states of the twentieth century. The literary-cultural criticism of these critics flourished in liberal democracy, though they often sharply criticized that democracy. No similar criticism was allowed to develop in Soviet Russia, in Nazi Germany, in Maoist China, or in any of the smaller outposts of totalitarianism.

Cultural criticism attempts to clarify the issues raised in public debate, but it also mediates between literature and the individual reader. Although this book has been devoted to U.S. cultural criticism, Gary Saul Morson's exposition of the Russian thinker Mikhail Bakhtin is relevant at this point. Morson's commentary underlines the difference between viewing literature as a source of precepts and literature as a vehicle of insight. Morson points out that Bakhtin, often presented as a Marxist contributor to cultural studies, in fact spent his life opposing the "theoretism" he discerned in both Saussurean linguistics and in Marxism. Morson emphasizes Bakhtin's insistence that "ethical choice is truly *momentous*" (207), that is to say, cannot be resolved by a predetermined formula. For Bakhtin and for Morson one of the great virtues of literature, and especially of the novel, is its capacity to convey the "momentousness" of human choices:

> In *Anna Karenina*, when Levin is challenged to say whether he would use violence to prevent a Turkish soldier from killing a Bulgarian baby, he replies that he does not know, that he would have to decide *at that very moment* on the basis of criteria he cannot enumerate in advance. His half-brother, a prominent intellectual, can only laugh at Levin's inability to state his principles, but for Tolstoy this sensitivity to real people and real particulars is the key to moral choice. In the hypothetical situation Levin is asked to face, the unforeseeable particularities are too important and the consequences of a wrong decision too terrible for him to abdicate choice to a set of abstract and easily describable rules. Or as Bakhtin stated this point: "There is no alibi for being." Theoretism cannot in any real sense appreciate the "non-alibi." ("Bakhtin and the Present Moment," 207)

Like Richard Rorty, Bakhtin believed that novels can provide insights denied to philosophy, but, unlike Rorty, he found in literature an affirmation of the supreme importance of moral choice:

> Bakhtin came to regard the novel as the highest art form—indeed, as the height of Western thought, more profound than abstract philosophy. . . . In novels we see moral decisions made moment by moment by inexhaustibly complex characters in unrepeatable social situations at particular historical times; and we see that the value of these decisions cannot be abstracted from these specifics. ("Prosaics," 526)

Lovejoy and Bakhtin are in agreement about the absence of any formulas to provide fixed rules for conduct, but neither shares the postmodernist skepticism that deprives ethical choices of all significance. The notion that the good life for human beings requires not innocence but, rather, prudent judgment, or practical wisdom, goes back at least to Aristotle. Wisdom is the fruit of personal experience but also may be enriched and extended through the absorption of the general human experience embodied in literature, philosophy, and religion. The humanist tradition in literary criticism—whose exemplars in the United States have included Lionel Trilling, H. L. Mencken, Irving Babbitt, Dwight Macdonald, Edmund Wilson, Diana Trilling, and Ralph Ellison—will continue as long as some at least believe that literature can aid human beings in what Lovejoy calls "the difficult art of life." Critics who make that aid available will demonstrate the assistance that cultural conservatism can offer to a society committed to political liberalism. For those who feel no need for such assistance there is always cultural studies.

Notes

Introduction

1. Leszek Kolakowski suggests that the history of ideas is always "to some extent an exercise in cultural self-criticism" (4). Kolakowski's use of the concept and its relevance to the present investigation is explored in chap. 14.

2. Trilling's selection of Hume's essay as a "charter" may seem arbitrary, given the amount of speculation and research since Hume on such questions, but his interpretation of the essay itself seems straightforward enough. Here are some quotations bearing on the points important for Trilling:

> The distinguishing between chance and causes must depend upon every particular man's sagacity, in considering every particular incident. But, if I were to assign any general rule to help us in applying this distinction, it would be the following, *What depends upon a few persons is, in a great measure, to be ascribed to chance, or secret and unknown cases: what arises from a great number, may often be accounted for by determinate and known causes.* (63)

> Those principles or causes, which are fitted to operate on a multitude, are always of a grosser and more stubborn nature, less subject to accidents, less influenced by whim and private fancy, than those which operate on a few only. (64)

> Though the persons, who cultivate the sciences with such astonishing success, as to attract the admiration of posterity, be always few, in all nations and all ages; it is impossible but a share of the same spirit and genius must be antecedently diffused through the people among whom they arise, in order to produce, form, and cultivate, from their earliest infancy, the taste and judgment of those eminent writers. The mass cannot be altogether insipid, from which such refined spirits are extracted. . . . The question, therefore, concerning the rise and progress of the arts and sciences is not altogether a question concerning the taste, genius, and spirit of a few, but concerning those of a whole people; and may, therefore, be accounted for, in some measure, by general causes and principles. (65)

Chapter 2

 1. One may agree with Trilling and Orwell in their view of intellectual life and still find serious flaws in Homage to Catalonia and in Trilling's interpretation of that book in "George Orwell and the Politics of Truth." For a critique of both Trilling's interpretation of *Homage to Catalonia* and Orwell's book itself, see my essay "Trilling's *Homage to Catalonia*."

Chapter 3

 1. The publication in 1990 of *The Diary of H. L. Mencken* raised again the question of Mencken's feelings toward blacks and Jews. (The "diary controversy" is reviewed by Fred Hobson in his 1994 biography of Mencken [544–46] and by Joseph Epstein in "Mencken on Trial" [222–25].) The editor of the diary, Charles A. Fecher, concluded that Mencken's attitude toward Jews deserves to be classified as anti-Semitic: "Let it be said at once, clearly and unequivocally: Mencken was an anti-Semite" (xix). After noting several examples of Mencken's regard for individual African Americans, Fecher also asserted that Mencken had an ineradicable prejudice against blacks:

> But neither the achievements of the black people he respected, nor his care for those he thought of as being in some sense his responsibility, could erase a deeply ingrained conviction that black people were by their very nature inferior to white. (xix)

Fecher proposed that Mencken's racism and anti-Semitism simply be recognized as an uncomfortable reality and then considered no further, as though any further discussion would amount to a defense of racism or anti-Semitism:

> When all is said and done, there probably is no defense. One cannot ask that he be forgiven, or even excused. About all one can do is ask the reader simply to accept the fact and pass on. (xxi)

A reader interested only in Mencken as a private person may find it possible "simply to accept the fact and pass on," but it is surely impossible for anyone interested in Mencken's cultural criticism to take the same attitude. As for Mencken the private individual, Fred Hobson's judgment that Mencken "could not completely escape the prejudices of his youth" (168), though he often transcended them in his writing and in his personal life, seems fair enough. Mencken had a good deal of evidence on his side, Hobson notes, in "consider[ing] himself, in his personal relations as well as his professional conduct, anything but anti-Semitic" (407). Hobson's study of Mencken's diary leads him to affirm "Mencken's essential respect for black Americans." Hobson notes, "Never in his discussion of individuals or of racial relations in Baltimore did he [Mencken] apply to blacks the kind of invective he heaped on poor whites" (456).

The key question, however, is not Mencken as an individual but, rather, Mencken as a writer. Hobson's characterization of Mencken's style does much to explain the diversity of opinion about Mencken's real ideas:

Rhetorically, at least, he lived life more dramatically than most other mortals, attempted more, risked more, said more, and said it more colorfully on a wider range of subjects than perhaps any other writer of his generation. The result, depending on what he came out with at any given time, was that he appeared to be both the best friend and the worst enemy of Jews, blacks, and numerous other segments of the population. (412)

Hobson's evocation provides an effective counter to Garry Wills's contribution to the controversy in a *New Republic* review of the diary. Arguing that Mencken "is best remembered now for his role at the evolution trial in Dayton in 1925" (34), Wills makes no attempt to consider Mencken as a writer. Since Mencken's bald opinions often seem mere vituperation outside the literary context of his essays, Wills has no difficulty assembling evidence that seems to justify branding Mencken "The Ugly American," the title of his review.

If style cannot be ignored, however, neither can style alone be made to answer the charges of racism and anti-Semitism. As Joseph Epstein points out, such accusations, if substantiated, affect our judgment of the work of a critic even more than our evaluations of a novelist or poet, e.g. T. S. Eliot:

But for a writer like Mencken, whose work deals directly in assertion and strong opinion, filled with craft but without the mediation of art, the charge of anti-Semitism or any other genuinely vicious prejudice constitutes a devastating blow against him. Those of a major poet's works that are not directly marred by anti-Semitism remain beautiful. But all of Mencken's views are suddenly in deepest doubt. (230–31)

A key consideration for Epstein is a striking omission in the World War II diary of any putative American anti-Semite. There are no entries railing about the Jews for bringing about World War II or for engineering United States involvement in the war:

Though greatly opposed to the conduct of World War II, and though detesting Franklin Delano Roosevelt, not once does Mencken blame American entry into the war on the Jews or Jewish pressure groups or on Jewish dealings *sub rosa*. For any sort of earnest anti-Semite . . . one would think the temptation to accuse the Jews would have been irresistible. Mencken resists . . . completely. (244)

Quoting from Mencken's last column for the *Baltimore Sun* before his World War II moratorium, a column urging aid to Jewish refugees from Hitler, Epstein suggests that "the following passages ought to be kept in mind alongside the charges of anti-Semitism against their author":

Either we are willing to give refuge to the German Jews, or we are not willing. If the former, then here is one vote for bringing them in by the first available ships, and staking them sufficiently to set them on their feet. That is the only way we can really help them, and that is the only way we can avoid going down into history as hypocrites almost as grotesque as the English.

The initiative should be taken by the so-called Christians who are now so free with weasel words of comfort and flattery, and so curiously stingy with practical aid. In particular, it should be taken by the political mountebanks who fill the air with hollow denunciations of Hitler, and yet never lift a hand to help an actual Jew. (231)

Epstein's verdict is that Mencken was not an anti-Semite. He is careful to state his opposing conclusion as clearly as Fecher:

To reverse Charles A. Fecher, let it be said at once, clearly and unequivocally: Mencken may have been tactless, he may have been foolhardy enough to think that a man could write what he pleased in his private diary, he may have been singularly unprescient in failing to realize that what he wrote sixty years ago would be read by an age as happy in its virtue and self-righteousness as our own. But H. L. Mencken was no anti-Semite, no enemy of the Jews. (245)

In considering the significance of Mencken's alleged racism for his cultural criticism, the testimony of Richard Wright and Ralph Ellison, among others, should be considered. Reviewing *The Diary of H. L. Mencken*, John Kenneth Galbraith remembered the impact of Mencken's published writings on his own generation:

What those of us who did read him long ago remember was his wonderfully explosive, some have said liberating, attack on an otherwise conventional, even stuffy world. . . . What he said about Roosevelt released us to say what we wanted to say about Herbert Hoover—and William Randolph Hearst. (41)

The classic example of Galbraith's point about the liberating impact of Mencken's writing on beginning writers is a passage in Richard Wright's *Black Boy*. Forbidden by law to check out books from the Memphis public library, Wright used a white person's card to check out some books by Mencken, whose name had drawn Wright's attention because of a recent attack on Mencken in an editorial in a Memphis newspaper. The following passage describes the impact of Mencken on the young Wright:

I was jarred and shocked by the style, the clear, clean, sweeping sentences. Why did he write like that? And how did one write like that? I pictured the man as a raging demon, slashing with his pen, consumed with hate, denouncing everything American, extolling everything European or German, laughing at the weaknesses of people, mocking God, authority. . . . Yes, this man was fighting, fighting with words. He was using words as a weapon, using them as one would use a club. Could words be weapons? Well, yes, for there they were. Then, maybe, perhaps, I could use them as a weapon? No. It frightened me. I read on and what amazed me was not what he said, but how on earth anybody had the courage to say it. (237)

I concluded the book with the conviction that I had somehow overlooked something terribly important in life. I had once tried to write, had once reveled in feeling, had let my crude imagination roam, but the impulse to dream had been slowly beaten out of me by experience. Now it surged up again and I hungered for books, new ways of looking and seeing. It was not a matter of believing or disbelieving what I read, but of feeling something new, of being affected by something that made the look of the world different. (237–38)

A letter to the *New York Review of Books* summed up the significance of the "diary controversy" persuasively:

> We wish to express our dismay at the overreaction to the *Diary* of H. L. Mencken. The *Diary* does indeed contain discourteous remarks about Jews and blacks. It also contains discourteous remarks about most races, nations and professions; in fact, Mencken's harshest words are directed at " 'the only pure Anglo-Saxons left in the United States' . . . a wretchedly dirty, shiftless, stupid and rascally people." Discourtesy was Mencken's style, as it was to a considerable degree the intellectual style of the 1920s. His hyperbole did not foreclose warm friendships with Jewish publishers, writers and doctors; no white editor of the day did more to seek out and encourage black writers; no editor did more to fight for freedom of expression for all Americans.
>
> Whatever Mencken's "prejudices"—the word he himself used to describe his essays—he was a tremendous liberating force in American culture, and should be so celebrated and remembered. (53)

The letter was signed by Louis Auchincloss, Ralph Ellison, John Kenneth Galbraith, John Hersey, Norman Mailer, Arthur Miller, Arthur Schlesinger Jr., William Styron, and Kurt Vonnegut.

2. The information about Babbitt's background is derived from the opening chapter of *Irving Babbitt* by Stephen C. Brennan and Stephen R. Yarbrough.

3. The phrase is excerpted from Russell Maloney's comment in the *New Yorker* about Babbitt's insistence on continuing to teach and work despite the effects of ulcerative colitis: "My family doctor tells me that for a man to continue his work during its last stage is 'definitely heroic'"(26). The passage from the *New Yorker* is quoted in John Yunck's wise essay, "Natural History of a Dead Quarrel: Hemingway and the Humanists" (37). Irving Babbitt's words are taken from William F. Giese's "Memoir" of his teacher. Here is Giese's conclusion:

> When I saw him for the last time, only a few weeks before his death, we had hardly been together a quarter-hour before he was extolling, with serene detachment from present circumstance, the luminous qualities of an article on Marcel Proust. . . . And all around him on his bed lay the scattered blue-books and reports of his graduate students, which he made it a matter of professional honor to read, though he could do so only in broken snatches. To my remonstrances he characteristically replied: "When a man has been hired to do a job, it's only decent to stick to it to the end." (25)

From *Irving Babbitt* I have derived not only factual information but also the point about Babbitt's "decency" in the face of death. Here is the relevant passage from Brennan and Yarbrough, which follows the previous quotation:

He finally died a miserable, indecent death, mumbling incoherently in a bed soaked with sweat. But his words to Giese recall an often-quoted passage from *Rousseau and Romanticism*: "After all to be a good humanist is merely to be moderate and sensible and decent . . . " (xx–xxi). It's easy to take this as a stultifying middle-class ethic or, as Edmund Wilson puts it, "the unexamined prejudice of a Puritan heritage." It wasn't though. To be decent is to be fitting and appropriate, and Babbitt tried to make his last days fitting and appropriate to the form of his life. (26–27)

Chapter 4

1. Michael Wreszin's sympathetic biography *A Rebel in Defense of Tradition* (1994) offers another image, that of Dwight Macdonald as a "rebellious, anti-authoritarian, anti-administrative" idealist (xiii). For Wreszin, Macdonald's judgments were sometimes mistaken but always driven by the highest principles; "Dwight," as Wreszin refers to subject throughout the biography, was sometimes a "holy fool"(xvii) and in his later years "a colorful, eccentric curmudgeon" (483,) but he was always, right or wrong, the "rebel who resists and says no to the intolerable absurdities of life, and by doing so makes an affirmative statement" (xvi).

In "The Politics of Dissent," a review of Macdonald's life prompted by the biography, Gertrude Himmelfarb finds Wreszin's portrait accurate enough but takes issue with the biography's positive assessment of Macdonald's congenital rebelliousness. Her critique is impressive:

> Consider the "intolerable absurdities" that Macdonald resisted: the war against Nazism, which was not only the greater evil but one of the most monstrous evils of modern times; or the creation of the state of Israel in the aftermath of the Holocaust; or the middlebrow culture of America, while embracing the counterculture of the New Left. And consider the kind of "affirmative statement" or "values" that emerged from this indomitable spirit of resistance: that bourgeois society is as degrading and dehumanizing as Soviet totalitarianism; or that the millennia-old Jewish culture is as provincial as Scottish culture; or that anarchism is the only alternative to capitalist politics, indeed the only moral position of the true intellectual. (37)

In *The Beginning of the Journey* Diana Trilling recorded both her affection for Macdonald and an assessment of his political judgment, which parallels Gertrude Himmelfarb's:

> Nothing was easier than to be angry at Macdonald, whether in or out of print, but it was difficult to stay angry with him; he was too childlike, too seemingly innocent. Certainly he was innocent of the consequences of his ideas. It says as much of the intellectual culture of his time as it does of him that he was never either then or later called to account for the positions he advocated in his wonderfully clear brisk prose. This "child" invited us to the grimmest of destinies, now class war, now anarchy. (303)

(This agreement between Gertrude Himmelfarb and Diana Trilling suggests that the gap between their politics is not as wide as Trilling insists in *The Beginning of the Journey*. See chapter 5.)

The works discussed in this chapter were chosen as examples of Macdonald's most impressive cultural criticism; they contain few examples of the posturing that Gertrude Himmelfarb rightly questions. "The Responsibility of Peoples," for example, does not palliate the evils of Nazism but makes no attempt to strike an ultramoral pose. Macdonald's point, indeed, is that our judgment of the ordinary German under Nazism must be informed by a willingness to imagine how we ourselves would have behaved had we been tested by similar circumstances. Macdonald's cultural criticism suggests a persona more difficult to grasp than that of "the rebel who resists and says no"; Michael Wreszin notes perceptively that Macdonald, at his best, embraced contraries. Macdonald's "anarchical anti-authoritarianism" was balanced by "a strong conservative streak":

> He called himself a "conservative anarchist.". . . He stood for standards. . . . He longed for the order and civilized limits of an elite community with respect for the traditions of the past. . . . Besides being a cultural conservative and self-proclaimed elitist, Dwight was a practicing egalitarian. (xv)

It is this latter, more complicated Macdonald who finds expression in his best writing and who is celebrated in this chapter.

2. Macdonald distances himself from Ortega's supposed desire "to rebuild the old class walls and bring the masses once more under aristocratic control" (69). But Ortega himself insisted, just as Macdonald does, on the distinction between a cultural or spiritual elite and an elite based on social or political power. Ortega makes the distinction explicitly in the first chapter of *The Revolt of the Masses*:

> The division of society into masses and select minorities is, then, not a division into social classes, but into classes of men, and cannot coincide with the hierarchic separation of "upper" and "lower" classes (15).

Chapter 5

1. Elaine Showalter does not provide a source for the striking phrase she quotes from Adrienne Rich characterizing the writing of some women (Susan Sontag and Elizabeth Hardwick are Showalter's own examples) as coming "from somewhere outside their female bodies." The phrase apparently derives from a passage in the "Afterword" of Rich's *Of Woman Born: Motherhood as Experience and Institution*:

> But the fear and hatred of our bodies has often crippled our brains. Some of the most brilliant women of our time are still trying to think from somewhere outside their female bodies—hence they are still merely reproducing old forms of intellection. (284)

2. Henry Dan Piper prefaces a quotation of the same passage from "The Crack-Up" quoted in this essay with these comments:

The secret of his [Fitzgerald's] art, won only after the painful act of self-discovery, had been his skill in writing about himself with objective detachment. Following the example of Keats, his favorite poet, he had learned how to cultivate a negative capability toward himself and his experience—believing that (as he said at the beginning of "The Crack-Up"). . . . (236)

Chapter 6

1. The judgment that *Patriotic Gore* is Wilson's finest work is not unanimous among writers on Wilson, but it is shared by a number of critics. In *Edmund Wilson's America* George H. Douglas calls *Patriotic Gore* "Edmund Wilson's finest work . . . a perfect manifestation of his literary methods, a showcase for his highest talents" (147). Charles P. Frank calls *Patriotic Gore* "Wilson's most satisfactory book" (67) in his study *Edmund Wilson*. David Castronovo offers somewhat more guarded praise, describing *Patriotic Gore* as "Wilson's most significant expression of his ideas about American power . . . one of Wilson's most impressive enterprises" (127–28). In his 1978 autobiographical work *New York Jew*, Kazin reaffirms the verdict of his 1962 review, calling the book Wilson's "masterpiece on the Civil War" (67), "a great book . . . the greatest single performance of Wilson's unique career as a man of letters" (248). (Kazin's comments in *New York Jew* also appear in his essay on Wilson as "The Great Anachronism" in John Wain's memorial volume.)

Patriotic Gore has been criticized for its lack of unity, even by critics who praise the book on other counts. George Douglas, for example, concedes that "its diversity perhaps accounts for many of its real or imagined weaknesses" (150). Janet Groh, in the most recent book on Wilson, does not risk a comment on the book's unity, but her chapter on *Patriotic Gore* is limited to a discussion of the chapter on Harriet Beecher Stowe as an independent entity. In his monograph *Edmund Wilson* Warner Berthoff finds *Patriotic Gore* marked by a "pattern of emphasis and omission" that seems "irregular and somewhat arbitrary" (39). Harry T. Moore reveals that he and the other judges on the 1962 National Book Award committee ruled out *Patriotic Gore* for consideration "because it was rather shapeless, a hodge-podge of various articles, however interesting and brilliant each of them was in itself" (viii). In an essay included in his 1964 collection *Doings and Undoings* Norman Podhoretz was willing to give *Patriotic Gore* credit for being "intermittently interesting," but found that the book "rambles along at what can only be called a self-indulgent pace, following where Wilson's idle curiosities and momentary enthusiasms happen to lead" (54). In a sympathetic consideration of Wilson's career Larzer Ziff suggests that "*Patriotic Gore* is akin to an anthology" (51) and compares it to Wilson's 1943 collection, *The Shock of Recognition*. No critic, to my knowledge, has made an argument for the work's unity along the lines suggested in this chapter.

The idiosyncracies of *Patriotic Gore* severely limit the book's achievement for both Norman Podhoretz and Leonard Kriegel. For Podhoretz in 1962 the "isolation and pessimism" of *Patriotic Gore* provided evidence that "we shall have to look elsewhere for the kind of guidance that it was once his [Edmund Wilson's] particular glory to give" (58). Leonard Kriegel's critique in his study *Edmund Wilson* is severe. Kriegel attacks Wilson for failing to emphasize "the brutalizing inhumanity of Negro slavery" (113). Wilson's

decision to write about Charlotte Forten seems perverse to Kriegel, since she "is so strikingly unrepresentative of the slave experience" that her diary often "appears to be the
work of a Southern belle with a dark skin" (110). Shocked by Wilson's omission of Frederick Douglass and W. E. B. Du Bois and the inclusion of Thomas Nelson Page, Kriegel
temporarily loses his grip on spelling, grammar, and chronology:

> Most shocking of all, there is no mention of either Frederick Douglas [sic] or W. E.
> B. Du Bois [born in 1868], each of whom authored autobiographies which shall
> [sic] live in the literature of the Civil War long after Thomas Nelson Page has been
> justly relegated to the position of a mere footnote in the literary history of the
> United States. (109)

For Kriegel *Patriotic Gore* is the most telling example of a decline that began in 1940:

> For when one examines the work Wilson has done since the publication of *To the
> Finland Station* in 1940, one finds that he has been guilty of creating his world at the
> expense of our reality. His magnificent loyalty to a conception of self that embod-
> ied both integrity and excellence has been matched, unfortunatly [sic], by a shrink-
> ing sense of human involvement and by an apparent withering away of his own
> sympathies. (124)

Such protests bear out Sherman Paul's admission that *Patriotic Gore* is "unsatisfactory if
one turns to it for a systematic or balanced presentation of the history or literature of the
period" (203). As a work of cultural self-criticism, however, dramatizing Edmund Wilson's "personal encounter with history" (203), *Patriotic Gore* only grows in importance;
Sherman Paul's 1965 exposition of the book remains one of the few discussions that illuminates the sources of its strange authority.

Chapter 7

1. Jerry Gafio Watts's *Heroism and the Black Intellectual: Ralph Ellison, Politics, and
Afro-American Intellectual Life* (1994) appeared after "The Example of Ralph Ellison" was
written. Though this chapter and Watts's book share a common respect for Ralph Ellison's intellectual and literary achievement, the difference in approaches and conclusions
is substantial. The chapter's approach is grounded in literary criticism, the book's rationale in the social sciences; the chapter finds Ellison's perspective exemplary, while the
book's final verdict is that Ellison's point of view "is humanistically disturbing" (120).
   Watts begins by thanking Ellison "for giving me and my generation an intellectual
presence and a corpus of work worthy of serious engagement" (xii). Deploring the
"uncivil and ad hominem attacks" (30) Ellison endured, Watts notes with some irony
that Ellison has "had the rare honor of being attacked by black leftists and black nationalists" (126). Watts himself rejects dogmas sacred to both leftists and nationalists. Black
intellectuals who focus on injustice are vulnerable to what Watts calls "the victim status
syndrome" (19), an outlook that, paradoxically, leaves one "utterly dependent on recognition from whites" (20). Watts regards the orientation of black identity around victim-

hood as "among the most crippling and pervasive ideological constructs that blacks have had to face" (16). Black nationalists, on the other hand, too easily fall into "black parochialism; cathartic/therapeutic, ethnic cheerleading; and sectarianism" (8). *Heroism and the Black Intellectual* credits Ellison with at least avoiding these errors.

Watts not only criticizes those who have attacked Ellison most harshly, he also explicitly accepts some of Ellison's key ideas. Ellison's thesis that "black Americans were culturally part white, and white Americans were culturally part black" may displease both black nationalists and white supremacists, but Watts asserts its truth while warning that it is "difficult to defend politically" (13). Praising Ellison for calling "blacks to a commitment to artistic/intellectual excellence," Watts declares that one of the most important aspects of Ellison's achievement is the way Ellison's "intellectual style embodies and protects the fundamental freedom of the black artist and intellectual to be an artist/intellectual without apology" (114).

The overall impact of *Heroism and the Black Intellectual*, however, is much less sympathetic to Ellison than such comments would lead one to expect. Although Watts once praises Ellison's commitment to excellence, he repeatedly characterizes Ellison as an elitist. According to Watts, Ellison is both a "meritocratic elitist" (47) and a "liberal establishmentarian elitist" (49), while Ellison's point of view is "an elitist nationalist vision" (107) and an "elitism of heroic individualism" (119). Given this emphasis on Ellison's supposed elitism, it is no surprise that Ellison harbors "rather blatantly antidemocratic views" (48), and his "vision is highly antidemocratic" (105). In summary, Watts concludes regretfully that Ellison is "not fundamentally democratically minded" (110).

A reading of *Heroism and the Black Intellectual* suggests that Watts's real objections to Ellison have less to do with any supposed elitism than with Ellison's unwillingness to share Watts' own leftist politics. As Watts tells it, once Ellison rejected "socialism as a normative political vision" (46), he became "obsessed with the issue of individual freedom" (55) and fell right into "the quagmire of bourgeois liberty" (57). Even more damning, Ellison became an "American patriot" (47).

The assumptions of Watts's own "sociological approach" (14) emerge strikingly when he charges that Ellison's political truancy "led him into a cul de sac from which the utter viciousness of racism and capitalism could not be comprehensively analyzed and attacked" (57). Ellison, a mere creative writer, apparently failed to note the moral equivalency Watts proposes between capitalism, an economic system ordinarily viewed as having both good and bad effects (the proportion of good to bad being a subject of extensive debate), and racism, a prejudice ordinarily considered wrong in itself. But then Watts, in fairness to Ellison, has stipulated that not merely Ellison himself but "most ambitious fine artists are not fundamentally democratically minded" (110).

Watts's own animus becomes most obvious in his harsh comments about two passages that most readers would find uncontroversial. Celebrating the genius of Charlie Christian and evoking the world of his own boyhood, Ellison contrasts his own memories of the world in which he and Charlie Christian grew up with the categories of the sociologist:

> This was an alive community in which the harshness of slum life was inescapable but in which the strength, the imagination of the people, was much in evidence. And yet you would have to say that it was indeed lower class, and lower-lower

class, and according to the sociologists utterly hopeless. (qtd. in *Heroism,* 106 from "What These Children Are Like," 72)

Watts assumes Ellison is not only wrong but culpably, perversely wrong in opposing his own memories of the neighborhood where he and Charlie Christian grew up to what Ellison would consider sociological reductionism. Watts, however, does not argue that Ellison is mistaken in believing that sociologists would classify the neighborhood as "utterly hopeless"; instead, he seems to argue that any sociologist who so classified it would have been right. For Watts Ellison's dispute with imaginary sociologists provides evidence that Ralph Ellison "is rhetorically willing to silence the pain and desperateness of Charlie Christian and his poor neighbors simply because of Christian's musical genius" (106).

In "The World and the Jug" Ralph Ellison challenged Irving Howe's seeming attempt to arbitrate the social conscience of black writers by recalling the fate of an English writer of an earlier generation:

I also know of another really quite brilliant writer who, under the advice of certain wise men who were then managing the consciences of artists, abandoned the prison of his writing to go to Spain, where he was allowed to throw away his life defending a worthless hill. I have not heard his name in years but I remember it vividly: it was Christopher Caudwell, né Christopher St. John Sprigg. (qtd. in *Heroism,* 144 from "The World and the Jug," 142)

In recalling a writer cut down before he could make his name memorable through his work, Ellison is not making a point about the Spanish Civil War but about the awesome responsibility assumed by those who would "manage the conscience" of writers or, indeed, of anybody else. Watts, however, is aroused to vituperation that seems as uncivil and ad hominem as any of those attacks that Watts himself had earlier decried:

Ellison would have us believe that a man who chose to fight against the spread of fascism in Spain threw his life away defending a worthless hill. In some respects, Ellison's disrespect and trivialization of those who have actually struggled against tyranny as opposed to those, like himself, who merely write about the human desire for freedom is [sic] myopic, selfish, and thoroughly disgusting. (Note 44, 144–45)

Watts's failure to respond more fully to Ellison's essays demonstrates how difficult it is for an approach grounded in the social sciences rather than the humanities to do justice to a writer of Ellison's talents.(When Watts does attempt to move from sociology to the humanities, as in his final verdict that Ellison's point of view "is humanistically disturbing," the phrasing itself suggests that the author is more at home in the social sciences than the humanities.) Watts's sociological orientation leads him to offer an explanation for the trajectory of Ellison's career that seems grossly inadequate: "It might well be the case that Ellison's outlandish ambitions have suffocated him artistically. If this is true, Ellison did not utilize a social marginality facilitator appropriate to his needs" (119). The problem may not be entirely intellectual, however; Charles Johnson has a point when he attributes the limitations of *Heroism and the Black Intellectual* to the absence of a quality for which even the "culturally enriched Marxism" (57) favored by Watts is no substitute:

> Although Ralph Ellison's body of work consists only of *Invisible Man* and two collections of essays, *Shadow and Act* and *Going to the Territory*, these works display insight and intellectual generosity rare in 20th-century American literature—a generosity I fear is missing from the pages of "Heroism and the Black Intellectual."
> (15)

Chapter 8

1. Harold Rosenberg's essay "Couch Liberalism and the Guilty Past" provides a representative example of an excoriation from Fiedler's own generation. The strategy of Rosenberg's essay is to establish the independence of left-liberals like himself by characterizing all communists or communist sympathizers as "fakers, fools and position seekers" (232), "scoundrels" (236), "middle-class careerists, closed both to argument and evidence, impatient with thought, psychopaths of 'radical' conformity" (236), and a "sodden group of Philistines" (237). Apparently, only by such name-calling can he make a case against Fiedler's argument that there was indeed a problematic relation between many liberals and Communism.

Adam Sorkin's essay "Politics, Privatism and the Fifties," criticizes Fiedler for implying that "the necessities of history deny idealism and call for informing! Adult responsibility requires confessing!" (70). There is no doubt that many readers have found exactly this message in Fiedler's essays on Hiss and the Rosenbergs. But I would argue that Fiedler rejected sentimentality rather than idealism and called on liberals not to confess—presumably, few had actually committed either perjury or espionage—but, rather, to reexamine the notion that liberal-left opinions guarantee personal innocence.

The historical verdict differs from the critical consensus. *Perjury*, by Allan Weinstein, concludes that Fiedler's assumption of Hiss's guilt was correct. Likewise, Weinstein shares Fiedler's view of the cultural significance of what might seem to be a simple question of fact:

> For anti-communists of the liberal left, accepting Hiss' guilt implied renouncing one's own earlier hopes concerning the Soviet Union, the American Communist Party, and the benefits that Communism supposedly held out for American society.
> (515)

Incidentally, Weinstein's undocumented statement that Fiedler "recanted" (551) his position on Hiss is not borne out by Fiedler's 1971 introduction to a new edition of *An End to Innocence*.

The Rosenberg File, by Ronald Radosh and Joyce Milton, argues convincingly that the Rosenbergs were indeed guilty of espionage but that the death sentence was unjustified—precisely Fiedler's point of view in his 1953 essay on the case. *The Rosenberg File*, in its analysis of the use of myth by both sides and in the examples it offers of the kind of "doublethink" by which the Rosenbergs's guilt was transmuted into innocence by some (xii–xiii, 329, 340)—points stressed by Fiedler—suggests that a full historical analysis only increases one's respect for Fiedler's essay. Radosh and Milton examine Dickstein's arguments against both Fiedler's essay and a similar analysis by Robert Warshow ("The 'Idealism' of Julius and Ethel Rosenberg" in *The Immediate Experience*) and conclude that "Dickstein's comments do not speak to the critique offered by both Fiedler and Warshow" (55).

The breakup of the Soviet Union and the consequent partial opening of KGB files have led to some sensational headlines about the Hiss and Rosenberg cases, but so far no study has provided evidence substantial enough to overturn the conclusions of either Weinstein or Radosh and Milton.

Chapter 9

1. This chapter focuses on some of Susan Sontag's major works but makes no attempt to consider her entire oeuvre. *Against Interpretation, Styles of Radical Will, Illness as Metaphor,* and *AIDS and Its Metaphors,* as well as two pieces from *Under the Sign of Saturn* collected in *A Susan Sontag Reader* are discussed, but *On Photography* is neglected, and there is no attempt to examine her novels or film scripts.

The difference between this chapter's view of Sontag's career and the perspective offered by Elizabeth Hardwick in her 1982 introduction to *A Susan Sontag Reader* is explained in part by the different times of writing and in part by the difference between a chapter and an introduction. Hardwick's introduction is, appropriately, a warm tribute to Sontag's "extraordinarily beautiful, expansive, and unique talent" (ix). Although this chapter is an analysis rather than a tribute, there is nothing in it that contradicts Elizabeth Hardwick's judgment about Susan Sontag's talent; a reading of Sontag's work after 1982 only confirms that evaluation, made "in the middle of her career" (xv). (Hardwick's generous, eloquent introduction to the anthology provides oblique evidence for Elaine Showalter's 1981 linking of Elizabeth Hardwick and Susan Sontag, mentioned in the chapter on Diana Trilling. Showalter was right in positing an elective affinity between these two gifted writers, though one may be pardoned for questioning whether she has done the connection justice by viewing the eminent pair through the angle of contemporary feminist criticism. According to Showalter, this "flowing confessional criticism" often "achieves the power and the dignity of art" and thus constitutes "an implicit rebuke" to the more constrained talents of writers such as Elizabeth Hardwick and Susan Sontag. In its light, Showalter assured us, the intellectual and stylistic brilliance for which the two are renowned diminishes to a shared "tight-lipped Olympian intelligence . . . arid and strained" [58].)

Chapter 10

1. Graff discusses the ways in which his views have changed since *Literature Against Itself* in his "Response" to Lorraine Clark's essay "Allan Bloom and Gerald Graff: On Mimesis as Freedom," which points out parallels between Allan Bloom's *The Closing of the American Mind* and *Literature Against Itself.* Clark's essay and Graff's rejoinder appear in *Beyond Cheering and Bashing: New Perspectives on* The Closing of the American Mind.

2. Marx ends the famous exposition of "the guiding principle of [his] studies" (20) in the preface to *A Contribution to the Critique of Political Economy* with the assertion that "the Bourgeois mode of production is the last antagonistic form of the social process of production . . . The prehistory of human society accordingly closes with this social formation" (21–2).

3. Tony Judt recalls Althusser's reputation at its height and offers a disillusioned retrospective analysis in reviewing the posthumous book *The Future Lasts Forever: A Memoir*, which Althusser wrote after emerging from a mental hospital, where he was confined for three years after being declared unfit for trial for strangling his wife:

> When I arrived in Paris as a graduate student in the late '60s . . . Althusser was touted by everyone I met as a man of extraordinary gifts, who was transforming our understanding of Marx and reshaping revolutionary theory. His name, his ideas, his books were everywhere. . . . Althusser was engaged in what he and his acolytes called a "symptomatic reading" of Marx, which is to say that they took from him what they needed and ignored the rest. Where they wished Marx to have said or meant something that they could not find in his writings, they interpreted the "silences," thereby constructing an entity of their own imagination. This thing they called a science, one that Marx was said to have invented and that could be applied, gridlike, to all social phenomena. (33)

Judt provides some suggestions about the sources of the appeal of Althusserian Marxism over the traditional, vulgar version:

> Althusser's special contribution was to remove Marxism altogether from the realm of history, politics and experience, and thereby to render it invulnerable to any criticism of the empirical sort. (33–34)

> In Althusser-speak, Marxism was a theory of structural practices: economic, ideological, political, theoretical. . . . Of particular significance was the notion of "theoretical practice." This oxymoronic phrase, which came to be chanted, mantralike, all over Europe in those years, had the special charm of placing intellectuals and intellectual activity on the same plane as the economic organizations and the political strategies that had preoccupied earlier generations of Marxists. . . . Althusser invented something that he and his followers called "Ideological State Apparatuses." . . . In Althusserian dogma the presence of these repressive and all-embracing ogres was held particularly responsible for the inconvenient stability and durability of liberal democracy. Of special note was the announcement that the university was, of all of these, the dominant one of our era. "Theoretical practice" in the academic arena was thus the site of ideological battle; and philosophy was absolutely vital as the "class struggle in theory." Scholars in their seminars were on the front line, and need feel guilty no more. (34)

Not surprisingly, Douglas Johnson, in the introduction to the version of Althusser's memoir published in the United States, sees things differently:

It has frequently been said that the tragedy of the Althussers was also the tragedy of Althusserianism. . . . But there are reasons for believing that this is not so. Althusser moved Marxism away from a mechanical evocation of economic principles. His description of the ideological state apparatus which manipulates people into positions of oppressor and oppressed, through education, the family, the media, has never been more relevant. (xvii)

But then Judt himself notes that, despite all the personal scandals and despite the worldwide collapse of Marxist governments, Althusser's influence on U.S. campuses is by no means exhausted:

In the United States, however, there are still university research centers that devote time and money to the study of Althusser's thought, and mount expensive conferences at which professors lecture one another earnestly about "Althusserianism" in everything from linguistics to hermeneutics. (36)

4. Lichtheim included himself among such intellectuals:

The somewhat paradoxical title *From Marx to Hegel* has been chosen in order to suggest that the central problem now before us is not so much to change the world (that is being done independently), but to understand it. (viii)

5. Lukács defends the special authority of the Communist Party on the basis that the party is simply "the organized form" of "the correct class consciousness of the proletariat," a thesis he presents in "Class Consciousness," an essay in his 1922 collection, *History and Class Consciousness* (75). The authority that Lukács is prepared to grant the party is absolute. In "Towards a Methodology of the Problem of Organization," the concluding essay of *History and Class Consciousness*, he called for

the conscious subordination of the self to that collective will that is destined to bring real freedom into being and that today is earnestly taking the first arduous, uncertain and groping steps toward it. This conscious collective will is the Communist Party. (315)

6. Freud uses the phrase to describe the mentality of primitive peoples, referring to "the now established omnipotence of thought among primitive races." Freud uncharacteristically fails here to recognize the appeal of such a belief in the modern world, arguing that "only in one field has the omnipotence of thought been retained in our own civilization, namely in art" (117).

7. Russell Jacoby brilliantly criticizes Jameson's discussion of the Bonaventure Hotel in *The Last Intellectuals* 169–172.

8. Jameson offers this phrase as part of a general "characterization of post-modern thought" (391). The characterization, however, is surely meant to apply to his own book *Postmodernism*.

Chapter 11

1. Said's point is not vitiated even if his own prose sometimes becomes similarly expansive, as in the following affirmations from "Orientalism Reconsidered" claiming "nothing less" than revolutionary significance for his own approach:

> Orientalism reconsidered in this wider and libertarian optic entails nothing less than the creation of new objects for a new kind of knowledge. (91)

> All of them ["analyses and theoretical projects undertaken out of similar impulses as those fueling the anti-Orientalist critique"] are interventionary in nature, that is, they self-consciously situate themselves at vulnerable conjunctural nodes of ongoing disciplinary discourses where each of them posits nothing less than new objects of knowledge, new praxes of humanist (in the broad sense of the word) activity, new theoretical models that upset or at the very least radically alter the prevailing paradigmatic norms. (104)

2. The chapter does not discuss either *Beginnings* or *Joseph Conrad and the Fiction of Autobiography*. Both works demand inclusion in any study of Said as a literary critic; their consideration may be omitted from a discussion of Said as a critic of culture and politics.

3. William E. Cain draws a similar conclusion:

> As his book progresses, Said depends on influential theorists and yet commits himself to values that these theorists expressly disallow. (210)

> Said's theoretical and human allegiances are at cross purposes (213).

Said has responded to criticisms in "Orientalism Reconsidered," but there is no reconsideration of this fundamental issue in that essay or, so far as I can tell, anywhere else in Said's work.

4. In *Covering Islam* Said tells the reader:

> I myself am neither religious nor of an Islamic background, although I think I can understand someone who declares himself or herself to be convinced of a particular faith. But insofar as I feel it is possible to discuss faith at all, it is in the form of *interpretations* of faith manifesting themselves in human acts that take place in human history and society. (41)

But this is just what Said refuses to do in "The Ideology of Difference"; he declares himself unable to discuss the relation between Zionist "interpretations" of Jewish faith and the actions of Israel.

5. A comparison of Said's treatment of Jane Austen with Ralph Ellison's comments on Jane Austen and the "nineteenth-century European novel" in "Society, Morality and the Novel" is instructive. Ellison sees the same connection between imperialism and the novel, including Jane Austen's fiction, that Said emphasizes so strongly, but he sees other things as well:

Perhaps we admire the nineteenth-century European novel today, in our time of frantic uncertainty, because we find it vibrant and alive and confidently able to confront good and evil in all their contradictory entanglement. In it was implicit the tragic realization that the treasure of possibility is always to be found in the cave of chaos, guarded by the demons of destruction. It is Abel Magwitch, the jailbird, who makes Pip's dream of a gentleman's life a reality in *Great Expectations*; just as it was the existence of human slavery and colonial exploitation which made possible many of the brighter achievements of modern civilization. And just as the muted insincerities and snobberies of Jane Austen's characters are but highly refined versions of those major insincerities and snobberies, connected with the exercise of power, which have led in our time to the steady crumbling of the empire upon which genteel English society has rested. In that moment of genteel stability, however, those who were most willfully aware of their destiny viewed freedom not simply in terms of necessity but in terms of possibility, and they were willing to take the risks necessary to attain their goals. It was the novel which could communicate their awareness of this sense of possibility along with its cost, and it was the novel which could, on the other hand, reconstruct an image of experience which would make it unnecessary for one to be aware of the true reality upon which society rested. Men, it is said, can stand reality in small doses only, and the novel, sometimes consciously, sometimes not, measured out that dosage.

This was the dark side of the novel's ability to forge images which would strengthen man's will to say No to chaos and affirm him in his task of humanizing himself and the world. It would, even while "entertaining" him, help create that fragile state of human certainty and stability (or the illusion of it at least, for perhaps illusion is all we ever have) and communion which is sometimes called love, brotherhood, democracy, sometimes simply the good life! And it could limit those who would share that life and justify our rejection of their humanity, and while condemning snobbery, could yet condone it, for society was admittedly hieratic and closed to pressure from below. (246–247)

Ellison's comment that Jane Austen's fiction helped to "reconstruct an image of experience which would make it unnecessary for one to be aware of the true reality upon which society rested" applies directly to Mansfield Park. He also, however, suggests that Jane Austen's presentation of "muted insincerities and snobberies" provides a critique of "those major insincerities and snobberies" connected with empire, an observation that also bears directly on *Mansfield Park*. For Said, Austen's complicity with imperialism diminishes, if it does not erase, the moral authority of both *Mansfield Park* and Jane Austen.

Ellison's skepticism is surely as profound as Said's, and his recognition of the links between literature and imperialism is as far-reaching. After emphasizing the complicity of the novel with power, however, Ellison suggests that nineteenth-century European novels, products of an imperialist era though they are, can still teach Americans of the late twentieth century some things worth knowing, such as the location of "the treasure of possibility" in "the cave of chaos" (246). Ellison notices both "the dark side" of fiction and its contribution to the never-ending "task of humanizing" (247). Said's discussion of *Mansfield Park* delineates the complicity but ignores the insights.

Ellison's perspective encourages one to draw out the political implications of Lionel Trilling's observation that *Mansfield Park* speaks "insistently for cautiousness and constraint, even for dullness" ("*Mansfield Park*," 184–85). This "cautiousness and constraint," summed up in the "self-denial and humility" that Sir Thomas Bertram finally realizes has been lacking, is surely antithetical to the belligerence and pride fostered by running an empire or a slave plantation. Jane Austen's willingness to dramatize the superiority of the former qualities over the latter has clear moral-political implications for those who are ready to see them.

Chapter 12

1. This is indeed an "admission," since, as Robert Stecker points out in reference to the passage, "This is precisely the sort of guidance of practice by theory that Fish tries to deny" (229).

2. The citations for Matthew Arnold's quotations of Edmund Burke list both the page number from Arnold's essay and the page number of the passage in the most recent collection of Burke's writings.

Chapter 13

1. Articles linking the two books appeared, for example, in the *Chronicle of Higher Education*, the *Nation*, *Parade*, and *Time*.

2. Surprisingly, the most vehement political denunciation occurred not in a U.S. journal but, instead, in the *Times Literary Supplement* (*TLS*). David Rieff, apparently unsatisfied with Kenneth Minogue's earlier, mildly sympathetic review in *TLS*, argued that the book was not "a scholarly argument about the fate of higher education in America and a lament over the decline of academic standards" but, rather, something "more disturbing" (950). In an article entitled "The Colonel and the Professor" Rieff found that Col. Oliver North and Prof. Allan Bloom typified "an age of pious bullies in America" (760). Rieff summed up the current (1987) American cultural-political scene this way:

> In the meantime, Nicaraguans on both sides die in a stupid war that the US government chooses to fight by that most cowardly of means, proxy, while, back home, men like Professor Bloom, their paychecks assured by right-wing foundations that have also been so active in supporting the Contras, publish books decent people would be ashamed of having written. (960)

3. In his *Nation* review Robert Pattison calls Hirsch's book "a carefully crafted bid to win friends and influence people" and adds:

> Few books published by an English teacher in recent years have been as solicitous of the educated community's good will as this one. Hirsch is more unctuous in his use of honorifics than a German innkeeper. (710)

4. There are stylistic parallels as well. Noting the influence of Marcuse and Adorno on the radicals of the 1960s, Bloom allows that

the activists had no special quarrel with the classic texts, and they were even a bit infected by their Frankfurt School masters' habit of parading their intimacy with high culture. (65)

Critics such as Robert Paul Wolff found Bloom vulnerable to the same charge of "parading." Wolff commented that the "most striking surface characteristic" of the book's "expository style" is

> an obsessive name-dropping that turns every page into a roll call of the Great Conversation. Consult the book at random (my copy falls open to pages 292——93), and one finds, within a brief compass, mention of Christopher Marlowe, Machiavelli (a Straussian buzzword, this), Bacon, Descartes, Hobbes, Leibniz, Locke, Montesquieu, Voltaire, Jacques Maritain, T. S. Eliot, Rousseau, Newton, Socrates, Moses, Cyrus, Theseus, Romulus, Swift, and Aristophanes. (65)

5. It would seem, for example, that only an "initiate" could recognize a "trace," one of Derrida's key concepts, given his warning that

> the trace is not more ideal than real, not more intelligible than sensible, not more a transparent signification than an opaque energy and *no concept of metaphysics can describe it.* (65)

6. In the conclusion of *The Next Left,* a book proposing strategies to bring about democratic socialism, Michael Harrington offers a more striking example of an enlistment of the "civil religion" on behalf of democracy than anything Hirsch mentions:

> In 1965, when Martin Luther King Jr. led thousands of marchers of different races and faiths and political persuasions through the empty streets of Montgomery, Alabama, the only spectators were the sullen and federalized national guardsmen, local people who had been forced to protect the lives of demonstrators they opposed. As a way of articulating the resentment of white, racist Montgomery, the city was everywhere decorated with Confederate flags. When we reached the statehouse—the birthplace of the Confederacy itself—we could see only a single American flag in the distance. At that point some genius among the marchers led us in a revolutionary anthem: "The Star Spangled Banner." We were dramatizing the fact that we represented the American tradition and not simply the claims of a black minority, that our cause was the cause of the entire society, not of an "interest group."

Harrington ends his book with this "true parable" because he believes that calling upon the ideals of the civil religion remains the best hope of the "democratic Left" (193).

Chapter 14

1. If it seems unfair to expect Jameson's April 1990 introduction to include a thoughtful response to the events of the previous fall and winter, then one might turn to

his contribution to *After the Fall: The Failure of Communism and the Future of Socialism,* an anthology organized specially to assess the significance of what editor Robin Blackburn calls "the debacle and disaster of Communism since 1989." Jameson's "Conversations on the New World Order," dated April 1991, opens with the bold thesis that the apparent triumph of capitalism demonstrates the theoretical insight of *Marxism*:

> It does not seem to make sense to talk about the bankruptcy of Marxism, when Marxism is very precisely the science and study of just that capitalism whose global triumph is affirmed in talk of Marxism's demise. (255)

Demonstrating the rhetorical flair to which he owes so much of his success, Jameson repeats the gambit of offering as evidence of success what seems catastrophic to mundane minds:

> As for Communism itself, what needs to be affirmed is that the most recent developments are due not to its failure but to its success. . . . The fact is that Stalinism was a success, fulfilling its modernizing mission, developing political and social subjects of a new type. (257)

Those who may blink in amazement at Jameson's ability to find theoretical gratification in historical failure are just not thinking dialectically:

> From a dialectical standpoint, to affirm that something is a success is also to posit the emergence of new contradictions, inherent in that very success. . . . It is just such an emergence that has to be posited on the occasion of the recent events. (257)

The entire article may be recommended to connoisseurs of a genre that might be called "defending the indefensible," a form that brings out the stylistic powers of its practitioners.

For an exemplary instance of cultural self-criticism by an American Marxist who became a Communist at fifteen and "although expelled from the party in 1950 at age twenty . . . remained a supporter of the international movement and of the Soviet Union until there was nothing left to support," see Eugene Genovese's essay "The Question" in the summer, 1994 issue of *Dissent.* Genovese declares soberly that

> we of the left have to answer to ourselves, to each other, to the movement to which we have devoted our lives, and especially to the millions of our comrades who were themselves slaughtered in a heroic effort to make the world a better place. (374)

Attempting to explain the attraction of Marxism to himself and others, Genovese asserts:

> The horrors did not arise from perversions of radical ideology but from the ideology itself. We were led into complicity with mass murder and the desecration of our professed ideals not by Stalinist or other corruptions of high ideals, much less

by unfortunate twists in some presumably objective course of historical development, but by a deep flaw in our very understanding of human nature—its frailty and its possibilities—and by our inability to replace the moral and ethical baseline long provided by the religion we have dismissed with indifference, not to say contempt. (375)

Genovese's reassessment, it should be noted, does not detour into Cynicism. Despite his willingness to face the worst about Communism and Marxism, he still believes that "The left has been right to fight for social justice. . . . Our indictment of class injustice, racism, and the denigration of women has not been rendered less urgent by the failure of socialism" (376). Such moral and political seriousness provides a standard by which to measure Jameson's response to the fall of Communism and the crisis of Marxism.

Chapter 15

1. In "Tolerance 101" Arthur Melzer has pointed out some limitations of "diversity" when the concept is used as the primary rhetorical device for opposing racism. He directs attention to "two new mutant strains of intolerance [that] have evolved today that are resistant to 'multiculturalism' precisely because they grow not from ignorance of diversity, but somehow from diversity itself." Arguing that people who live in an atmosphere of "great skepticism and diversity" often "learn not to think at all," he suggests that where diversity is the norm, prejudice may be reduced, but "the vital pressure to use others' beliefs to criticize and enlarge one's own" is also reduced. Thus, "self-criticism turns to self-satisfaction. And that is how diversity itself becomes a force for complacency and prejudice." The atmosphere may discourage "systematic persecution," but, Melzer suggests, the "new breed of intolerance—a lazy, easygoing loutishness—thrives on 'diversity' and will not be dispelled by more of it" (11)

Melzer also warns about "a second new strain of intolerance that tends to arise precisely in a multicultural society." He notes:

Moral and religious doctrines, under the pressure of an environment of heightened skepticism and diversity, tend to mutate into dogmatisms, hardened against outside influence. . . . This reaction against diversity is the true source of the cults, New Wave superstitions, and narrower forms of religiosity . . . that have been proliferating in recent years.

How, asks Melzer, "can more diversity as such be the cure for this strain of intolerance, any more than the first?" (11)

Offering diversity as an ideal in itself is not as likely to minimize prejudice as "a direct, rational defense of the ideal of tolerance," Melzer argues (11). A "rational, enduring commitment to the ideal of liberal tolerance," he concludes, provides the best hope for creating a climate in which meaningful respect for a diversity of opinions and cultures can flourish (12).

Works Cited

Abrams. M. H. "How to Do Things with Texts." *Partisan Review* 46 (1979): 566–88. Rpt. in *Doing Things with Texts: Essays in Criticism and Critical Theory,* ed. Michael Fischer, 269–96. New York: Norton, 1989.

Adorno, Theodor. "Cultural Criticism and Society." *Prisms.* Trans. Samuel and Shierry Weber. Cambridge: MIT P, 1981. 19–34.

———. *Negative Dialectics.* 1966. Trans. E. B. Ashton. New York: Seabury P, 1973.

Althusser, Louis. *The Future Lasts Forever: A Memoir.* 1992. Ed. Olivier Corpet and Yann Moulier Boutang. Trans. Richard Veasey. Intro. by Douglas Johnson. New York: New P, 1993.

Arnold, Matthew. "The Function of Criticism at the Present Time." *Lectures and Essays in Criticism.* Vol. 3 of *The Complete Prose Works of Matthew Arnold,* ed. R. H. Super, 11 vols., 258–85. Ann Arbor: U of Michigan P, 1962.

———. "The Study of Poetry." *English Literature and Irish Politics.* Vol. 9 of *The Complete Prose Works of Matthew Arnold,* ed. R. H. Super. 11 vols., 161–88. Ann Arbor: U of Michigan P, 1973.

Auchincloss, Louis, Ralph Ellison, John Kenneth Galbraith, John Hersey, Norman Mailer, Arthur Miller, Arthur Schlesinger Jr., William Styron, and Kurt Vonnegut. Letter. *New York Review of Books,* 15 Mar. 1990, 53.

Austen, Jane. *Mansfield Park.* 1814. Ed. Tony Tanner. London: Penguin, 1966.

Babbitt, Irving. "Buddha and the Occident." *The Dhammapada.* Trans. Irving Babbitt, 65–121. New York: Oxford UP, 1936. Rpt. in *Irving Babbitt: Representative Writings,* ed. George A. Panichas, 224–70. Lincoln: U of Nebraska P, 1981.

———. *Democracy and Leadership.* Boston: Houghton Mifflin, 1924.

———. "English and the Discipline of Ideas," *English Journal* 9 (Feb. 1920): 61–70. Rpt. in *Irving Babbitt: Representative Writings,.* ed. George A. Panichas, 61–70. Lincoln: U of Nebraska P, 1981.

———. *Literature and the American College: Essays in Defense of the Humanities.* 1908. Washington, D.C.: National Humanities Institute, 1986.

———. "Matthew Arnold." *Irving Babbitt: Representative Writings,* ed. George A. Panichas, 103–15. Lincoln: U of Nebraska P, 1981.

———. *Rousseau and Romanticism.* Boston: Houghton Mifflin, 1919.

———. "What I Believe: Rousseau and Religion." In *Spanish Character and Other Essays,* ed. Frederick Manchester, Rachel Giese, and William F. Giese, 225–48.

Boston: Houghton Mifflin, 1940. Rpt. as "What I Believe" in *Irving Babbitt: Repre-sentative Writings,* ed. George A. Panichas, 3–18. Lincoln: U of Nebraska P, 1981.

Baldwin, James. *Nobody Knows My Name: More Notes of a Native Son.* New York: Dial, 1961.

———. *Notes of a Native Son.* 1955. Boston: Beacon P, 1984.

Balzac, Honoré de. *Old Goriot.* Trans. Marion Crawford. Middlesex, Eng.: Penguin, 1951.

Baraka, Imamu Amiri (LeRoi Jones). *Blues People: Negro Music in White America.* New York: Morrow, 1963.

Barzun, Jacques. "Reckoning with Time and Place." In *The Culture We Deserve,* ed. Arthur Krystal, 75–86. Middletown, Conn.: Wesleyan UP, 1989.

Bellah, Robert N. *The Broken Covenant: American Civil Religion in Time of Trial.* New York: Seabury, 1975.

———. "Civil Religion in America." Daedalus: Journal of the American Academy of Arts and Sciences 96 (1967): 1–21.

Bellow, Saul. Foreword. *The Closing of the American Mind: How Higher Education Has Failed Democracy and Impoverished the Souls of Today's Students,* by Allan Bloom, 11–18. New York: Simon and Schuster, 1987.

Berthoff, Warner. *Edmund Wilson.* University of Minnesota Pamphlets on American Writers 67. Minneapolis: U of Minnesota P, 1968.

Blackburn, Robin. Preface. In *After the Fall: The Failure of Communism and the Future of Socialism,* ed. Robin Blackburn, ix–xvi. London: Verso, 1991.

Blankfort, Michael. *A Time to Live.* Harcourt Brace, 1943.

Bloom, Allan. *The Closing of the American Mind: How Higher Education Has Failed Democracy and Impoverished the Souls of Today's Students.* Foreword by Saul Bellow. New York: Simon and Schuster, 1987.

Bowen, Ezra. "Are Student Heads Full of Emptiness?" *Time,* 17 Aug. 1987, 56–57.

Brennan, Frederick. *Memo to a Firing Squad.* New York: Knopf, 1943.

Brennan, Stephen C. and Stephen R. Yarbrough. *Irving Babbitt.* Boston: Twayne, 1987.

Brookfield, Stephen D. "E. D. Hirsch's 'Cultural Literacy': A Cocktail-Party View of Higher Education." *Chronicle of Higher Education,* 16 Sept. 1987, B2.

Buchanan, James P. "Allan Bloom and 'The Closing of the American Mind': Conclusions Too Neat, Too Clean, and Too Elite." *Chronicle of Higher Education,* 16 Sept. 1987, B2.

Burke, Edmund. *Reflections on the Revolution in France. The French Revolution 1790–1794.* Ed. and intro. L. G. Mitchell. Vol. 8 of *The Writings and Speeches of Edmund Burke,* 53–293. Oxford: Oxford UP, 1989.

———. *Thoughts on French Affairs. The French Revolution 1790–1794.* Ed. and intro. L. G. Mitchell. Vol. 8 of *The Writings and Speeches of Edmund Burke,* 338–86. Oxford: Oxford UP, 1989.

Cain, William E. *The Crisis in Criticism: Theory, Literature, and Reform in English Studies.* Baltimore: Johns Hopkins UP.

Castronovo, David. *Edmund Wilson.* New York: Ungar, 1984.

Clark, Eleanor. *The Bitter Box.* Garden City, NY: Doubleday, 1946.

Clark, Lorraine. "Allan Bloom and Gerald Graff: On Mimesis as Freedom." In *Beyond Cheering and Bashing: New Perspectives on* The Closing of the American Mind, ed.

James Seaton and William K. Buckley, 151–60. Bowling Green, Ohio: Bowling Green SU Popular P, 1992.

Cleaver, Eldridge. *Soul on Ice.* New York: McGraw-Hill, 1968.

Derrida, Jacques. *Of Grammatology.* Trans. Gayatri Chakravorty Spivak. Baltimore: Johns Hopkins UP, 1974.

Dickstein, Morris. *Gates of Eden: American Culture in the Sixties.* New York: Basic, 1977.

Douglas, George H. *Edmund Wilson's America.* Lexington: UP of Kentucky, 1983.

Eagleton, Terry. *Literary Theory: An Introduction.* Minneapolis: U of Minnesota P, 1983.

Eliot, T. S. "Francis Herbert Bradley." *Essays Ancient & Modern,* 45–61. London: Faber and Faber, 1936.

Ellison, Ralph. *"An American Dilemma:* A Review." *Shadow and Act,* 303–317.

———. "Blues People." *Shadow and Act,* 247–58.

———. "Brave Words for a Startling Occasion." *Shadow and Act,* 102–6.

———. "An Extravagance of Laughter." *Going to the Territory,* 145–97.

———. *Going to the Territory.* 1986. New York: Vintage, Random House, 1987.

———. *Invisible Man.* 1952. New York: Vintage, 1972.

———. "The Little Man at Chehaw Station." *Going to the Territory,* 3–38.

———. "The Myth of the Flawed White Southerner." *Going to the Territory,* 76–87.

———. "Perspective of Literature." *Going to the Territory,* 321–38.

———. *Shadow and Act.* 1964. New York: Vintage, Random House, 1972.

———. "Twentieth-Century Fiction and the Black Mask of Humanity." *Shadow and Act,* 24–44.

———. "What These Children Are Like." *Going to the Territory,* 64–75.

———. "The World and the Jug." *Shadow and Act,* 107–43.

Emerson, Ralph Waldo. "The Conservative." *Ralph Waldo Emerson: Essays and Lectures.* Ed. Joel Porte, 171–90. New York: Library of America, 1983.

Epstein, Joseph. "Mencken on Trial." *Pertinent Players: Essays on the Literary Life,* 222–45. New York: Norton, 1993.

Fairbanks, Charles H., Jr. "The Nature of the Beast." *National Interest* (Spring 1993): 46–56.

Farrell, James A. Introduction. *Prejudices: A Selection,.* by H. L. Mencken. Ed. James A. Farrell, v–xviii. New York: Knopf, 1955.

Fecher, Charles A. Introduction. *The Diary of H. L. Mencken,* by H. L. Mencken. Ed. Charles A. Fecher, vii–xxvii. New York: Knopf, 1990.

Fiedler, Leslie. "Afterthoughts on the Rosenbergs." *An End to Innocence: Essays on Culture and Politics,* 25–45.

———. *An End to Innocence: Essays on Culture and Politics.* 1955. 2nd ed. New York: Stein and Day, 1972.

———. *Being Busted.* New York: Stein and Day, 1969.

———. *Fiedler on the Roof: Essays on Literature and Jewish Identity.* Boston: Godine, 1991.

———. "Hiss, Chambers, and the Age of Innocence," *An End to Innocence: Essays on Culture and Politics,* 3–24.

———. "In Every Generation." *Fiedler on the Roof: Essays on Literature and Jewish Identity,* 159–81.

———. *Inadvertent Epic.* Intro. Barrie Hayne. New York: Simon and Schuster, 1979.

———. *Love and Death in the American Novel.* New York: Criterion, 1960.

———. "McCarthy and the Intellectuals." *An End to Innocence: Essays on Culture and Politics,* 46–87.

———. *No! in Thunder.* Boston: Beacon P, 1960.

———. *What Was Literature? Class Culture and Mass Society.* New York: Simon and Schuster, 1982.

Fish, Stanley. "Anti-Foundationalism, Theory Hope, and the Teaching of Composition." *Doing What Comes Naturally: Change, Rhetoric, and the Practice of Theory in Literary and Legal Studies,* 342–55.

———. "Anti-Professionalism." *Doing What Comes Naturally: Change, Rhetoric, and the Practice of Theory in Literary and Legal Studies,* 215–46.

———. "Appendix. Fish Tales: A Conversation with 'The Contemporary Sophist.'" Interview with Gary A. Olson. *There's No Such Thing as Free Speech, and It's a Good Thing, Too,* 281–307.

———. "Critical Self-Consciousness, Or Can We Know What We're Doing?" *Doing What Comes Naturally: Change, Rhetoric, and the Practice of Theory in Literary and Legal Studies,* 436–67.

———. *Doing What Comes Naturally: Change, Rhetoric, and the Practice of Theory in Literary and Legal Studies.* Durham: Duke UP, 1989.

———. "Fish v. Fiss." *Doing What Comes Naturally: Change, Rhetoric, and the Practice of Theory in Literary and Legal Studies,* 120–40.

———. "Force." *Doing What Comes Naturally: Change, Rhetoric, and the Practice of Theory in Literary and Legal Studies,* 503–24.

———. "Introduction: Going Down the Anti-Formalist Road." *Doing What Comes Naturally: Change, Rhetoric, and the Practice of Theory in Literary and Legal Studies,* 1–33.

———. "Jerry Falwell's Mother, or What's the Harm?" *There's No Such Thing as Free Speech, and It's a Good Thing, Too,* 120–33.

———. "The Law Wishes to Have a Formal Existence." *There's No Such Thing as Free Speech, and It's a Good Thing, Too,* 141–79.

———. Preface. *Doing What Comes Naturally: Change, Rhetoric, and the Practice of Theory in Literary and Legal Studies,* ix–x.

———. Preface. *There's No Such Thing as Free Speech, and It's a Good Thing, Too.* New York: Oxford UP, 1994.

———. "Speaking in Code, or, How to Turn Bigotry and Ignorance into Moral Principles." *There's No Such Thing as Free Speech, and It's a Good Thing, Too,* 89–101.

———. *There's No Such Thing as Free Speech, and It's a Good Thing, Too.* New York: Oxford UP, 1994.

———. "Why Literary Criticism Is like Virtue." *London Review of Books,* 10 June 1993, 11–16.

———. "Why No One's Afraid of Wolfgang Iser." *Doing What Comes Naturally: Change, Rhetoric, and the Practice of Theory in Literary and Legal Studies,* 68–86.

Fitzgerald, F. Scott. "The Crack-Up." *The Crack-Up.* Ed. Edmund Wilson, 69–84. New York: New Directions, 1945.

———. "You Can Only Fight Discrimination with Discrimination." *There's No Such Thing as Free Speech, and It's a Good Thing, Too,* 70–79.

———. *The Great Gatsby.* 1925. New York: Charles Scribner's Sons, 1953.

————. "The Rich Boy." *The Stories of F. Scott Fitzgerald*. Ed. Malcolm Cowley, 177–208. New York: Charles Scribner's Sons, 1951.

Frank, Charles P. *Edmund Wilson*. New York: Twayne, 1970.

Freud, Sigmund. *Civilization and Its Discontents*. 1930. Trans. Joan Riviere. Garden City, NY: Doubleday, 1958.

————. *Totem and Taboo*. Trans. A. A. Brill. New York: Random, 1918.

Fukuyama, Francis. "The End of History?" *National Interest* 16 (1989): 3–18.

————. *The End of History and the Last Man*. 1992. New York: Avon Books, 1993.

Galbraith, John Kenneth. "Viva Mencken!" Review of *The Diary of H. L. Mencken*, by H. L. Mencken. *New York Review of Books* 28 June 1990, 41.

Genovese, Eugene. "The Question." *Dissent* 41 (1994): 371–76.

Giese, William F. "Memoir." In *Irving Babbitt: Man and Teacher*, ed. Frederick Manchester and Odell Shepard, 1–25. New York: Putnam's, 1941.

Graff, Gerald. *Literature against Itself*. Chicago: U of Chicago P, 1970.

————. "Response." In *Beyond Cheering and Bashing: New Perspectives on "The Closing of the American Mind,"* ed. James Seaton and William K. Buckley, 161–63. Bowling Green, OH: Bowling Green SU Popular P, 1992.

Griffin, Robert J. "Ideology and Misrepresentation: A Response to Edward Said." *Critical Inquiry* 15 (Spring 1989): 611–25.

Groh, Janet. *Edmund Wilson: A Critic for Our Time*. Athens: Ohio UP, 1989.

Habermas, Jürgen. *The Philosophical Discourse of Modernity*. Trans. Frederick Lawrence. Intro. Thomas McCarthy. Cambridge: MIT P, 1987.

Hardwick, Elizabeth. Introduction. In *The Susan Sontag Reader*, 1982. Susan Sontag. Rpt.. New York: Random House, 1983.

————. *Seduction and Betrayal: Women and Literature*. New York: Random House, 1974.

Harrington, Michael. *The Next Left: The History of a Future*. New York: Holt, 1986.

Hayne, Barrie. Introduction. *The Inadvertent Epic: From Uncle Tom's Cabin to Roots*, by Leslie A. Fiedler, vii–xi. New York: Touchstone–Simon and Schuster, 1979.

Hegel, G. W. F. *Reason in History: A General Introduction to the Philosophy of History*. Ed. and trans. Robert S. Hartman. New York: Liberal Arts P, 1953.

Hemingway, Ernest. "A Natural History of the Dead." *Winner Take Nothing*, 97–106. 1933. Rpt. New York: Scribner's, 1970.

Himmelfarb, Gertrude. "On Looking into the Abyss." *On Looking into the Abyss: Untimely Thoughts on Culture and Society*, 3-26.

————. *On Looking into the Abyss: Untimely Thoughts on Culture and Society*. New York: Knopf, 1994.

————. "The Politics of Dissent." *Commentary*, (July 1994): 32–37.

Hirsch, E. D., Jr. *Cultural Literacy: What Every American Needs to Know*. Boston: Houghton Mifflin, 1987.

Hobson, Fred. *Mencken: A Life*. New York: Random House, 1994.

Hume, David. "Of the Rise and the Progress of the Arts and Sciences." *Essays, Literary, Moral, and Political*, 63–79. 1748. Rpt. London: Ward, Lock and Bowden, 1875.

Jacoby, Russell. *The Last Intellectuals: American Culture in the Age of Academe*. New York: Basic Books, 1987.

James, Henry. *Hawthorne*. 1872. In *Literary Criticism: Essays on Literature, American Writ-*

ers, English Writers, ed. Leon Edel with Mark Wilson, 315–474. New York: Library of America, 1984.

Jameson, Fredric. "Conversations on the New World Order." In *After the Fall: The Failure of Communism and the Future of Socialism,* ed. Robin Blackburn, 255–68. London: Verso, 1991.

———. *The Political Unconscious.* Ithaca: Cornell UP, 1981.

———. *Postmodernism, or, The Cultural Logic of Late Capitalism.* Durham: Duke UP, 1991.

Johnson, Charles. "Race, Politics and Ralph Ellison." Review of *Heroism and the Black Intellectual: Ralph Ellison, Politics, and Afro-American Intellectual Life,* by Jerry Gafio Watts. *New York Times Book Review* 5 Feb. 1995: 15.

Johnson, Douglas. Introduction. *The Future Lasts Forever: A Memoir,* by Louis Althusser. 1992. Ed. Olivier Corpet and Yann Moulier Boutang, vi–xviii. Trans. Richard Veasey. New York: New P, 1993.

Johnson, Samuel. "Preface, 1765." In *Selections from Johnson on Shakespeare,* ed. Bertrand H. Bronson with Jean M. O'Meara, 8-60. New Haven: Yale UP, 1986.

Judt, Tony. "The Paris Strangler." Review of *The Future Lasts Forever: A Memoir,* by Louis Althusser. *New Republic* 7 Mar. 1994, 33–37.

Kazin, Alfred. "The Great Anachronism: A View from the Sixties." In *Edmund Wilson: The Man and His Work,* ed. John Wain, 11–27. New York: New York UP, 1978.

———. *On Native Grounds: An Interpretation of Modern American Prose Literature.* 1942. Rpt. New York: Anchor, 1956.

———. *New York Jew.* New York: Knopf, 1978.

———. "Our American Plutarch." *Reporter,* 24 May 1962, 43–46.

Keats, John. "To George and Tom Keats." 22 Dec. 1818. Letter 45 in *The Letters of John Keats 1814–1821,* ed. Hyder Edward Rollins, I: 191–94. 2 vols. Cambridge: Harvard UP, 1958.

Kellner, Douglas. "Toward a Multiperspectival Cultural Studies," *Centennial Review* 36, no. 1 (1992): 5–41.

Koestler, Arthur. *Thieves in the Night: Chronicle of an Experiment.* 1946. Rpt. London: Hutchinson, 1965.

Kolakowski Leszek. *The Founders.* Trans. P. S. Falla. Oxford: Oxford UP, 1978. Vol. 1 of *Main Currents of Marxism: Its Origins, Growth and Dissolution.* 3 vols. Oxford: Oxford UP, 1978.

Kriegel, Leonard. *Edmund Wilson.* Pref. Harry T. Moore. Cross Currents-Modern Critiques. Carbondale, IL: Southern Illinois UP, 1971.

Kundera, Milan. *Life Is Elsewhere.* Trans. Peter Kussi. New York: Viking Penguin, 1986.

Lasch, Christopher. *The Culture of Narcissism: American Life in An Age of Diminishing Expectations.* New York: Warner, 1979.

———. *The New Radicalism in America, 1889–1963: The Intellectual as a Social Type.* 1965. Rpt. New York: Norton, 1986.

Lichtheim, George. *From Marx to Hegel.* New York: Herder and Herder, 1971.

Lincoln, Abraham. "Speech on the Dred Scott Decision at Springfield, Illinois, June 26, 1857." *Speeches and Writings, 1832–1858.* Ed. Don E. Fehrenbacher, 390–403. New York: Library of America, 1989.

Lovejoy, Arthur O. *The Great Chain of Being: A Study of the History of an Idea.* 1936. Rpt. New York: Harper Torchbooks–Harper and Brothers, 1960.

Lukács, George. "Class Consciousness." *History and Class Consciousness: Studies in Marxist Dialectics,* 46–82.

———. *History and Class Consciousness: Studies in Marxist Dialectics.* 1922. Trans. Rodney Livingstone. Cambridge: MIT P, 1971.

———. "Toward a Methodology of the Problem of Organization." *History and Class Consciousness: Studies in Marxist Dialectics,* 295–342.

Macdonald, Dwight. *Against the American Grain: Essays on the Effects of Mass Culture.* 1962. Rpt. New York: Da Capo, 1983.

———. "Comment." *Politics* (July 1945): 207–9.

———. *Dwight Macdonald on Movies.* Englewood Cliffs, NJ: Prentice–Hall, 1969.

———. "*Massachusetts v. Mailer.*" *Discriminations: Essays and Afterthoughts, 1938–1974,* 194–209. New York: Grossman/Viking, 1974.

———. "My Favorite General." *Memoirs of a Revolutionist: Essays in Political Criticism,* 92–100.

———. *Memoirs of a Revolutionist: Essays in Political Criticism.* 1957. Rpt. New York: Meridian, 1958.

———. "Trotskyism I: 'The Only Really Moral People.'" *Memoirs of a Revolutionist: Essays in Political Criticism,* 272–75.

———. "Trotskyism II: Revolution, Ltd." *Memoirs of a Revolutionist: Essays in Political Criticism,* 275–83.

———. *Politics.* Vol. 2 (1945). Radical Periodicals in the United States, 1890–1960. New York: Greenwood Reprint Corp., 1968.

———. Untitled reply to Guenter Reimann. *Politics* (May 1945): 155–156.

———. "The Responsibility of Peoples." *Memoirs of a Revolutionist: Essays in Political Criticism,* 33–72.

McKenney, Ruth. *Jake Home.* New York: Harcourt, Brace, 1943.

MacLeish, Archibald. "Ars Poetica." *Streets in the Moon,* 37–38. Boston: Houghton Mifflin, 1926. Rpt. in *New and Collected Poems, 1917–1976,* 106–7. Boston: Houghton Mifflin, 1976.

Mailer, Norman. *The Armies of the Night: History as a Novel, the Novel as History.* New York: New American Library, 1968.

Maloney, Russell. "A Footnote to a Footnote." *New Yorker,* 15 July 1939, 26.

Mann, Thomas. "A Brother." *Order of the Day: Political Essays and Speeches of Two Decades,* 153–161. New York: Knopf, 1942.

———. *Confessions of Felix Krull, Confidence Man (The Early Years).* Trans. Denver Lindley. 1955. Rpt. Vintage–Random House, 1969.

———. *Doctor Faustus: The Life of the German Composer Adrian Leverkuhn as Told by a Friend.* Trans. H. T. Lowe-Porter. New York: Random House, 1948.

———. *Reflections of a Nonpolitical Man.* 1918. Trans. Walter D. Morris. New York: Ungar, 1983.

Marcuse, Herbert. *Eros and Civilization.* 1955. Rpt. New York: Vintage–Random House, 1961.

———. *One-Dimensional Man: Studies in the Ideology of Advanced Industrial Society.* Boston: Beacon P, 1964.

―――. "Repressive Tolerance." In *A Critique of Pure Tolerance*, Robert Paul Wolff and Barrington Moore Jr., 81–123. Boston: Beacon P, 1965.

―――. "Philosophie und kritische Theorie," *Zeitschrift für Sozialforschung*, 6 (1937): 631–647. Rpt. as "Philosophy and Critical Theory." *Negations: Essays in Critical Theory*. Trans. Jeremy J. Shapiro, 134–58. Boston: Beacon P, 1968.

Marx, Karl. *A Contribution to the Critique of Political Economy*. Ed. Maurice Dobb. Trans. S. W. Ryazanskaya. Moscow: International Publishers, 1970.

Melzer, Arthur M. "Tolerance 101." *New Republic*, 1 July 1991, 10–12.

Mencken, H. L. *The American Language: An Inquiry into the Development of English in the United States*. 1919. 4th ed. New York: Knopf, 1937.

―――. "On Being an American." *Prejudices: Third Series*, 9–64. New York: Knopf, 1922. Rpt. in *Prejudices: A Selection*, 89–125.

―――. *In Defense of Women*. New York: Knopf, 1918.

―――. *The Diary of H. L. Mencken*. Ed. Charles A. Fecher. New York: Knopf, 1990.

―――. *The Gist of Nietzsche*. Boston: Luce, 1910.

―――. "On Living in Baltimore." *Prejudices: Fifth Series*, 237–43. New York: Knopf, 1926. Rpt. in *Prejudices: A Selection*, 206–10.

―――. *Minority Report: H. L. Mencken's Notebooks*. New York: Knopf, 1956.

―――. "The National Letters." 1920. *Prejudices: Second Series*, 9–101. New York: Knopf, 1920. Rpt. in abridged form in *The Vintage Mencken*, ed. Alistair Cooke, 85–106. New York: Vintage, 1955.

―――. *The Philosophy of Friedrich Nietzsche*. 1913. 3d ed. Port Washington, NY: Kennikat P, 1967.

―――. *Prejudices: A Selection*. Ed. James T. Farrell. 1955. Rpt. New York: Vintage–Random House, 1958.

―――. "Roosevelt: An Autopsy." *Prejudices: Second Series*, 102–35. New York: Knopf, 1920. Rpt. in *Prejudices: A Selection*, 47–69.

Mill, John Stuart. "Bentham." In *Mill's Essays on Literature and Society*, ed. J. B. Schneewind, 240–89. New York: Collier, 1965.

―――. "Coleridge." In *Mill's Essays on Literature and Society*, ed. J. B. Schneewind, 290–347. New York: Collier, 1965.

Minogue, Kenneth. "The Graves of Academe." *Times Literary Supplement*, 24 July 1987, 786.

Moore, Harry T. Preface. *Edmund Wilson*, by Leonard Kriegel, vii–x. Cross Currents–Modern Critiques. Carbondale: Southern Illinois UP, 1971.

Morson, Gary Saul. "Bakhtin and the Present Moment." *American Scholar* 60 (1991): 201–22.

―――. "Prosaics: An Approach to the Humanities." *American Scholar* 57 (1988): 515–28.

Myrdal, Gunnar. *An American Dilemma: The Negro Problem and Modern Democracy*. 1944. 20th anniversary ed. New York: Harper and Row, 1962.

Netanyahu, Benjamin, ed. *Terrorism: How the West Can Win*. New York: Farrar, 1986.

Newman, John Henry Cardinal. *Apologia Pro Vita Sua*. 1864. New York: Image, 1956.

Ortega Y Gasset, José. *The Revolt of the Masses*. 1930. Rpt. New York: Norton, 1957.

Pattison, Robert. "On the Finn Syndrome and the Shakespeare Paradox." *Nation*, 30 May 1987, 710–20.

Paul, Sherman. *Edmund Wilson: A Study of Literary Vocation in Our Time.* Urbana: U of Illinois P, 1965.

Piper, Henry Dan. *F. Scott Fitzgerald: A Critical Portrait.* New York: Holt, Rinehart and Winston, 1965.

Podhoretz, Norman. "Edmund Wilson—Then and Now." *Doings and Undoings: The Fifties and After in American Writing,* 30–58. New York: Farrar, 1964.

Radosh, Ronald, and Joyce Milton. *The Rosenberg File.* New York: Holt, 1983.

Real, Michael. *Mass-Mediated Culture.* Englewood Cliffs, NJ: Prentice-Hall, 1977.

Rich, Adrienne. *Of Woman Born: Motherhood as Experience and Institution.* New York: Norton, 1976.

Rieff, David. "The Colonel and the Professor." *Times Literary Supplement,* 4 Sept. 1987, 950+.

Rieff, Philip. *Fellow Teachers.* New York: Harper, 1973.

Rorty, Richard. *Consequences of Pragmatism (Essays: 1972–1980).* Minneapolis: U of Minnesota P, 1982.

———. *Contingency, Irony, and Solidarity.* Cambridge: Cambridge UP, 1989.

———. "Cosmopolitanism without Emancipation: A Response to Jean-François Lyotard." *Objectivity, Relativism, and Truth: Philosophical Papers Volume 1,* 211–22.

———. "De Man and the American Cultural Left." *Essays on Heidegger and Others: Philosophical Papers, Volume 2,* 129–39.

———. "On Ethnocentrism: A Reply to Clifford Geertz." *Objectivity, Relativism, and Truth: Philosophical Papers, Volume 1,* 203–10.

———. *Essays on Heidegger and Others: Philosophical Papers, Volume 2.* Cambridge: Cambridge UP, 1991.

———. "Freud and Moral Reflection." *Essays on Heidegger and Others: Philosophical Papers Volume 2,* 143–63.

———. "Habermas and Lyotard on Postmodernity." *Essays on Heidegger and Others: Philosophical Papers Volume 2,* 164–76.

———. "Heidegger, Kundera, and Dickens." *Essays on Heidegger and Others: Philosophical Papers Volume 2,* 66–82.

———. "Introduction: Antirepresentationalism, Ethnocentrism, and Liberalism." *Objectivity, Relativism, and Truth: Philosophical Papers Volume 1,* 1–17.

———. "Introduction: Pragmatism and Philosophy." *Consequences of Pragmatism (Essays: 1972–1980),* xiii–xlvii.

———. "Just One More Species Doing Its Best." Review of *The Later Works, 1925–1953. Vol. XVII: Miscellaneous Writings, 1885–1953,* by John Dewey. Ed. Jo Ann Boydston. *The Later Dewey,* by J. E. Tiles. *John Dewey and American Democracy,* by Robert Westbrook. *Beloved Community: The Cultural Criticism of Randolph Bourne, Van Wyck Brooks, Waldo Frank and Lewis Mumford,* by Casey Blake. *London Review of Books,* 25 July, 1991, 3–7.

———. *Objectivity, Relativism, and Truth: Philosophical Papers Volume 1.* Cambridge: Cambridge UP, 1991.

———. "Nineteenth-Century Idealism and Twentieth-Century Textualism." *Consequences of Pragmatism (Essays: 1972–1980),* 139–59.

———. "Philosophy as a Kind of Writing: An Essay on Derrida." *Consequences of Pragmatism (Essays: 1972–1980),* 90–109.

———. "Pragmatism, Relativism, Irrationalism." *Consequences of Pragmatism (Essays: 1972–1980)*, 160–75.

———. "Pragmatism without Method." *Objectivity, Relativism, and Truth: Philosophical Papers, Volume 1*, 63–77.

———. "The Priority of Democracy to Philosophy." *Objectivity, Relativism, and Truth: Philosophical Papers, Volume 1*, 175–96.

———. "Professionalized Philosophy and Transcendentalist Culture." *Consequences of Pragmatism (Essays: 1972–1980)*, 60–71.

———. "Two Cheers for the Cultural Left." *South Atlantic Quarterly.* 89 no. 1 (1990): 227–34.

———. "Unger, Castoriadis, and the Romance of a National Future." *Essays on Heidegger and Others: Philosophical Papers, Volume 2*, 177–92.

Rosenberg, Harold. "Couch Liberalism and the Guilty Past." *The Tradition of the New*, 221–40. New York: McGraw-Hill, 1965.

Ryan, Michael. "Are Our Universities Letting Us Down?" *Parade Magazine*, 24 Jan. 1988, 8–10.

Said, Edward W. *Beginnings: Intention and Method.* 1975. Rpt. New York: Columbia UP, 1985.

———. *Blaming the Victims: Spurious Scholarship and the Palestinian Question.* Ed. Edward W. Said and Christopher Hitchens. London: Verso, 1988.

———. "Conclusion: Religious Criticism." *The World, the Text, and the Critic*, 290–94.

——— *Covering Islam: How the Media and the Experts Determine How We See the Rest of the World.* New York: Pantheon, 1981.

———. "Criticism between Culture and System." *The World, the Text, and the Critic*, 178–225.

———. *Culture and Imperialism.* New York: Knopf, 1993.

———. "The Essential Terrorist." *Blaming the Victims*, 149–58.

———. *Identity, Authority and Freedom: The Potentate and the Traveller.* 31st TB Davie Memorial Lecture, 22 May 1991. Cape Town, S. Africa: U of Cape Town P, 1991.

———. "An Ideology of Difference." *Critical Inquiry* 12 (1985): 38–57.

——— "Introduction: Secular Criticism." *The World, the Text, and the Critic*, 1–30.

———. *Joseph Conrad and the Fiction of Autobiography.* Cambridge: Harvard UP, 1966.

———. "Michael Walzer's *Exodus and Revolution*: A Canaanite Reading." *Blaming the Victims: Spurious Scholarship and the Palestinian Question*, 161–78.

———. *Musical Elaborations.* The 1989 Wellek Library Lectures. New York: Columbia UP, 1991.

———. *Orientalism.* 1978. Rpt. New York: Vintage, 1979.

———. "Orientalism Reconsidered." *Cultural Critique* 1, no. 1 (1985): 89–107.

———. *The Question of Palestine.* New York: Times Books, 1979.

———. "Raymond Schwab and the Romance of Ideas." *The World, the Text, and the Critic*, 248–67.

———. "Reflections on American 'Left' Literary Criticism." *The World, the Text, and the Critic*, 158–77.

———. "Representing the Colonized: Anthropology's Interlocutors." *Critical Inquiry* 15 (Winter 1989): 205–25.

———. "Response." *Critical Inquiry* 15 (1989): 634–46.

————. "Traveling Theory." *The World, the Text, and the Critic*, 226–47.

————. *The World, the Text, and the Critic*. Cambridge: Harvard UP, 1983.

Santayana, George. *The Genteel Tradition: Nine Essays by George Santayana*. Ed. Douglas L. Wilson. Cambridge: Harvard UP, 1967.

————. "The Genteel Tradition in American Philosophy." *Winds of Doctrine*, 186–205. New York: Scribner's, 1913. Rpt. in *The Genteel Tradition: Nine Essays by George Santayana*, 37–64.

————. *The Genteel Tradition at Bay*. New York: Scribner's, 1931. Rpt. in *The Genteel Tradition: Nine Essays by George Santayana*, 153–95.

Seaton, James. "Trilling's *Homage to Catalonia*." *Salmagundi: A Quarterly of the Humanities and Social Sciences*. 94–95 (1992): 142–56.

Seghers, Anna. *The Seventh Cross*. Boston: Little Brown, 1942.

————. *Transit*. Boston: Little Brown, 1944. Pub. in German as *Transit: Roman*. Konstanz: C. Weller, 1948.

Showalter, Elaine. "Feminist Criticism in the Wilderness." In *Feminist Criticism*, ed. Elaine Showalter, 125–43. . New York: Pantheon, 1985. Rpt. in *Contemporary Literary Criticism: Literary and Cultural Studies*, ed. Robert Con Davis and Ronald Schleifer, 51–71. 3d ed. New York: Longman, 1994.

Simon, John. Introduction. *Against the American Grain: Essays on the Effects of Mass Culture*, by Dwight Macdonald, v–viii. 1962. Rpt. New York: Da Capo, 1983.

Smith, J. Allen. "*Job* and the Anguish of the Legal Profession: An Example of the Relationship of Literature, Law and Justice." *Rutgers Law Review* 32 (1979): 661–75.

Sontag, Susan. "The Aesthetics of Silence." *Styles of Radical Will*. 3–34. Rpt. in *A Susan Sontag Reader*, 181–204.

————. *AIDS and its Metaphors*. New York: Farrar, 1989. Rpt. in *Illness as Metaphor and AIDS and Its Metaphors*, 89–183. New York: Doubleday, 1990.

————. "Against Interpretation." *Against Interpretation and Other Essays*, 3–14.

————. *Against Interpretation and Other Essays*. New York: Farrar, 1966.

————. "The Anthropologist as Hero." *Against Interpretation and Other Essays*, 69–81.

————. "Camus' Notebooks." *Against Interpretation and Other Essays*, 52–60.

————. "Fascinating Fascism." *Under the Sign of Saturn*, 73–105. New York: Farrar, 1980. Rpt. in *A Susan Sontag Reader*, 305–25.

————. "Godard's *Vivre Sa Vie*." *Against Interpretation and Other Essays*, 196–208.

————. "Going to theater, Etc." *Against Interpretation and Other Essays*, 140–62.

————. *Illness as Metaphor*. New York: Farrar, 1978. Rpt. in *Illness as Metaphor and AIDS and Its Metaphors*, 1–87. New York: Doubleday, 1990.

————. "Ionesco." *Against Interpretation and Other Essays*, 115–22.

————. "The Literary Criticism of Georg Lukács." *Against Interpretation and Other Essays*, 82–92.

————. "Marat/Sade/Artaud." *Against Interpretation and Other Essays*, 163–74.

————. "Nathalie Sarraute and the Novel." *Against Interpretation and Other Essays*, 100–111.

————. "Notes on 'Camp.'" *Against Interpretation and Other Essays*, 275–92. Rpt. in *A Susan Sontag Reader*, 105–19.

————. *On Photography*. New York: Farrar, 1977.

———. "On Style." *Against Interpretation and Other Essays*, 15–36. Rpt. in *A Susan Sontag Reader*, 137–55.

———. "One Culture and the New Sensibility." *Against Interpretation and Other Essays*, 293–304.

———. "Piety without Content." *Against Interpretation and Other Essays*, 249–55.

———. "The Pornographic Imagination." *Styles of Radical Will*, 35–73. Rpt. in *A Susan Sontag Reader*, 205–33.

———. "Psychoanalysis and Norman O. Brown's *Life Against Death.*" *Against Interpretation and Other Essays*, 256–62.

———. "Sartre's *Saint Genet.*" *Against Interpretation and Other Essays*, 93–99.

———. "Simone Weil." *Against Interpretation and Other Essays*, 49–51. Rpt. in *A Susan Sontag Reader*, 91–93.

———. *Styles of Radical Will*. 1969. Rpt. New York: Anchor-Doubleday, 1991.

———. *A Susan Sontag Reader*. 1982. Intro. Elizabeth Hardwick. New York: Random House, 1983.

———. "Spiritual style in the Films of Robert Bresson." *Against Interpretation and Other Essays*, 177–95.

———. "What's Happening in America (1966)." *Styles of Radical Will*, 193–204.

———. "Women, the Arts, and the Politics of Culture: An Interview with Susan Sontag." With Maxine Bernstein and Robert Boyers. *Salmagundi* 31–32 (Fall 1975–Winter 1976): 29–48. Rpt. and abridged as "The *Salmagundi* Interview." *The Susan Sontag Reader*, 329–46.

Sorkin, Adam J. "Politics, Privatism and the Fifties: Ring Lardner Jr.'s *The Ecstasy of Owen Muir.*" *Journal of American Culture* 8, no.3 (1985): 59–73.

Stecker, Robert. "Fish's Argument for the Relativity of Interpretive Truth." *Journal of Aesthetics and Art Criticism* 48 (1990): 223–30.

Tate, Allen. "The Fallacy of Humanism." In *The Critique of Humanism: A Symposium*, ed. C. Hartley Grattan, 131–166. New York: Brewer and Warren, 1930.

Trilling, Diana. "After the Profumo Case." *Claremont Essays*, 1–19.

———. *The Beginning of the Journey: The Marriage of Diana and Lionel Trilling*. New York: Harcourt, 1993.

———. *Claremont Essays*. New York: Harcourt, 1964.

———. Introduction. *The Portable D. H. Lawrence*. Ed. Diana Trilling. New York: Viking, 1947.

———. "A Memorandum on the Hiss Case." *Claremont Essays*, 65–86.

———. *Mrs. Harris: The Death of the Scarsdale Diet Doctor*. New York: Harcourt, 1981.

———. "The Other Night at Columbia: A Report from the Academy." *Claremont Essays*, 153–73.

———. *Reviewing the Forties*. Intro. Paul Fussell. New York: Harcourt, 1978.

———. "On the Steps of Low Library." *We Must March My Darlings: A Critical Decade*, 75–153.

———. "Two Symposiums: 1. Liberal Anti-Communism Revisited. 2. What's Happening to America?" *We Must March My Darlings: A Critical Decade*, 39–73.

———. *We Must March My Darlings: A Critical Decade*. New York: Harcourt, 1977.

Trilling, Lionel. *Beyond Culture: Essays on Literature and Learning*. 1965. The Works of Lionel Trilling, uniform ed. New York: Harcourt, 1978.

————. "The Fate of Pleasure." *Beyond Culture: Essays on Literature and Learning,* 50–76.

————. "The Function of the Little Magazine." *The Liberal Imagination: Essays on Literature and Society,* 89–99.

————. "George Orwell and the Politics of Truth." *The Opposing Self: Nine Essays in Criticism,* 133–51.

————. *The Last Decade: Essays and Reviews, 1965-75.* Ed. Diana Trilling. The Works of Lionel Trilling, uniform ed. New York: Harcourt, 1979.

————. *The Liberal Imagination: Essays on Literature and Society.* 1950. The Works of Lionel Trilling, uniform ed. New York: Harcourt, 1979.

————. "Manners, Morals, and the Novel." *The Liberal Imagination: Essays on Literature and Society,* 193–209.

————. "Mansfield Park." *The Opposing Self: Nine Essays in Criticism,* 181–202.

————. *Matthew Arnold.* 1939. The Works of Lionel Trilling, uniform ed. New York: Harcourt, 1977.

————. "Mind in the Modern World." First Thomas Jefferson Lecture in the Humanities of the National Endowment for the Humanities. 1972. Published as *Mind in the Modern World.* New York: Viking, 1973. Rpt. in *The Last Decade: Essays and Reviews, 1965–75,* 100–128.

————. "On the Teaching of Modern Literature." *Beyond Culture: Essays on Literature and Learning,* 3–27.

————. *The Opposing Self: Nine Essays in Criticism.* 1955. The Works of Lionel Trilling, uniform ed. New York: Harcourt, 1978.

————. "The Poet as Hero: Keats in His Letters." *The Opposing Self: Nine Essays in Criticism,* 3–43.

————. ."*The Princess Casamassima.*" *The Liberal Imagination: Essays on Literature and Society,,* 56–88.

————. "Reality in America." *The Liberal Imagination: Essays on Literature and Society,* 3–20.

————. *Sincerity and Authenticity.* Cambridge: Harvard UP, 1972.

————. "The Sense of the Past." *Partisan Review* 45 (1942): 229–41. Rpt. in *The Liberal Imagination: Essays on Literature and Society,* 172–86.

————. "William Dean Howells and the Roots of Modern Taste." *The Opposing Self: Nine Essays in Criticism,* 67–91.

Twain, Mark. *Adventures of Huckleberry Finn.* 1885. Rpt. Berkeley: U of California P, 1985.

Wald, Alan. *The New York Intellectuals: The Rise and Decline of the Anti-Stalinist Left from the 1930s to the 1980s.* Chapel Hill: U of North Carolina P, 1987.

Walzer, Michael. *The Company of Critics: Social Criticism and Political Commitment in the Twentieth Century.* New York: Basic, 1988.

Warshow, Robert. "The 'Idealism' of Julius and Ethel Rosenberg." *The Immediate Experience: Movies, Comics, Theatre & Other Aspects of Popular Culture,* 69–81. Garden City NY: Doubleday, 1962.

Watts, Jerry Gafio. *Heroism and the Black Intellectual: Ralph Ellison, Politics, and Afro-American Intellectual Life.* Chapel Hill: U of North Carolina P, 1994.

Weinstein, Allen. *Perjury: The Hiss-Chambers Case.* New York: Knopf, 1978.

West, Robin. "Authority, Autonomy and Choice: The Role of Consent in the Moral and Political Visions of Franz Kafka and Richard Posner." *Harvard Law Review* 99 (1985): 384–428.

White, Hayden. "The Politics of Historical Interpretation: Discipline and De-Sublimation." *Critical Inquiry* 9 (1982): 113–37. Rpt. in *The Politics of Interpretation,* ed. W. J. T. Mitchell, 119–43. Chicago: U of Chicago P, 1983.

White, James Boyd. *When Words Lose Their Meaning: Constitutions and Reconstitutions of Language, Character, and Community.* Chicago: U of Chicago P, 1984.

Whitman, Walt. "Democratic Vistas." 1892. *Walt Whitman: Complete Poetry and Collected Prose.* Ed. Justin Kaplan, 929–94.. New York: Library of America, 1982.

Williams, Tennessee. *A Streetcar Named Desire.* New York: New Directions, 1947.

Wilson, Edmund. "The Aftermath of Mencken." *The Devils and Canon Barham: Ten Essays on Poets, Novelists and Monsters,* 92–104. Farrar, 1973.

———. "The Author at Sixty." *A Piece of My Mind: Reflections at Sixty,* 208–39. New York: Farrar, 1956. Rpt. in *The Portable Edmund Wilson.* Ed. Lewis M. Dabney, 20–44. New York: Viking, 1983.

———. *Patriotic Gore: Studies in the Literature of the American Civil War.* 1962. Rpt. New York: Galaxy–Oxford UP, 1966.

———, ed. *The Shock of Recognition: The Development of Literature in the United States Recorded by the Men Who Made It.* 1943. 2d. ed. New York: Farrar, 1955.

———. "Summary as of 1940." *To the Finland Station: A Study in the Writing and Acting of History,* 475–484. 1940. Rpt. Garden City, NY: Anchor-Doubleday, 1953.

———. *To the Finland Station: A Study in the Writing and Acting of History.* 1940. New York: Farrar, 1972.

Wills, Garry. "The Ugly American." Review of *The Diary of H. L. Mencken,* by H. L Mencken. Ed. *New Republic,* 19 Feb. 1990, 31–34.

Wolff, Robert Paul. Review of *The Closing of the American Mind: How Higher Education Has Failed Democracy and Impoverished the Souls of Today's Students,* by Allan Bloom. *Academe* (Sept.–Oct. 1987): 64–65.

Wreszin, Michael. *A Rebel in Defense of Tradition: The Life and Politics of Dwight Macdonald.* New York: Basic-HarperCollins, 1994.

Wright, Richard. *Black Boy (American Hunger). Black Boy,* 1945. *American Hunger,* 1977. *Later Works.* Ed. Arnold Rampersad, 1–365. New York: Library of America, 1991.

Yunck, John A. "The Natural History of a Dead Quarrel: Hemingway and the Humanists." *South Atlantic Quarterly* 62 no.1 (1963): 29–42.

Ziff, Larzer. "The Man by the Fire: Edmund Wilson and American Literature." In *Edmund Wilson: The Man and His Work,* ed. John Wain, 43–59. New York: New York UP, 1978.

Index

Abelard, Peter, 235

Abrams, M. H., 22, 23; "How to Do Things with Texts," 23

Adams, Henry, 46–47, 210 (*Education of Henry Adams*)

Adorno, Theodor, 10, 121, 148–49, 203–4, 258–59n.4

Althusser, Louis, 147, 254–55n.3

Anticommunism, 6, 65-66, 71, 76, 78, 105-6, 114, 252n.1; Leslie Fiedler and, 105-6, 114, 252n.1; Diana Trilling's, 6, 65-66, 71, 76, 78. *See also* Communism

Armstrong, Louis, 204

Arnold, Matthew, 1, 2–4, 11, 29–30, 117, 121–30, 131, 134, 188–89; cultural criticism, example of, 1; Terry Eagleton, criticized by, 2; T. S. Eliot, allies with, 11; Leslie Fiedler, compared to, 117; self-criticism, admires in Edmund Burke, 188–89; Susan Sontag, criticized by, 121–22; Susan Sontag, key difference with, 134; Susan Sontag, parallels with, 122–30, 131, 134; Lionel Trilling, influenced by, 2, 29–30; works: "Function of Criticism at the Present Time," 2–4, 188–89; "Study of Poetry," 125, 134

Artaud, Antonin, 124, 127

Auchincloss, Louis, 245n.1

Austen, Jane, 116, 179–81, 185, 256–58n.5

Babbitt, Irving, 1, 5, 6–7, 21, 39–40, 48–55, 157, 158, 221, 222–23, 224–25, 237, 239, 245–46n.3; criticism, significance of, 1, 5, 39–40, 53–54, 221, 224–25, 239; death, courage facing, 53, 245–46n.3; early life, 48; Emersonianism, opposition to, 6–7, 21; humanism, positive and critical, 49–50;

humanitarianism, contrasted with humanism, 39, 51–52; imperialism, critique of, 50–51; Fredric Jameson, comparison with, 157-58; H. L. Mencken, criticized by, 39, 222–23; H. L. Mencken, parallels with, 5, 39–40, 53–54; New Humanism and, 47–48, 53; unionist tradition affirmed by, 237; works: "Buddha and the Occident," 53; *Democracy and Leadership*, 5, 49, 50, 51, 52–53; "English and the Discipline of Ideas," 49, 225; *Literature and the American College*, 48, 49, 50, 51; "Matthew Arnold," 157; *Rousseau and Romanticism*, 246n.3; "What I Believe," 49, 50, 52, 158, 225

Babeuf, François-Noel ("Gracchus"), 80

Baldwin, James, 97, 228

Balzac, Honoré de, 143, 145–46

Baraka, Imamu Amiri (LeRoi Jones), 100–101

Barzun, Jacques, 1–2

Bellah, Robert, 18, 209–10

Bellow, Saul, 210

Benjamin, Walter, 121

Bentham, Jeremy, 26, 162, 173–74

Berthoff, Warner, 248n.1

Beyond the Valley of the Dolls, 106

Bismarck, Otto von, 81

Blackburn, Robin, 260n.1

Blankfort, Michael (*A Time to Live*), 71–72

Bloom, Allan (*Closing of the American Mind*), 9–10, 171, 197–98, 201-8, 210–12, 217, 253n.1, 258n.2, 258–59n.4; approach, significance of, 9–10, 212, 217; *Closing* and *Cultural Literacy*, 9–10, 197–98, 201, 208, 210, 217; *Closing* and *Great Gatsby*, 210–12; *Closing* and *Literature Against Itself*, 253n.1; *Closing* and *Philosophical Discourse of Moder-*

version of, 251–52n.1; Edmund Wilson on, 80–81. *See also* Communism; Lenin; Mao Zedong; Marx, Karl; Stalin
McCarthy, Eugene, 77
McCarthy, Joseph, 76, 77, 78, 105
McKenney, Ruth (*Jake Home*), 71–72
Melville, Herman, 112, 114 (*Bartleby*)
Melzer, Arthur M. ("Tolerance 101"), 261n.1
Mencken, H. L., 1, 5, 6–7, 21, 23, 39–47, 52, 53–54, 155, 157–58, 214, 221, 222–24, 226, 237, 239, 242–45n.1; anti-Semitism of, accusations of, 242–45n.1; Irving Babbitt and, 5, 39–40, 52, 53–54, 222–23; criticism, significance of, 1, 5, 221, 222–24, 239; Ralph Ellison defends, 244–45n.1; Ralph Waldo Emerson and, 6–7, 21; Joseph Epstein on, 242–44n.1; James T. Farrell and, 40; Fredric Jameson, compared to, 155, 157–58; Dwight Macdonald, compared to, 5, 226; racism, accusations of, 242–45n.1; Richard Rorty and, 6–7, 23; Garry Wills on, 243n.1; Richard Wright on, 244–45n.1; works: *American Language*, 40–41, 223; "On Being an American," 40–41, 223–24; *In Defense of Women*, 41–44, 45; *Diary of H. L. Mencken*, 242–45n.1; *Gist of Nietzsche*, 40; "On Living in Baltimore," 41, 45–47; *Minority Report*, 224; "The National Letters," 52; *Philosophy of Friedrich Nietzsche*, 40; *Prejudices*, 40; "Roosevelt: An Autopsy," 41, 44–45, 46, 158
Mill, John Stuart, 173–74
Miller, Arthur (*After the Fall*), 124
Milton, Joyce, 252–53n.1
Minogue, Kenneth, 258n.2
Moore, Harry T., 248n.1
More, Paul Elmer, 47
Morson, Gary Saul, 238
Multiculturalism, 232, 235, 261n.1
Mussolini, Benito, 16, 19, 52. *See also* Fascism
Myrdal, Gunnar, 96–97

Nagel, Thomas, 24
Nathan, George Jean, 40
Nazism, 6, 16–17, 24–25, 53, 69–73, 118, 134, 135, 150–51, 226, 237; Irving Babbitt and, 53; Gertrude Himmelfarb on Dwight Macdonald's treatment of, 246–47n.1; Fredric Jameson and, 150–51; Leszek Kolakowski

on Thomas Mann's treatment of, 214; Georg Lukács and, 150–51; Dwight Macdonald on, 6, 57–58, 246–47n.1, Thomas Mann and, 118, 214 (*Dr. Faustus*); Richard Rorty on, 16–17, 24–25; Susan Sontag and, 134, 135; Diana Trilling and, 6, 69–73, 226. *See also* Fascism; Hitler, Adolf
Neoconservatism, 65, 67–68, 191
Netanyahu, Benjamin, 165
Newman, John Henry Cardinal, 169, 171–72, 173
Nietzsche, Friedrich, 40, 45, 47, 53, 135, 137, 176, 179, 202, 206–7; Irving Babbitt on, 53; Allan Bloom and, 202, 206–7; H. L. Mencken and, 40, 45, 47; Edward Said and, 176, 179; Susan Sontag and, 135, 137
North, Oliver, 258n.2
Nostromo, 176

Oliver, Sy, 116
O'Neill, Eugene (*Marco Millions*), 122
Orlovsky, Peter, 73
Ortega Y Gasset, José, 56, 247n.2
Orwell, George, 17 (*1984*), 31, 87, 242n.1 (*Homage to Catalonia*)

Page, Inman, 98
Parker, Charlie 93, 98–99
Parrington, V. L., 156
Partisan Review, 157
Pattison, Robert, 258n.3
Patton, George, 57
Paul, Sherman, 249n.1
Piper, Henry Dan, 247–48n.2
Plato, 20, 203, 212, 234, 237
Podhoretz, Norman, 248n.1
Political correctness, 34, 69, 99
Porter, Cole, 116
Posner, Richard, 184
Postmodernism, 8, 15–16, 21–24, 27, 32, 33, 65, 141, 143, 153–58, 219–21, 232, 233, 238, 255n.8; Mikhail Bakhtin does not share skepticism of, 238; cultural studies and, 21; Jacques Derrida and, 16; Ralph Ellison differs from, 27; Stanley Fish and, 15; Fredric Jameson and, 15, 255n.8; Douglas Kellner favors openness to, 232; Arthur Lovejoy does not share skepticism of, 238; H. L. Mencken differs from, 27; *Postmodernism*, 8, 141, 143, 153–58, 219–21, 255n.8; Richard